# Fiction, Philosophy and the Ideal of Conversation

# Fiction, Philosophy and the Ideal of Conversation

Erin Elizabeth Greer

EDINBURGH
University Press

Edinburgh University Press is one of the leading university presses in the UK. We publish academic books and journals in our selected subject areas across the humanities and social sciences, combining cutting-edge scholarship with high editorial and production values to produce academic works of lasting importance. For more information visit our website: edinburghuniversitypress.com

© Erin Elizabeth Greer 2024, 2025

Edinburgh University Press Ltd
13 Infirmary Street,
Edinburgh, EH1 1LT

First published in hardback by Edinburgh University Press 2024

Typeset in 10.5/13 Adobe Sabon by
IDSUK (DataConnection) Ltd

A CIP record for this book is available from the British Library

ISBN 978 1 3995 2021 8 (hardback)
ISBN 978 1 3995 2022 5 (paperback)
ISBN 978 1 3995 2023 2 (webready PDF)
ISBN 978 1 3995 2024, 2025, 2025 9 (epub)

The right of Erin Elizabeth Greer to be identified as the author of this work has been asserted in accordance with the Copyright, Designs and Patents Act 1988, and the Copyright and Related Rights Regulations 2003 (SI No. 2498).

# Contents

| | |
|---|---|
| *Acknowledgements* | vi |
| *Abbreviations* | ix |
| Introduction: Conversation as Worldmaking in Literature, Philosophy and Criticism | 1 |
| 1. Perfectionism and the Conversation of Justice: Austen and Cavell | 31 |
| 2. Performative Conversation and Acknowledgement: Meredith, Austin and Cavell | 63 |
| 3. Conversation and Common Sense: Woolf, Russell and Kant | 95 |
| 4. Public Conversation and Judgement: Rushdie and Arendt | 121 |
| 5. Digital vs Political Conversation: Ali Smith, Arendt and Wittgenstein | 162 |
| Afterword | 186 |
| *Notes* | 193 |
| *Bibliography* | 215 |
| *Index* | 229 |

## *Acknowledgements*

Writing these acknowledgements, I feel a kind of vertiginous, looping gratitude: thankful to the people who have helped make the book possible, and thankful to the book for helping make possible and shaping many personal and intellectual connections. In most straightforward terms, this book began as my PhD dissertation in the English programme at UC Berkeley. My first thanks go to my generous and incisive dissertation committee, and above all to my supervisor and mentor at Berkeley, Elizabeth Abel. Elizabeth responded to every turn of phrase and thought, in person and on the page, with remarkable care, attention to detail and insight. Moreover, she fostered community among her advisees, bringing us together to discuss each other's work over bagels, for instance, and providing several kinds of sustenance in the process. I'm deeply grateful for the example she set as a mentor and reader. I am also thankful to have had the opportunity to work closely with the rest of my committee members: Kent Puckett's responses to my work were simultaneously challenging, reassuring and inspiring; conversations with Anne-Lise François unfailingly prompted me to rethink, in the most pleasurable ways, assumptions about how or why I was reading; and it was in a wonderful class with Michael Lucey that I first read many of the sociolinguistic and philosophical perspectives on 'talk' that have informed this book, indirectly but crucially, from my qualifying exams to the present. I must also give special thanks to Grace Lavery, who, although she was not on my committee, provided dauntingly sharp feedback on the project's animating ideas and on the book proposal at several key moments: acts of abundant generosity. I am a better thinker, reader, writer and teacher because of each of these mentors, and the consequences stretch beyond my scholarly work and into ordinary life. Thank you.

The seeds for this project were planted when I was an undergraduate and first took a class with Toril Moi. I took as many courses as possible with Toril after that first, and in my final year she supervised my senior honours thesis. Toril introduced me to Stanley Cavell's work, but even more, she introduced me to a form of life: it was through this combination of experiences – reading, talking and writing about literature and philosophy with her guidance – that I discovered and began to cultivate the passion and practical habits that have become the foundation of my career. I remain humbled and grateful for this best of possible initiations.

Since filing my dissertation, this project and I have gone through many stages, all of which were supported and influenced in countless ways by the community of scholars and friends I have found at the University of Texas at Dallas. I am especially grateful to Ashley Barnes, Charles Hatfield and Davis Smith-Brecheisen for invigorating conversations about the state and stakes of literary studies, which I'd wager (also with gratitude) are unlikely to come to a definitive end any time soon. I am also thankful for the brilliant and lucid feedback Ashley and Charles have given me on drafts of this project – and additional thanks are due to Dan Wickberg, Eric Schlereth, Shilyh Warren, Annelise Heinz and Josef Nguyen for reading and commenting with insight and encouragement on portions of the manuscript. Heartfelt thanks are due to Anne Gray Fischer, whose wisdom, warmth and friendship shaped this project both directly and indirectly. Annie is the walking companion of any thinker's dreams (among many other virtues). For keeping the community flame burning even as the coronavirus pandemic turned our lives upside down, I thank everyone I've mentioned so far in these acknowledgements, plus Jon Malesic, Will Meyers, Linda Smith-Brecheisen, Whitney Stewart, Ben Wright, Janet Hendrickson, Amy Freund, Sean Cotter and Kimberly Hill. Elizabeth Ingleson left Dallas too soon for my taste, but it was a joy and a timely source of personal and intellectual renewal to reunite in London while I was in the final stages of revising this book. Longer-distance friends from my Berkeley years, who taught me a lot about politics, ethics and the joy of talking about the world, include Steven Kotz, Alex Brostoff, Michaeljit Sandhu, Margaret Mary Downey, Paul Bissember, César Bowley Castillo, Ryan McWilliams, Tyleen Kelly, Marianne Kaletzky, Shannon Ikebe, Laurel Fish, Christopher Chandler, Wonjun and Amanda Lee, Ionas Porges-Kiriakou, Eva Kersey, Scott Kinder and Xander Lenc.

I am thrilled that this project brought me into contact with Ingeborg Löfgren, Viktor Johansson and, through them, the Nordic Ordinary Language Criticism group. Thanks are due to NOLC for the opportunity to discuss this work shortly before I submitted the final manuscript. Not only am I grateful for all participants' rich engagement with the project – traces of which are inscribed in the afterword – but I am heartened by the existence of this dynamic, warm intellectual community. Thanks are also due to David Rudrum, whose support for the project and (to cite Ingeborg) 'social genius' made my first in-person conference in several years a powerful reminder of the pleasure and fruitfulness of thinking with others.

I want to thank everyone at Edinburgh University Press for believing in this project and offering helpful guidance and support at each stage. Special thanks are due to Emily Sharp and Elizabeth Fraser, a great editorial team, and to the two readers whose responses to the work immensely improved its final form.

My parents, Margaret Gaffney and Charles Greer, inspired my early loves for both talking and reading, and I cannot imagine having written this book without their love, friendship and confidence in me and this project. The first readers of each chapter's drafts were my mom and stepdad, Matthew Galvin, and their questions, suggestions and support have undoubtedly made this a better book. The book has likewise benefited from innumerable conversations sitting on the deck or walking in the woods with my dad, and from the warm friendship of my stepmom, Kathy Greer. My aunt Carol Gaffney has been another crucial, constant loving presence in my life. I am astonished at my great fortune in having the family (or, families) I do.

Finally, and every day, I am grateful to Daniel Scott. Our partnership is the same age as this project, I recently realised, and I cannot think of a better description of Dan's mode of living than Cavell's gloss on the key to exemplary conversation: 'articulate responsiveness, expressiveness'. Dan's responsiveness, to me and to the world, is part of every word of this book.

# Abbreviations

'Concept'   Hannah Arendt. 'The Concept of History: Ancient and Modern'. In *Between Past and Future: Eight Exercises in Political Thought*, 41–90. New York: Viking Press, 1968.
'Crisis'    Hannah Arendt. 'The Crisis in Culture: Its Social and Its Political Significance'. In *Between Past and Future*, 197–226. New York: Viking Press, 1968.
CHU         Stanley Cavell. *Conditions Handsome and Unhandsome: The Constitution of Emersonian Perfectionism*. Chicago: University of Chicago Press, 1990.
Cities      Stanley Cavell. *Cities of Words: Pedagogical Letters on a Register of the Moral Life*. Cambridge, MA: Harvard University Press, 2005.
CR          Stanley Cavell. *The Claim of Reason: Wittgenstein, Skepticism, Morality, and Tragedy*. New York: Oxford University Press, 1979.
CT          Stanley Cavell. *Contesting Tears: The Hollywood Melodrama of the Unknown Woman*. Chicago: University of Chicago Press, 1996.
HC          Hannah Arendt. *The Human Condition*. Chicago: University of Chicago Press, 1958.
IQO         Stanley Cavell. *In Quest of the Ordinary: Lines of Skepticism and Romanticism*. Chicago: University of Chicago Press, 1994.
LMT         Hannah Arendt. *The Life of the Mind*, vol. 1, *Thinking*. New York: Harcourt, 1978.
LKPP        Hannah Arendt. *Lectures on Kant's Political Philosophy*. Chicago: University of Chicago Press, 1989.
MWM         Stanley Cavell. *Must We Mean What We Say?* Cambridge, UK: Cambridge University Press, 1976.

| | |
|---|---|
| *PDAT* | Stanley Cavell. *Philosophy the Day After Tomorrow.* Cambridge, MA: Harvard University Press, 2006. |
| *Pitch* | Stanley Cavell. *A Pitch of Philosophy: Autobiographical Exercises.* Cambridge, MA: Harvard University Press, 1994. |
| *Pursuits* | Stanley Cavell. *Pursuits of Happiness: The Hollywood Comedy of Remarriage.* Cambridge, MA: Harvard University Press, 1981. |
| TP | Hannah Arendt. 'Truth and Politics'. In *Between Past and Future*, 227–264. New York: Viking Press, 1968. |

# Introduction: Conversation as Worldmaking in Literature, Philosophy and Criticism

In her 2011 novel *There But For The*, Ali Smith warns that 'we're forgetting how to know what's real', that we are swayed instead by the 'so-called truth' offered on the Internet.[1] Smith's 'Brexit' novel, *Autumn* (2016), gives voice through one of its characters to another truism of the twenty-first century, frequently linked to the first in popular imagination, if not explicitly in Smith's work: 'it is the end of dialogue', she reflects, a 'time of people saying stuff to each other and none of it actually ever becoming dialogue'.[2] The character formulates the political implications of the supposed end of dialogue with a vivid image: 'it's like democracy is a bottle someone can threaten to smash and do a bit of damage with' (112). A post-dialogue era is a post-democratic and illiberal era, she implies, in which democracy degrades into electoral outcries, angry and destructive referenda rather than ongoing conversation.

Placed together, these passages evoke the widespread and rather hazy intuitions about conversation this book seeks to clarify. *Fiction, Philosophy and the Ideal of Conversation* argues that the premises of the passages above – that shared access to 'truth' is contingent on our modes of communication, and that healthy collective life depends on conversation and similarly open-ended forms of talk – are interwoven in a complex philosophical and literary outlook worth elucidating. For centuries, long in advance of digital-age formulations, writers have linked conversation to our capacity to 'know what's real' about the world, other people and ourselves. Doubting this capacity is known in philosophy as scepticism, and this book originates from the observation that conversation plays a vital, under-appreciated role in compelling responses to philosophical scepticism offered by works of ordinary language philosophy, political philosophy and British fiction. I show that there is a suggestive interplay between conversation's function in exemplary philosophical responses to scepticism and depictions of communication – and its failures – in novels by authors spanning from Jane Austen through Salman Rushdie and Ali Smith. Moreover, I argue that a conversational reading practice inspired by Stanley Cavell, one of the main proponents of conversation in this context, allows us to gain a sharper view of the implications of the idea of conversation for ethical, political and literary-critical forms of life.

Three arguments thus interweave in the pages that follow: there is, across various works of philosophy, a persistent and compelling view of conversation as a response to scepticism; this view is both shared and complicated by works of fiction; and a reading practice inspired by this vision of conversation allows us to delineate the contours of the idealisation of conversation, as well as the resources it provides for ethics, politics and criticism seeking to respond to the uncertainties of the twenty-first century. Cavell describes one of his intellectual guides, J. L. Austin, as having broached a 'new literary-philosophical criticism', referring to the creativity of Austin's writing and thinking, but his own work embraced a hyphenated, conversational mode of enquiry far more profoundly.[3] I am not the first to observe Cavell's idealisation of conversation – indeed, it is for some of his readers a shortcoming – nor the first to see its traces in his idiosyncratic reading practices, which consistently interweave philosophical, literary and other aesthetic works.[4] Yet the significance of conversation to his work merits further attention on its own terms and as a resource for contemporary literary studies. In addition to Cavell's work, Hannah Arendt's formulation of political speech and judgement will be crucial to my elaboration of the political ramifications of the idea of conversation expressed in the philosophical and literary texts, as well as in conversational criticism. I draw my novels from the post-Romantic British canon, a scope that helps illuminate links between representations of communication, developments in narrative form, and sceptical uncertainties that reflect local political and social conditions. I imagine, however, that texts from different traditions might provide similarly useful resources. I'll revisit this supposition and its place in a conversational reading project shortly.

It is a commonplace to describe interdisciplinary work as 'conversational', and exchanges between literature and philosophy are as old as the idea of distinct literary and philosophical traditions. The very ordinariness of this metaphor suggests we might benefit from clarifying what we mean when we describe interdisciplinary 'conversation', or when – as is especially true in much of the meta-disciplinary 'post-critique' writing so prominent in contemporary literary studies – scholars call for more conversation, less suspicion, or more generous modes of engaging with our texts and other scholars.[5] Cavell's 'literary-philosophical criticism' and ordinary language philosophy's general dedication to the everyday and ordinary uses of language indeed complement the current embrace of modes of reading with rather than against, or in scepticism towards, works of literature.[6] The clarified picture of conversation this book develops supports such work by shining light on the tacit presuppositions and stakes of what many of us who write at the intersections of literary criticism and other fields already do.[7] So, I hope this book feeds not only the current interest in the relationship between ordinary language philosophy and literature, but also the field's broader interest in linking literary criticism to affirmative projects within and beyond the discipline.

Yet, I'll also pause to note that although this book's reading practice manifests an ethos often associated with 'post-critique' – responsiveness to the words on the page, learning through attentive encounters with texts, not proceeding under the assumption that texts 'hide' things from us – I do not think this ethos is necessarily post-critical, nor that it is at odds with critical theory.[8] As I hope to make clear in this introduction and throughout this book, the originality of the kind of reading Cavell models, and which I attempt to practise as well, lies not in a new way of engaging with the words on the page, but in a different understanding of how and why we might bring the fruits of that familiar interpretive labour – call it close reading – into conversation with other voices, which may, at times, offer theoretical or critical claims. In short, clarifying and continuing Cavell's conversational criticism, these pages strive to provide a richer context for grappling with conditions branded today as 'post-truth', while also offering a new way to articulate the value of including the 'voice' of literature, as Cavell puts it, in broader conversations defining our times.

Conversation has long been a promiscuous ideal. From antiquity forwards, European and Anglo-American writers have repeatedly invoked conversation and similarly open-ended modes of talk as both a symbol and the practical foundation of marriage and ethics, politics, and philosophy itself. One of the earliest visions of marriage as friendship in the British tradition arrives via John Milton's seventeenth-century assertion that 'a meet and happy conversation is the chiefest and the noblest end of marriage'.[9] This idea reappears in various guises in nineteenth-century courtship novels, Hollywood films that Cavell deems inheritors of Milton's view, and, broadened beyond the conjugal, in contemporary warnings about the consequences of digital media's erosion of face-to-face conversation. Sherry Turkle's best-selling 2015 book, *Reclaiming Conversation: The Power of Talk in a Digital Age*, for instance, warns that the digital era's displacement of ordinary conversation threatens our 'capacity for empathy, friendship, and intimacy'.[10] Another variant of the conversational ideal moves from the coffee houses and chatty periodicals of early modern Britain, through Jürgen Habermas's seminal account of their role in forming the liberal public sphere, to a platitude among contemporary pundits, encapsulated by Barack Obama in a 2016 interview with *The New Yorker* in which he remarks that social media 'sharply polarize the electorate and make it very difficult to have a common conversation'.[11] A third conceptual thread stretches from the Socratic dialogue, through Immanuel Kant's account of the 'public use of one's reason' as the engine of enlightenment and Richard Rorty's description of his aim in philosophy as 'continuing the conversation of the West', to contemporary formulations of 'cancel culture' as a threat not only to 'free speech' but also to our collective intellectual progress.[12] Hans-Georg Gadamer's *Truth and Method* proposes textual hermeneutics modelled on conversation. Emmanuel Levinas and Maurice Blanchot build an ethical programme around the 'primordial' encounter of face-to-face conversation, and according to Dorothy Hale's *The Novel and the New Ethics*, this vision casts a powerful influence on contemporary understandings of the ethical value of literature, expressed by poststructuralist literary critics as well as by contemporary novelists such as Zadie Smith and J. M. Coetzee. The sociologist credited with planting the seeds of empirical studies of conversation, Erving Goffman, described conversation in evocatively aesthetic terms as 'a period of idling felt to be an end in itself', 'the bridge that people build to one another' that 'creates [. . .] a world and a reality that has other participants in it'.[13] More profoundly than romantic love, Goffman concludes, conversation 'lights up the world'.[14]

The hasty sketch above suggests a combination of loftiness and vagueness, which some have deemed a liability. In the late 1990s, the literary critic David Simpson denounced a 'cult of conversation' in the humanities, which he posited allowed scholars dazzled or seduced by poststructuralism to avoid staking themselves in definitive judgements, while simultaneously invoking nostalgic associations with a 'civilised' and erudite, pre-professional ruling class.[15] In political discourse, politicians frequently call for 'conversation' as a means of dodging demands for policy action or accountability. Mari Boor Tonn recounts a darkly humorous example from Tony Blair's days as the British Prime Minister: in 2003, Blair's government launched 'The Big Conversation', by many accounts as a cynical response to 'mounting criticism of his indifference to public opinion on issues ranging from the Iraq war to steep tuition hike proposals'.[16] The initiative solicited public opinion, but its website only featured edited and censored extracts. A similarly named website began to receive and post the uncensored views of British citizens who confused the sites. The contrast was humiliating for the government and underscored what a charade the 'big conversation' was. Tonn suggests that although the primary scandal was the bogus pretence of civic engagement, the starting premise was itself problematic: the government invited 'conversation' precisely because it already knew it was unpopular but had no intention of changing its policies, as though the theatre of democratic participation would function as a release valve rather than a channel of popular will.

I could trace additional routes travelled by the conversational ideal, but my purpose here is only to establish the outlines of a backdrop against which my readings take place: conversation is at once an ordinary practice we engage in constantly, and a synecdoche for a range of cherished ideas about how we should relate to others, the pursuit of knowledge, and the world itself. This book focuses on a specific set of uses of conversation in responses to philosophical scepticism, a predominating preoccupation of modern European and Anglo-American philosophy, which I understand to reverberate in today's preoccupations with the linked breakdowns of common reality and conversation associated with the rise of the Internet. At its core, scepticism warns that our senses, our reason, or an evil spirit might deceive us in our understandings of the world or other people. It is, in Kant's words, the 'scandal of philosophy and human reason', insisting as it does 'that the existence of things outside us [. . .] should have to be assumed merely on faith'.[17] This notion is understandably also a 'scandal' for ethical and political life: if we cannot be sure of the existence of things or minds outside ourselves, why bother with ethics or democratic politics? In Cavell's interpretation, the ordinary language philosopher's commitment to 'the ordinary' and 'the everyday' is a refusal not of scepticism, but of the panic or despair scepticism might prompt. As we'll see, the significance of conversation for Cavell is closely connected to his sense that language is the best, and only, tool by which we can offer one another 'articulate responsiveness, expressiveness', despite doubts we cannot put definitively to rest. Accepting the truth of scepticism, Cavell argues, allows us to enter 'the field of serious and playful conversation or exchange'.[18]

A similar recourse to conversation appears in Hannah Arendt's political thought. Arendt, who like many traces the origins of modern philosophical scepticism to René Descartes's dubious encounter with wax in the seventeenth century, argues that the 'scandal' is not so much doubt itself, but rather the Cartesian 'solution', *cogito ergo sum*. The *cogito* argument, she claims, is one of the founding disasters of

Western modernity. It reassures us only of our own cognition, our doubting subjective existence, and we turn inward. 'What men now have in common', Arendt writes, 'is not the world but the structure of their minds, and this they cannot have in common, strictly speaking'.[19] 'Reality', she warns, 'cannot be derived' from Descartes's starting point, and 'the Cartesian doubt' is ultimately 'a sophisticated and veiled form of rejection' of reality.[20] By this view, 'post-truth' politics is simply the latest developmental stage of the cognitive despair Arendt declares definitive of the European 'modern age', now close to 400 years old. Yet, for Arendt – as for the ordinary language philosophers and novelists I bring together – conversation promises something of a reprieve. It does not 'defeat' sceptical doubt, but instead turns such doubt on its head.

Borrowing one of Wittgenstein's descriptions of the general project of ordinary language philosophy, we can say that for the writers in this book, conversation can help 'turn' us 'round [. . .] the fixed point of our real need'.[21] We cannot be certain that we share a common reality, or that our knowledge of others' minds is accurate, and this absence of certainty is precisely why we talk. (It is also through talking that we discover the extent to which we constitute a 'we', a point I'll return to repeatedly, which is crucial to distinguishing the stakes of normative claims in ordinary language philosophy.) Conversation, like the common world in Arendt's work, 'relates and separates' us at the same time (*HC*, 52). Our 'incessant talk', in another of her phrases, is evidence of our imperfect knowledge and, simultaneously, the primary medium by which we learn to see whatever we *do* glimpse of one another and our shared world.[22]

This work, however, is fraught with paradoxes and challenges, as the novels help us see. The central novels assembled here – by Jane Austen, George Meredith, Virginia Woolf, Salman Rushdie and Ali Smith – span roughly 200 years of British literary and political history, and on the surface their formal and conceptual concerns differ greatly. Yet each depicts scepticism of one form or another, threats to a common sense of 'what's real' that range from class bias, patriarchy and racism to modernist scepticism and the rise of the Internet. Each novel, moreover, connects these threats to language use in scenes of literal conversation as well as scenes I read in dialogue with metaphorical invocations of conversation to describe democratic public life and digital social media. Read together, and with philosophers whose interests they share, the novels suggest a complex and complementary vision of language use, in which conversation is a worldmaking practice: a generative source of common ground, at once serious and playful, improvisational and normative, which paradoxically draws power from our underlying sceptical doubts about such mutual understanding.²³ Conversation, in this view, is performative. It mitigates scepticism because speech *acts*, forming and transforming our forms of life. This vision of conversation underscores the interplay between the creative openness that in ordinary language distinguishes conversation from discussion or debate, and the normative conventions that underwrite our capacities to communicate at all.

I refer to this vision as the 'conversational outlook', a phrase that adapts Cavell's description of moral perfectionism as an 'outlook or dimension of thought embodied and developed' by a range of texts. As I explain in more detail below, this description of perfectionism – a central theme in Cavell's work, in which conversation plays a major part – has helped me understand the figurative career of conversation. Although I distinguish conversation from 'discussion', 'debate' and more restricted modes of communication, I do not seek to define or theorise conversation. A key element of my approach is the understanding that invocations of conversation do not coalesce into a singular idea that might be encapsulated in a theory or definition, but this does not mean that the figurative range of conversation is arbitrary. It is, to borrow from Wittgenstein, an ideal with 'blurred edges', its uses 'not everywhere circumscribed by rules', yet sharing 'family resemblances' that my readings strive to make intelligible (*PI*, §71, §68, §67). As Wittgenstein writes, an ordinary language philosopher begins by describing rather than theorising; when we find we 'don't know [our] way about', describing the ways in which we use language can help us gain a 'clear view' of the grounds on which we stand (*PI*, §123, §122). This practice can release us from a 'picture' that has 'held us captive' by bringing to light what we already know or believe – the 'agreement not only in definitions but also (queer as this may sound) in judgments', which underlies our mutual understanding (*PI*, §115, §242).²⁴ Philosophy, he claims, 'cannot give [. . .] foundation' to language: 'it can in the end only describe it' (*PI*, §124).

As any reader of Wittgenstein or Cavell knows, careful description can be extremely generative, clearing muddled thoughts and revolutionising our outlooks.²⁵ Disclosing what we understand of the world exercises and potentially expands our capacity for mutual attunement. In this sense, the practice of ordinary language philosophy, and of literary criticism undertaken in its spirit, enacts the curiously descriptive yet creative power I argue the writers in this book implicitly ascribe to conversation. My readings, then, enact the 'conversational outlook' not only by staging conversations between works of literature and philosophy, but by modelling how this work transforms the common objects of study, just as the conversational outlook implies that talking with others transforms, and generates, our common world. Thus, as this book's readings 'describe' conversation as a response to scepticism, they also create a new vision of conversation: the outlook is not 'buried' in the texts, but rather coalesces when the texts are read in relation to one another.

In the rest of this introduction, I elaborate on this reading practice and sketch the gist of the conversational outlook, focusing on its expression in the work of Cavell and Arendt, with whom my literary readings are most persistently in conversation. While Cavell's work gives strongest expression to the 'conversational outlook', Arendt – and the readings undertaken in dialogue with her work – clarifies its political implications. After establishing the resonances between their treatments of conversation and scepticism below, I briefly outline the chapters. By way of concluding – and of opening into the rest of the book – I return to the idea of conversational reading, expanding on the ethical and political implications of such literary criticism. Here and throughout this book, my ambition is to show that literature, read in conversation with philosophy, can help us address one of the most pressing 'real needs' facing us outside of literary studies. In other words, the book makes a new case for how and why we might use literature in this way, while retaining a sense of the distinctiveness of the voice of literature.

## Conversational Criticism

The word 'after' appears in the subtitles of two recent works that, like this book, link literary studies to ordinary language philosophy. 'After' expresses both temporality and influence, an affirmed family resemblance. For Toril Moi, whose book *Revolution of the Ordinary* bears the subtitle *Literary Studies After Wittgenstein, Austin, and Cavell*, literary studies should transform after encountering ordinary language philosophy, because the latter should put to rest – or release us from the captivating pictures of – fruitless metaphysical debates about the nature of language or textual objects. The long shadow of poststructuralism and deconstruction lingers, and it interferes with the work we do best, Moi argues, which is simply reading. Cavell's work informs Moi's project both for its contributions to dispelling a haze of textual metaphysics, and for its provision of a model of reading that sidesteps debates about the surfaces and depths of texts, their presence to us or their endless deferral of meaning, author intentionality, and so forth. Moi proposes we leave behind such questions and undertake reading as a practice of acknowledgement, responding to our texts as Cavell describes good conversationalists responding to one another. In short, for Moi, literary studies 'after' ordinary language philosophy becomes 'a conversation between the work and the reader'.[26] I wholeheartedly agree, and unpacking this idea is one of my aims in this introduction and throughout the book. For Karen Zumhagen-Yekplé in *A Different Order of Difficulty: Literature after Wittgenstein*, the task at hand is to discern powerful correspondences between canonical modernist literary works and Wittgenstein's *Tractatus Logico-Philosophicus*, itself arguably understood best when approached as a modernist literary work. Reading Woolf after Wittgenstein (or rather, after one of his influential interpreters, Cora Diamond), for instance, Zumhagen-Yekplé provides a new account of the philosophical dimensions of Woolf's portrait of 'the difficulty of reality'. Like Zumhagen-Yekplé, I reinterpret canonical novels by tracing their shared concerns with ordinary language and other philosophers writing before, contemporaneously with, and after the novelists. Like Moi, I find in Cavell's understanding of conversation a powerful model for my own readings, but one that stands to benefit from clarification.

Before turning to the details of Cavell's conversational criticism, I want to briefly address the ways in which this book inherits and resembles, without quite reproducing, the orientations of other studies of conversation in British fiction. Most scholarship on conversation in fiction, especially in British fiction, focuses on the historical and narratological functions of represented speech. Jon Mee's *Conversable Worlds*, for instance, tracks the rich correspondences between eighteenth- and nineteenth-century texts and a broader culture of conversation in early modern and Romantic era Britain, the culture of clubs, bookshop sociability and conversationally toned periodicals that Habermas would argue planted seeds for the political public sphere of liberal Britain. Amanda Anderson's *Bleak Liberalism* shows how representations of character dialogue in exemplary novels reflects ambivalence about the norms of liberal discourse in the nineteenth and twentieth centuries. In two recent works, *Someone: the Pragmatics of Misfit Sexualities* and *What Proust Heard: Novels and the Ethnography of Talk*, Michael Lucey demonstrates the resources that the fields of linguistic anthropology, pragmatics and sociological 'conversation analysis' provide for literary studies, using social science to reveal new dimensions of critique and language analysis in scenes of talk in French novels, with wider implications for literary historians in general.[27] Elizabeth Alsop's *Making Conversation in Modernist Fiction* offers a formalist analysis of speech in fiction, arguing that the 'very *structures* of talk' in works of modernist fiction 'bear meaning' and suggest 'ideas in excess of their semantic content'.[28] We can link Alsop's study – as she in fact does – to Mikhail Bakhtin's canonical work characterising the novel as a literary genre itself structured by talk. Bakhtin's account of the 'heteroglossic', 'polyphonous', 'internally dialogized' form of the novel is itself an exemplary expression of what I call the conversational outlook: according to Bakhtin, a novel's world emerges through the 'interanimation' of voices and perspectives, just as this book describes an outlook according to which our common world takes shape through the incessant talk of people occupying different standpoints.[29] A novel, Bakhtin claims, is constituted through the circulation of many voices and points of view that never resolve into a final, fixed voice or perspective on reality, and as we'll see, this account of the poetics of the novel matches the alleged poetics of common ground in conversation.

Scholarship on conversation and fiction is above all historicist. Even Bakhtin's cosmopolitan formalism, after all, casts the European novel as a quintessentially modern genre whose poetics match the heteroglossic world made by global exchanges of people and goods. The present book partially shares the implied view that it's no coincidence the modern novel's development in Anglophone and European literature runs parallel to the development of the modern, liberal state, and that this parallel informs the representations of talk in British fiction (I'll argue that several of the novels I study also allude to this literary-historical view, with compelling ambivalence). Scholars have advanced various causal narratives relating these coinciding *bildungs*, and this is perhaps especially the case in studies of British literature and culture, where since Ian Watt's *The Rise of the Novel* it has been argued that the modern novel has either reflected or directly promoted the development of liberalism.[30] The novel, it is held, has naturalised (and thus occluded the historical specificity of) a new vision of the private, individual subject.[31] As Nancy Armstrong puts it, rather strongly, 'the history of the novel and the history of the modern subject are, quite literally, one and the same'.[32] The numerous versions of this narrative have been challenged in many ways, of course, which we can distil into one central contention: there is no singular history of 'the novel', because there is no singular object we should call 'the novel'.[33] Stories about the 'rise of the novel' can seem like 'just so' stories, post hoc descriptions that imply inevitability and trajectory where the record is in fact far messier and more contingent. They also risk reproducing an imperial vision in which European (or British) culture is the standard of modern culture as such.[34]

We can rephrase this challenge to 'rise of the novel' discourse in terms from ordinary language philosophy: narratives about 'the novel' evince a 'craving for generality' apt to lead us astray.[35] The same might be said of Bakhtin's declarations about 'novelistic discourse'. I share this wariness towards generalisation, and historicising 'the British novel' – if there is such a thing – is not my central ambition. Nonetheless, one of my aims in what follows is to show that the novels I have assembled link sceptical doubts to specific, historically contingent circumstances. Readers will notice that the expressions of scepticism in the novels I focus on are themselves reflections of familiar touchpoints in the historical trajectory of liberal culture in Britain: the novels render class division, patriarchy, interwar scepticism about society writ large, postcolonial racism and digital new media in terms that resonate with philosophical scepticism, linking these sources of social division to doubts about shared perception. To study conversation as a trope through which these novels work out the ethical and political stakes of scepticism is thus, simultaneously, to study how select canonical works of fiction respond to the shifting culture and politics of Britain over a period in which liberal democracy ascended, imperfectly, and arguably fell apart. My focus is not, however, on this parallel, which would hardly be news. Woolf, for instance, is famously sceptical of language and claims of inclusive community, political or otherwise, and any reader of the novel studied in Chapter 4, Rushdie's *The Satanic Verses*, is bound to discern its criticisms of the policing of 'common sense' and political discourse in Thatcher-era Britain. So, although my readings supplement familiar narratives about correspondences between British fiction and the development and contestation of liberalism, and underscore a connection between these correspondences and philosophical scepticism, this book provides something other than a new history of British fiction. It tries, rather, to reorient what we do with fiction. I do not claim that the novels I have brought together represent stages of 'the British novel' but rather that they offer exemplary investigations of how language use shapes and is shaped by our common world, and that reading them in a 'conversational' manner inspired by ordinary language philosophy allows us to draw insights that extend beyond the specific cases studied, to shine light on any efforts to make a shared world in the shadow of grave doubts. When I call their investigations exemplary, I mean that the novels' explorations of language use and scepticism add valuable dimensions to the outlook on conversation this book develops. Further, these specific novels contain moments of self-consciousness about their links to literary tradition and history, moments I'll draw on as part of my ongoing consideration of the pertinence of imaginative fiction to interdisciplinary ethical and political enquiry.

A reader might understandably ask why the novels I've chosen for this book are all *British*, if neither Britishness nor 'the British novel' is my central interest. Here I offer two responses. The first is to note a parallel between British fiction and the Hollywood films to which

Cavell repeatedly returned. For Cavell, the films he calls 'comedies of remarriage' express American self-understanding as the birthplace of a new kind of democracy enabling – even urging – individual 'pursuits of happiness'. Analogous claims have been made of novels and national narratives of 'Britishness', linking the genre of the novel to Britain's self-understanding as the birthplace of liberalism in markets and politics. Indeed, as I have mentioned, the novels gathered in this book are responsive to the shifting politics of Britain, as well as to this literary-historical account of British fiction. I do not stress this parallel between my project and Cavell's, however. One reason is that his work on film is invested in exploring an idea of 'America', in addition to the ideas about conversational responsiveness I draw upon from that work, and this book is not equivalently interested in the idea of 'Britain'. My second explanation for this book's Britishness is riskier, more frank, and potentially more provocative in implication: I have simply turned to the body of literature I know best, as a teacher and scholar of British literature. As should become increasingly clear as this book proceeds, in a 'conversational' project whose main object of study is extra-literary, there is no pre-existing or abstract set of criteria by which to select primary texts. The Britishness of my examples serves more as an enabling constraint, like language, than a motivating interest. The test of my examples is their usefulness, the degree to which the chapters themselves prove compelling. Like conversation in the outlook it describes, this book is the outcome of a mixture of contingency, improvisation and convention.

As I have said, my readings draw formal inspiration from Cavell's literary-philosophical criticism, while seeking to clarify and extend such work. Conversation is both a fundamental subject and something like a method for Cavell (I'll return to my hesitation about calling it a method, outright, later in this introduction). Throughout his career, Cavell repeatedly draws on plays by Shakespeare, Beckett and Ibsen, Romantic poetry, Hollywood films, and a wide range of other works of art, treating them not as objects or illustrations of philosophy, but as contributors to a collective enquiry into the 'life form of talkers'.[36] As Michael Fischer observes in the first book to explicitly connect Cavell to academic literary criticism, '[i]n Cavell's work, literature is always bringing to mind philosophy, and philosophy is always opening itself to literature, generating a dialogue that transforms each one'.[37] This captures part of my meaning when I describe my readings, and Cavell's, as conversational: the encounters between works of literature and philosophy transform each. Neither serves as a key to unlock or expose the hidden depths of the other. But the shape and ambition of this 'dialogue', for Cavell as for me, deserve further attention. A good place to begin looking is in Cavell's account of moral perfectionism, the source of my language for describing this book's task as elucidating a conversational outlook.

Cavell calls his work on perfectionism a 'project of reading and thematization', in which he traces how the features or insights of diverse texts contribute to a perfectionist 'outlook'.[38] Outlook, here, serves as an alternative to 'definition' or 'theory':

> A definition of what I mean by perfectionism, Emersonian or otherwise, is not in view in what follows. Not only have I no complete list of necessary and sufficient conditions for using the term, but I have no theory in which a definition of perfectionism would play a useful role. I emphasize accordingly [. . .] an open-ended thematics, let me call it, of perfectionism [. . .] This project, in its possible continuations, itself expresses the interest I have in the idea. That there is no closed list of features that constitute perfectionism follows from conceiving of perfectionism as an outlook or dimension of thought embodied and developed in a set of texts spanning the range of Western culture, a conception that is odd in linking texts that may otherwise not be thought of together and open in two directions: as to whether a text belongs in the set and what feature or features in the text constitute its belonging. (*CHU*, 4)

We will return to the particulars of Cavell's perfectionism in Chapter 1, where I show that Austen's *Persuasion* provokes especially critical 'continuations' of the perfectionist outlook. For now, I'll summarise Cavell's perfectionism as an understanding of moral development as prompted by conversation with an exemplary other, who might be a friend, a stranger, a lover, a teacher, and so on. This conversation prompts us to reassess our lives and our place in the world, as we discover through our encounter with the other that we are 'enchained, fixated', but also that we can 'turn (convert, revolutionize [our]self)' (*CHU*, 6–7). The imagery here recalls Wittgenstein's 'rotation' on our real need, and, indeed, Cavell shows that Wittgenstein's *Investigations* is a text full of perfectionist scenes of education, as I'll revisit at the end of Chapter 2.[39] The opening moment of perfectionist self-discovery is not a radical uprooting, but rather the start of a 'revolutionary' transformation, turning or revolving away from one set of preoccupations and ways of living, and in the process becoming a 'further' version of oneself. There is no end to this perfectionist process; there is always a further self to discover and become through new conversations, or new stages of ongoing conversations.[40]

The passage above encapsulates Cavell's sense, with Wittgenstein, that we ought to consider specific examples, looking carefully and describing our outlook – our foundation of shared, ordinary language, for Wittgenstein, or a shared understanding of moral development, for perfectionism – before we develop a generalising account of whatever commonalities might unite the particulars. In this explanation of his reading practice, Cavell also immediately invites his reader into conversation. Not only are we tacitly invited to participate in further 'continuations' of his thematisation of perfectionism – enlisting additional texts or amending the open list of features associated with the perfectionist outlook – we also might pause to wonder, in what kind of intellectual project would a definition of perfectionism play a 'useful role'? Perhaps one that aims to categorise texts as either perfectionist or not perfectionist, or as falling on a perfectionist spectrum: a matter of matching texts with categories. Perhaps an effort of theorisation that presupposes that the purpose of reading is to discover rules to live by, or categories to know by.

Cavell's aim is not to theorise or categorise, but to explore, to think with a set of texts he finds congenial. His work on perfectionism draws together 'voices' and 'sometimes only a fragment' of many different texts that he claims have been 'left out (forgotten?) in characteristic philosophical discussions about how we might live, voices that will enter other conversations, more urgent ones to my mind, about how we do live' (*CHU*, 5–6). As Wittgenstein describes the ordinary language philosopher's task, Cavell 'assembl[es] reminders for a particular purpose', in this case, for the purpose of thinking about how we live, and how conversations with others sometimes inspire us to transform our lives (*PI*, §127). Elucidating an 'outlook' rather than delineating a theory or definition authorises him to gather 'reminders' without the restraints of historical periodisation, generic specificity or ideological affiliation. Attending to the 'voices' well, of course, means keeping such specificities in mind, and Cavell historicises the perfectionism and responses to scepticism he finds in Shakespeare, the Romantics, and so on.[41] Yet he is guided primarily not by historical criteria but by his own judgement, his perception of a project and set of insights shared by authors he admires, ranging from Plato through Jane Austen and Ralph Waldo Emerson, Shakespeare through Friedrich Nietzsche, Henrik Ibsen, the Hollywood remarriage comedies, and a related, bleaker genre he calls 'melodramas of the unknown woman'.

In effect, Cavell suggests that moral perfectionism is rather like a topic of conversation, or more precisely, a topic that takes shape through conversation. 'Suppose that there is an outlook intuitively sketched out (sometimes negatively) in some imaginary interplay among the following texts', he writes, in the key of exploration and invitation. A lengthy parenthetical note follows: '(I ask almost nothing from the idea of this interplay. It is not meant to do more than momentarily activate the fantasy, perhaps it vanishes early, that there is a place in the mind where the good books are in conversation, among themselves and with other sources of thought and pleasure)' (*CHU*, 4). In this parenthesis, we have an illuminating, albeit indirect, synopsis of Cavell's style of reading, which is also my style of reading. The clause 'other sources of thought and pleasure' suggests how the critic's own interests play a role in interpretation. The momentary fantasy implies that critical insights emerge through a 'conversation' among texts that becomes audible to the critic because of the critic's habits of interest and attention.

The fantasy I've just cited encapsulates, to my mind, Cavell's larger project: across his career, his writing gives public expression to conversations he learns to hear in his mind, conversations that prove to be interlinked and whose continuations he remains acutely attuned for, as he continues to read philosophy, literature and film. This fantasy is subtly different from the conservative 'great conversation' idea expounded by figures like Michael Oakeshott, for whom 'western civilization' is an ongoing conversation – a fantasy recovered in a more progressive register by Richard Rorty's aspiration to write philosophy that 'continu[es] the conversation of the West'. Cavell suggests the 'conversation' does not simply exist in the idealised public sphere of 'western civilization': it exists if and when critics render audible a specific 'conversation' within their heads. In other words, the critic does not merely overhear and translate the 'great conversation' of canonical texts; the critic *makes* a public conversation by drawing texts – which may or may not be canonical – into generative interrelation. This vision of criticism as an act of making conversation places additional ethical and political demands on the critic, as I'll discuss in greater detail at the end of this introduction.

In my view, the idea of conversation is more foundational to Cavell's thought than his major themes of marriage, perfectionism, ordinary or everyday life, and scepticism, insofar as this idea is central to his efforts to work through these other subjects of interest. As the early chapters which follow demonstrate, tracking *his* conversational outlook illuminates subtle interrelations between his ideas about moral perfectionism, marriage and scepticism, as well as democratic politics. He touches on the latter sometimes directly but mostly obliquely, and I'll argue that Arendt's writings about democratic political speech and judgement provide a manner of 'continuing' Cavell's conversations in a more explicitly political key.

## The Conversational Outlook

Here the metaphor of an 'outlook' proves to be useful for understanding the use of conversation not only in Cavell's thought, but in all the readings I bring together in this book. An outlook is a fixed spot, like a rocky ledge protruding above a canyon. To say that certain texts or people share an outlook – perfectionist or conversational or otherwise – is to say that they share a foundation, an initial bedrock. They might nonetheless turn in different directions, taking in different views. As I've alluded, imagery similar to Cavell's 'outlook' is central to Wittgenstein's description of ordinary language philosophy as a project of describing the 'foundation' on which we currently stand, the 'real need' we are to turn round. In Cavell's thematisation of perfectionism, the texts he draws together share a foundational understanding of moral development through conversation. Yet each text Cavell reads directs our gaze differently, and thereby helps us see different aspects of the vista visible from the perfectionist outlook. Plato helps us formulate ideas about pedagogy via conversation, for instance. Ibsen helps us see that sometimes a relationship must come to an end, if a person is to continue to find their further selves (this is Nora's revelation at the end of *A Doll's House*: she needs to converse with someone other than her husband). In the Hollywood remarriage films, a relationship can resume when the lovers discover that they still draw forth each other's further selves in conversation. In each of these directions, there are additional horizons that other texts might illuminate. There are innumerable additional directions in which we might turn. I'll revisit the implications of this metaphor for reading in the final section of this introduction.

The conversational outlook is similarly rooted and expansive, and the readings in the chapters that follow elaborate only several of the many aspects we might glimpse from this outlook. The conversational outlook in fact proposes that conversation's performative link to 'what's real' is a function of a similar dialectic between rooted constraints and expansive possibilities. An interchange between openness and convention or normativity is key to the function of conversation in Cavell's account of acknowledgement, which releases us from sceptical panic about unknowable 'other minds', as well as in Arendt's parallel account of conversation as a political practice haunted by the scepticism it simultaneously holds at bay. Chapters 2 and 4 develop these ideas most extensively, but I'll establish several key points of overlap here.

For both Cavell and Arendt, the 'scandal of scepticism' is not sceptical doubt itself, but rather our common responses to it. Cavell argues that Wittgenstein makes a crucial intervention, here, by showing us that 'skepticism is (not exactly true, but not exactly false either; it is the name of) a standing threat to, or temptation of, the human mind' (*CT*, 89). According to his reading, Wittgenstein does not try to 'defeat' scepticism but instead rotates our relation to doubt, a movement which Cavell's own work extends. *Of course* we cannot read each other's minds, and nothing short of a leap of faith can relieve sincere fears that our 'world' might be a dream, or the work of evil spirits. The problem arises when we catastrophise, or when we go to great lengths to deny these ordinary uncertainties. Scepticism, Cavell argues, is a scandal when it tempts us to deny responsibility for what we *can* know, or do, or say. We must 'accept' the existence of the world, he writes, which entails also accepting that its existence is beyond 'the function of knowing' (*MWM*, 324). In the case of other people, we must 'acknowledge' them, which means accepting their separate, unknowable existence and nonetheless responding to them, talking to them, despite and because of our understanding that talk will never close the gap between us (*MWM*, 324). Moreover, we must endlessly repeat these acts of acceptance and acknowledgement. According to Cavell's readings of Wittgenstein, it is telling that *Philosophical Investigations* repeatedly stages its own relapse into worry and doubt, enacting for the reader the inescapability of *both* certain kinds of uncertainty and resistance to these kinds of uncertainty.

Acknowledgement depends on accepting the contingencies and 'merely conventional' nature of language, its 'publicness' and by implication, its imperfection. Language cannot perfectly express our feelings, especially when we take the perspective on language that ordinary language philosophy urges. Language is a 'form of life', a phrase with which Wittgenstein indicates that language is not a system of 'crystalline purity', underwritten by a fixed vocabulary and set of rules, nor by metaphysical links between signified and signifier (*PI*, §108). Language exists in practice, in use, as he emphasises by characterising different uses of language as 'language-games' (for example, telling a story, giving someone directions, and so on). Many of our words and concepts are 'blurred', their various invocations sharing 'family resemblances' rather than a rigorous underlying logic. Wittgenstein's best-known example of this is the word 'game', which we use in reference to the Olympics, card games, playing with children and a range of other loosely related activities. We 'learn and teach words in certain contexts, and then [. . .] project them into further contexts', Cavell observes, underscoring our capacity to improvise and use language in the unpredictable course of daily life (*MWM*, 52). To project effectively, meaningfully, we must share a form of life with others, and Cavell describes learning a language as a process of 'initiation', in which we do not memorise dictionary definitions and grammar rules, but rather grow to share with others a 'mutual attunement' towards 'the objects and persons of our world'.[42] When we 'project' our words into further contexts, 'nothing insures that this projection will take place [successfully] (in particular, not the grasping of universals nor the grasping of books of rules), just as nothing insures that we will make, and understand, the same projections' (*MWM*, 52). Lacking hard rules to protect us from misunderstanding, Cavell supposes, we may 'begin to feel, or ought to, terrified that maybe language (and understanding, and knowledge) rests upon very shaky foundations – a thin net over an abyss' (*CR*, 178). (The threat of this sort of sceptical fear, I'll argue in Chapter 2, drives the plot of Meredith's *The Egoist*.) One of the signature moves of ordinary language philosophy is to remind us, repeatedly, that we nonetheless generally *do* understand each other, which is testament to our shared forms of life. In Cavell's gloss, forms of life are 'nothing more and nothing less' than our shared 'routes of interest and feeling, modes of response, senses of humor and of significance and of fulfillment' (*CR*, 168; *MWM*, 52).[43]

The twin moves counselled by ordinary language philosophy in response to scepticism – accepting the world, acknowledging other persons – are not light tasks. They entail a difficult 'humbling' of 'the intellect' that functions somewhat like an inoculation: a dose of sceptical humility pre-empts a fully-fledged flight from reason and the pursuit of knowledge or intimacy, and it thus prepares us for the 'responsibility of responsiveness'.[44] Acknowledgement, Cavell writes, 'goes beyond knowledge', entailing that we not only accept the other's unknown presence, but that we respond to the other and recognise the relationship is reciprocal. We must 'put ourselves in [the other's] presence [. . .] allowing ourselves to be seen' (*MWM*, 332–333). As we'll see, conversation exemplifies the work of acknowledgement. To talk entails accepting 'separateness' as the 'logic of human intimacy' and hence the 'field of serious and playful conversation or exchange' (*CT*, 221). Every conversation tests and potentially expands our shared routes of feeling, but every conversation also presupposes – is conditioned and limited by – pre-existing criteria. We must accept the 'thin net' of shared conventions in both its fragility and its constraining norms, if we are to undertake the kinds of conversations Cavell admires, which he describes in his studies of Hollywood remarriage comedies as 'forms of life' characterised by 'articulate responsiveness, expressiveness'.[45]

Arendt's political thought offers a similar account of conversation as a form of life thinly, vulnerably, warding off an 'abyss'.[46] The 'public realm', 'space of appearance', or 'common world' – three phrases she uses mostly interchangeably – is, she claims, the performative effect of speaking in public. She distinguishes this collective space from the given or earthly context of biological life, claiming that the common, public world only comes into existence when and where we gather 'in the manner of speech and action' (*HC*, 199). 'The reality of the public realm relies on the simultaneous presence of innumerable perspectives and aspects in which the common world presents itself', she writes, and our shared sense of the common world 'ris[es] out of the sum total of aspects presented by one object to a multitude of spectators' (*HC*, 57). What we understand as conversation, and not only speeches by politicians, is essential to the generation of this shared reality out of many aspects: 'incessant talk', she argues, teaches us 'that the world we have in common is usually regarded from an infinite number of different standpoints' ('Concept', 51). We learn through conversation 'to see the same in very different and frequently opposing aspects', to recognise 'that the same object [we see] also appears to others though its mode of appearance may be different' ('Concept', 51; *LMT*, 50). A conversation, like an artwork, brings us together by directing our attention towards the same object, from our separate standpoints. In the process – and only for as long as we are talking – we generate the shared world in which we talk.

This view contains scepticism within it, like the ordinary language philosophy view of language. Arendt considers our human form of life to be intertwined with speech. We have collective experience – a shared, public world – only as long as we converse, and unfortunately, we are least likely to converse when our common world is most vulnerable. She develops these ideas against the backdrop of scepticism and its 'scandal' for democratic political life, warning that beginning in the latter half of the twentieth century, new forces have increasingly threatened the common world: the rise of mass culture – where conformity rather than 'innumerable perspectives' reigns – and totalitarianism – where dogma must be repeated if a person is to survive. As we'll see in the final chapter, her descriptions imply that twenty-first-century digital technologies have radicalised these forces, and her commentary thus helps me reframe our current concerns about the common world.

We cannot predict the conversations that will shape and reshape our worlds. This unpredictability is part of the picture of language use shared by ordinary language philosophers and, in somewhat more abstract terms, Arendt. In Arendt's political thought, the non-necessity of logical rigour in public life is essential: it is not only 'reasonable' discourse that shapes the common realm, but all speech in public. This is a main point of disagreement between Arendt and liberal political philosophers like John Rawls or Jürgen Habermas, and I suspect this accounts for her resurgent popularity in an era that seems increasingly illiberal or postliberal. As I discuss at length in Chapter 4, not only does Arendt argue that political views are not susceptible to change via logical argument, but her understanding of democracy requires a commitment to 'newness' excluded by conventional liberal accounts of public discourse. Political life, especially in a democracy, will lead to unprecedented events, and newcomers will continually arrive (through birth or immigration), bringing to light new 'aspects' of 'reality'. The openness and improvisation of conversation, as opposed to rational discussion, figuratively accommodates this integral link between newness and democratic politics. Yet this same openness gives rise to a further question, which might tempt perilous scepticism anew: How do we judge events and political claims that arise in such a shifting and unpredictably open arena? We cannot have politics without judgement; the challenge, according to Arendt and the outlook developed in this book, is to integrate an open, conversational ethos with a practice that is essentially normative, but not based on shared logical or empirical commitments. Arendt's response is to turn to Kant's aesthetic judgement, which I'll argue is continuous with her earlier work on public life as conversational, and an invaluable route towards reconciling democratic conversation and political judgement today.

Arendt's turn to Kantian aesthetics is another noteworthy connection between her work and ordinary language philosophy. As Cavell and others have noted, the appeal to 'what we say' in ordinary language philosophy is similar to the appeal to universal 'communicability' in Kant's aesthetic theory. Kant's *Critique of Judgement* is, among other things, an investigation of 'what we say' when we see something beautiful, and what 'agreements in our criteria' these responses imply. It is a work founded – as Sianne Ngai has observed – on a 'turn to ordinary conversation, to the codified expressions used in our compulsive sharing of judgment'.[47] Moreover, ordinary language philosophy understands language to be flexible rather than rule-bound, its criteria endlessly changing as we speak, as if conversation proceeds like aesthetic judgement in Kant's account: 'without the mediation of a concept'.[48] Indeed, Cavell invokes Kantian aesthetics when describing the conversations of the film couples who exemplify acknowledgement, writing that they 'achieve purposefulness without purpose' (*Pursuits*, 89). In a passage of *Conditions Handsome and Unhandsome* that pronounces the couples' conversations models of perfectionist friendship, in addition to acknowledgement, he again 'adapt[s] a rhetorical discovery of Kant's', writing: 'A recurrent point of the conversation that constitutes the friendship' is 'the finding of mutual happiness without a concept' (*CHU*, 32). Here Cavell casts exemplary conversations as aesthetic achievements. In Kant's words, they exhibit 'merely formal purposiveness' or 'purposiveness without purpose', and participants in them cannot explain their pleasure by reference to external criteria such as usefulness or an abstract concept like 'beauty' (*CJ*, §15, 62). In Cavell's view, good conversation similarly generates its own criteria, discovering and 'articulat[ing] its basis' as it proceeds (*CHU*, 32).

The overlap between ethical and political uses of conversation, against the backdrop of epistemological scepticism, comprises the shared foundation I call the conversational overlook. Its bedrock, as it were, is inscribed in the word's Latin roots, *con* or *com* (with) and *vertĕre* (to turn). According to the imagery conjured by the word's etymology, we 'turn together' towards the same object or world or subject matter. It is an image of togetherness premised on separateness, reminiscent of acknowledgement. It emphasises a shared perceptual and embodied experience – turning together, rather than pursuing a definite aim, as is implied in discussion or debate.[49] In this sense, it evokes Arendt's account of the public realm, which indicates that it is through 'incessant talk' that we learn we are 'turning' towards the same world, and through this twofold conversation generate its shared, many-faceted reality. It also evokes the perfectionist emphasis on 'turning', in conversation, towards new horizons visible from one's outlook.

Etymology, of course, does not hold the key to the 'essence' of conversation.[50] That would be anathema to the picture of language use I share with ordinary language philosophy, in which there is no 'essence' of a word apart from its uses. But Cavell himself alludes repeatedly to this etymology in his work on perfectionism, both in his references to 'turning' and in his playful use of words that share the root *vertĕre*: conversion, revolution and aversion. Aversive conversation, he writes, is political critique carried on as a '*continual turning away* from society', which, because it is sparked by an aspiration for society's further possibility, is also 'thereby a continual turning *toward* it. Toward and away' (*CHU*, 59). Such conversation is crucial in democracy understood as a perfectionist, never-finished political conversation: another commonality between Cavell and Arendt.[51] I am not prepared to claim that Wittgenstein intentionally alludes to the same etymology, but his accounts of turning our examination around, and rotating on our real need, certainly evoke it. The *OED* reports that to 'converse' originally meant 'to turn oneself about, to move to and fro, pass one's life, dwell, abide, live somewhere, keep company with'.[52] In this case, etymology offers not metaphysical essence, but a 'reminder' useful for the particular purpose of helping us see an outlook shared by the texts in this book and, I believe, by many today who invoke conversation as an imperilled, essential art.

## Outline of Chapters

The book's chapters are arranged to track the ideal of conversation as it scales from interpersonal, literal conversation to scenes of interaction more metaphorically evocative of conversation. In Cavell's work, this projection from interpersonal, ethical conversation to democratic political life is explicit. In Arendt's, the link between interpersonal and political conversation lacks the mediating ethical strain, but her treatment of political talk nonetheless invokes and thereby reframes in a sharper political register many of the features Cavell ascribes to conversation. Readers will note that the chapter arrangement is also chronological, according to the publication dates of the literary works. As I have stressed, the ambitions guiding my readings are conceptual before they are historical, but this does not mean I ignore history. Indeed, I hope the chronological arrangement highlights the correspondence between shifting political and aesthetic forms, without implying a theory about the nature of the connection between historical forces and aesthetic form.

The first two chapters focus primarily on the ethical implications of the conversational outlook, but they remind us in various ways that our language – our form of life – cannot be disentangled from our political conditions. In Chapter 1, I show that reading Jane Austen's *Persuasion* (1817) alongside Cavell's work on moral perfectionism allows us to trace links between acknowledgement, perfectionism and broader issues of justice, here situated in tensions Austen subtly notes between class inequality, emergent liberal values, and the habits of mind and perception associated with reading. This encounter between Austen and Cavell raises surprising, provocative questions about the ways that literature itself attunes us to reality. As we'll see, literary attunement has world-restricting consequences in the novel, hampering its heroine's perfectionist development and excluding lower classes from the world she's able to perceive. *Persuasion*, I'll claim, thereby draws us – Austen's readers and the readers of this book – into an aversive conversation about the stakes of literary study, the ways our 'routes of interest and feeling' are shaped and reshaped in readings like those I offer in this book.

Chapter 2 further examines the limits and possibilities of ethical responsiveness in an unequal society, turning with George Meredith's *The Egoist* (1879) to the difficulty of acknowledgement within a form of life that systematically denies and distorts women's voices. *The Egoist*'s central drama turns on what J. L. Austin calls the performative or illocutionary dimension of language, and I show that its study of the implications of speech performativity in an unjust world at once affirms and complicates the treatment of linguistic scepticism by ordinary language philosophers. Performativity, the novel suggests, is a key asset and liability in conversations haunted on one end by scepticism about other minds, and on the other end by injustice that might provoke its own, more historically contingent scepticism about women's capacity for self-expression. Moreover, the novel culminates in a stunningly prescient examination of conversation that performatively strips observers of any confidence they share a reality, or form of life. Meredith, read alongside Cavell and Austin, dramatically tests the ethical and epistemological implications of the 'shaky foundations' of our mutual understanding.

The middle chapter serves as a bridge between the book's early readings of scenes of literal exchanges of speech, and the final two chapters' consideration of conversation in increasingly figurative terms, as a trope for political and digital life. It begins with a study of key passages in Virginia Woolf's *To the Lighthouse* (1927), focusing especially on the elaborate scene of dinner-table conversation depicted as an art directed by Mrs Ramsay. I then turn to *The Waves* (1931), the text I argue most vividly articulates the conversational outlook in both form and philosophy. Woolf's lyrical 'play-poem' records something like a lifelong conversation between six friends. Reading the text alongside the aesthetic and epistemological philosophy that influenced Woolf and the Bloomsbury set, I develop Woolf's implicit vision of aesthetically charged conversation as a means of relieving sceptical doubt about our external world. *The Waves*, I show, converges the ordinary and etymological senses of 'conversation' in scenes of talk in which the characters generate what one calls a 'many-sided substance', and another a 'dwelling-place', by 'turning together' towards objects of common interest. The curious style of *The Waves* formally manifests the twofold sense of conversation these scenes dramatise: it is itself a 'many-sided substance' that emerges through voices 'turning together'. In this sense, I suggest, Woolf's many-sided substance prefigures the vision of conversation that informs Hannah Arendt's political thought.

Chapter 4 develops the political implications of this vision of conversation by reading Arendt alongside Salman Rushdie's *The Satanic Verses* (1988) and theorists of 'counterpublics' comprised of people who have been forcibly excluded from the official 'space of appearance'. My reading of the novel's depiction of an 'undercity' – its word for a community of South Asian and Afro-Caribbean Londoners who rise up against police violence – corrects for infamous limitations in Arendt's treatment of racial prejudice and other forms of inequality. I also extend the work on political judgement interrupted by her death, developing a conversational framework for political life that integrates generative, unpredictable newness with the normativity of judgement, modelled after aesthetic experience. Like the ethical conversation studied in the book's first half, the public realm in this framework depends on a dynamic exchange between norms and openness. It is a 'shaky foundation' whose shakiness is not only its condition of possibility, but also one of its chief recommendations. This conversational view of public life retains indisputable elements of scepticism, which are in fact fundamental to democratic forms of life: we cannot be absolutely certain in our political judgements, because the political realm is constitutively unsettled, and disputes cannot be adjudicated with finality by referring to criteria outside themselves. Simultaneously, this conversational view allows us to make a shared world: we can speak and judge together according to procedures learned in aesthetic experience. The magical-realist form of *The Satanic Verses* moreover transforms the practice of reading into an analogue for the mode of political judgement Arendt argues is essential, if we want to comprehend (as Rushdie puts it) 'how newness enters the world'.

The book's final chapter turns with Ali Smith's *There But For The* to the digital realm. I read the novel's mysterious central premise as an allegory for the language-games, in Wittgenstein's sense, of meme circulation on social media. Before the narrative opens, a man named Miles has locked himself in a guest bedroom during a dinner party. He remains there for months and gains global celebrity, while 'fans' proclaim disparate meanings of his action, undeterred by the fact that he remains silent about his intentions. I read the various 'uses' of Miles as a memetic language-game exemplary of the forms of digital life allegedly threatening 'common conversation' today. Returning via Smith to Wittgenstein's picture of language use, and reading both in relation to the prior chapter's account of Arendt's political thought, Chapter 5 offers a new framework for understanding social media's impact on politics. This framework entails a comparison, invited by the novel, between the criteria of memetic language-games and the criteria involved in writing and reading imaginative literature: the novel resolves its memetic situation through an exchange of conversation and written stories. My reading of this closing sequence becomes a meditation on the relationship between conversation, interpreting fiction, and the modes of thinking conducive to public conversation. An afterword draws this meditation to a close, reasserting yet qualifying the analogy between the conversational readings of this book and modes of conversation, interpretation and judgement essential to sustaining a shared reality.

A reader inclined to generalise from the chronological arrangement of chapters might speculate that British fiction itself scales its interests outwards – or that I mean to imply that the preponderance of domestic dramas and courtship plots in the nineteenth century gives way to modernist scepticism, which has afterlives in the acute political scepticism of postwar, postcolonial and now digital-era Britain. Insofar as this hasty sketch of British literary and political history is accurate, it suggests that the book's examples reflect the development of the novel, which itself happens to echo the conceptual projection of the conversational outlook from interpersonal talk to increasingly abstract modes of communication. Such a conclusion runs into obstacles as soon as we recall that many nineteenth-century British novels were at least as interested in politics and the 'condition of England' as they were in courtship. There is no shortage of nineteenth-century fiction that grapples with questions surrounding public expression in scenes of argument, protest and rioting.[53] My use of Rushdie's text to unpack the affordances of 'conversation' for understanding public life reflects my judgement that it offers resources that George Eliot's *Felix Holt* or Thomas Carlyle's *Chartism*, for instance, do not: among other reasons, the hybrid, magical-realist style of *The Satanic Verses* offers formal and conceptual means of bridging 'conversation' to democratic judgement, and its attention to race in addition to class resonates with contemporary political needs. Yet I readily acknowledge that *Felix Holt*, in turn, offers resources *The Satanic Verses* does not. I also acknowledge that others may wish to draw firmer historical conclusions from the encounters between these works of literature and philosophy. These acknowledgements lead me back to the issue of what, precisely, conversational criticism entails and enables, and the responsibilities of the critic engaged in interdisciplinary work on the model described in this book.

## The Ethics and Politics of Conversational Criticism

In his introduction to *Pursuits of Happiness*, the book about Hollywood remarriage comedies, Cavell reflects on an accusation that might be made against my work as well as his, the accusation that he projects philosophical insight onto texts that do not in fact reward this kind of attention. He resists the charge. 'In my experience', he writes, 'people worried about reading in, or overinterpretation, or going too far, are, or were, typically afraid of getting started, of reading as such, as if afraid that texts – like people, like times and places – mean things and moreover mean more than you know' (35). 'Most texts', he continues, 'like most lives, are underread, not overread' (35).

This claim becomes especially compelling, and plausible, if we reconceive of reading as aspiring to something *in addition* to interpretation as it is typically conceptualised. I believe that there's truth to the argument – at times expressed by Cavell – that the meaning of a work of art is a function of intention and autonomous from its uses; intention, here, need not be a conscious idea in the head of an author, but it needs to be an expressiveness rooted in a text, something that we can claim exists by pointing to the arrangement of details in the text.[54] The meaning of a text is, to speak with Kant, signified in its inner purposiveness. Cavell's interpretations mostly complement this idea – he points out patterns, images and telling lacunae that he often considers with generosity, arguing that in fact these lacunae can deepen our sense of what the text means on its own terms. But such interpretation is not the horizon of Cavell's work: he does more than say what a text means on its own terms, autonomous from the 'interplay' or conversation he stages. He says what the text means in conversation with other texts, or rather, what the conversation itself means once the voices in it have been made audible. When he writes that he tries to allow 'a work of art [to] have a voice in what philosophy says about it' – or that he wishes to remind us of the voices of art forgotten by philosophy – he means that he wishes to let their voices enter into a conversation.[55] This implies that they speak for more than themselves, and that what they have to say reverberates with significance they cannot alone control. The meaning of one's words in conversation always partly depends on their uptake. This is not a poststructuralist 'birth of the reader' situation, nor a freewheeling interdisciplinary project that occludes the distinct kinds of expertise and objects of study associated with different disciplines. It is an account of literary-philosophy as a practice of bringing 'conversations' into an audible frequency, in which it is equally important to attend to the specific voices of each participant – to interpret them on their own terms, using our best tools to attend to their voices – and to attend to what happens when those voices or interpretations meet others. As David Rudrum has observed, Cavell's style of reading literature cannot be summarised as employing a 'method' or distinctive 'approach'. His writings evince a 'constant and ceaseless refusal [. . .] to nail his colours to a procedural, methodological, or theoretical mast', and this 'is perhaps the most refreshing, original, and worthwhile aspect of his work, since he thereby liberates himself from the confines of a particular and specific approach to his subject'.[56] I would add that this liberation allows him to offer to his texts and subjects the 'articulate responsiveness' that he finds in the best film conversations.

By this view, conversational criticism commits a literary-philosophical critic to responsibility on at least three registers. First, we are responsible for our interpretations. Second, we are responsible for – and should have some account of – our selection of which voices to invite into conversation. This selection, I claim, is worldmaking in the sense that Arendt and to a lesser extent Cavell find conversation to be worldmaking. Third, we are responsible for our rendering of that conversation, for giving public form to the 'interplay' Cavell describes as existing first in a literary-philosopher's mind.

The first responsibility can be phrased in terms that Toril Moi has recently put forward: reading, as I mentioned above, becomes a practice of acknowledgement, of responding with care and humility to the voice of the text. As I've noted, acknowledgement stands for the 'articulate responsiveness' we should offer others despite the voice of scepticism, which continually tells us how little certainty we have about their deepest feelings and thoughts. Acknowledgement also entails revealing oneself, 'put[ting] oneself in the other's presence' and disclosing something of ourselves in our responses. When Cavell supposes that 'most texts, like most lives, are underread' owing to fear of reading as such, he subtly links reading and scepticism, and thus reading, conversation and acknowledgement. Drawing on Cavell's account of acknowledgement, Moi writes that our primary responsibility is to attend carefully to the text and express our responses. In the process, as Moi claims, we cannot help but reveal something of ourselves. She writes, 'we must do justice both to the work and ourselves. Just as I try not to impose my own theories on the work, I need to acknowledge my own investments, interests, and reactions. After all, if they drive me toward this particular work, I need to account for them, too. Understood as a practice of acknowledgment, reading becomes a conversation between the work and the reader' (*Revolution*, 217).

Moi offers a compelling reason to avoid describing literary criticism (any, not just Cavell's) as employing a 'method'. She argues:

> In my view, literary criticism – by which I mean what we now call 'reading' – doesn't have anything we can plausibly call competing methods, at least not in the sense widely used in the sciences and social sciences: a set of explicit – and repeatable – strategies for how to generate new knowledge. This is why literary critics often have trouble explaining their 'method' to colleagues in other disciplines. (178)

One reason our readings are not repeatable is that our readings enact our own specific responses to texts: this is what it means to approach reading as a practice of acknowledgement. I am the one who responds to *Persuasion* the way I do in the first chapter. This does not mean that my responses are merely personal, nor that they are heroically original.

It means that I see my reading as an encounter between myself and a text, and the work of criticism as an effort to give a public description of this encounter, which invites the reader – my reader, you – to test the persuasiveness of what I describe. What might be 'repeatable' is a perception and interpretation, once delineated in words, but not the initial encounter that brought me to that perception.

I risk something personal when I say what I believe a text means, and – to cite Cavell – I invite you to 'look and find out whether you can see what I see, wish to say what I wish to say' (*MWM*, 95–96). In this way, interpretations are like the appeal to 'what we say' in ordinary language philosophy, which, as I've noted, is similar to the search for universal validity in aesthetic judgement. (The difficulty of this search is a key theme in Chapter 4.) As Cavell argues, such appeals do not refer to authority and the status quo, but rather, like aesthetic judgement, are opportunities to discover whether or not we are in community, how much of our form of life – or outlook – we share. The 'we' is tentative, an invitation. Such testing might extend or contract our sense of community by revealing and possibly altering how extensive or narrow our shared outlook is, and with whom we share it.[57] Writing in a similar vein in a 2020 *PMLA* 'Theories & Methodologies' essay cluster, Robert Chodat casts the work of literary criticism in Cavellian terms as 'testing our attunements'.[58] Interpretations, Chodat writes, are perlocutionary or 'passionate' utterances, speech acts revisited in the second chapter of this book, which reveal desire and conviction, in this case exposing what we're most responsive to in works of literature. Also drawing on Cavell's description of perlocutionary utterances, Andrew H. Miller claims he tries to write 'implicative' rather than 'conclusive' criticism, criticism that draws the reader into the project, inviting continuation by showing the critic's process of thinking with texts.[59]

The second responsibility I mentioned above concerns the political and poetic aspect of conversational criticism: we bear responsibility for our choices of voices to include in the conversations we bring into being. As we know, certain voices skew conversation; silences do, as well. This common-sense idea implicitly drives debates about literary canons, important efforts to diversify what we think of as 'great books' or to question the premise of shared curricula in the first place. There are parallels between the 'canon wars' that persist and debates between liberal theorists of public discourse and advocates of counterpublic theory and practice. Thus, while the ethical responsibilities and challenges of conversational criticism are reflected most directly in Chapters 1 and 2, the political responsibilities are reflected in the analyses of worldmaking conversation and political judgement in the latter three chapters. Just as I'll argue that a specific kind of 'reality' – the common, shared world – emerges and transforms in conversation that brings into view the 'sum total of aspects' of items of mutual interest, a specific kind of critical reality comes into existence, and transforms, through the conversational criticism that brings into relation specific voices and the 'aspects' of the world they express. Here, I should note, I've flipped the outlook metaphor, or insisted on a dual usage: in this book conversation is a shared foundation underwriting the texts' perspectives on our form of life as talkers, and it is also the central object towards which the texts I've brought together turn, from their somewhat different perspectives, thereby illuminating different aspects of the shared object. This dual or recursive use of conversation as an outlook and as the object viewed from different outlooks echoes one of the recursive aspects of conversation highlighted in this book: its power is a function of its chiastic structure, of the relay between constraint and improvisation, material conditions and expressive, worldmaking experiments.[60]

Here is another reason conversational criticism requires humility and a willingness for endless 'continuation'. Different voices enable and constrain different conversations. Not only is it impossible for any singular person to bring all the 'right' voices into conversation, but there is no static set of 'right' voices. We must exercise judgement, and we must be willing to revise our judgements as new voices emerge or come to our attention. This has political implications, as the parallel to disputes over literary canons insists, but it also has conceptual implications. I can imagine books about conversation in British fiction, or texts from other traditions, that would draw on different texts and thus yield a different account of how conversation helps us inhabit a common world. I can imagine books about the relation between fiction, talk and democratic worldmaking conceived as a global or cosmopolitan project. There are many novels, poems and plays I'd love to draw on to illuminate additional 'aspects' of conversation, different horizons visible from the bedrock of our forms of life as talkers. There are many scholars and students I'd love to witness doing the same. I am responsible for having chosen (or enlisted) these books for this conversation, and for drawing the present book to a close such that others can pick it up. I have neither illusion nor the wish to have sketched all there is to see of, and from, the conversational outlook.

The third responsibility I mentioned above is what we might call craft, which here mixes ethics, politics and poetics. Among the challenges I've grappled with while writing this book, a central one has been the challenge of writing in a style that allows the voices of literature, philosophy and my own to balance and interweave with one another, taking on appropriate accents. This third challenge blurs with the ethical and political challenges. I hope I've done justice to the aesthetic and philosophical affordances of each of the texts brought together in these pages, as well as to the many-sided substance their voices make when brought together. I hope the voices I've selected make something, together, that others find worth making. But also, I hope that this book is what Miller calls 'implicative', Chodat calls 'passionate', and Cavell represents as an invitation to conversation. In the chapters that follow, I disclose commitments that are at once aesthetic, political and ethical. I disclose what I see in the texts and what I see when their various lights are brought to bear on a common object, an interest I claim to share with them. And in doing so, I appeal at once to community – Do you see what I see? – and continuation: What else do you see? Where else might we turn, together, to broaden and clarify the reality we share?

Chapter 1

# Perfectionism and the Conversation of Justice: Austen and Cavell

It may seem inevitable that a book about the significance of conversation in British fiction opens with Jane Austen, an author who has been dubbed 'the doyenne of conversation in the English novel'.[1] Indeed, Austen set both formally and ethically rigorous standards for fictional talk, as becomes especially clear when her work is read alongside that of Stanley Cavell. In *Philosophy the Day After Tomorrow*, Cavell describes coming to Austen's fiction late in his career and discovering a core feature of the perfectionist outlook in 'the turn and texture of every scene' of her novels: the 'craving for a life lived from [. . .] the further self, glimpsed from the perspective of what they picture as life's higher moments – perfectionist moments' (*PDAT*, 122). Not only do Austen's heroines frequently exhibit perfectionist cravings, but the novels propose that conversation is the central activity through which we grow into our 'further' selves. This, too, is a core feature of the perfectionist outlook, and its point of overlap with the conversational outlook.

My interest in Austen, however, is driven less by her anticipation of Cavellian themes, than by a striking deviation from these themes in *Persuasion*, the novel that otherwise appears to be the closest precursor to the films Cavell calls the Hollywood 'comedies of remarriage'. As he writes of the remarriage films, *Persuasion*'s 'drive [. . .] is not to get the central pair together, but to get them *back* together, together *again*', eight years after Anne Elliot broke off her engagement with Frederick Wentworth (*Pursuits*, 2). This narrative trajectory allows *Persuasion* to map its specific vision of the foundations of good marriage, marriage that exemplifies compatibility and (again citing Cavell's account of the films) 'the reciprocity or equality of consciousness between a woman and a man' (*Pursuits*, 17). The novel culminates in a mature recommitment, just as the remarriage films frequently feature an older pair, seasoned and independent before deciding it is worthwhile to recommit. Finally, to get back together, *Persuasion*'s couple must overcome internal rather than external obstacles, such as the objections of others, a process Cavell aligns with the perfectionist 'transfiguration of their way of life' (*Cities*, 421).

Yet there is a glaring difference between *Persuasion* and the remarriage films, which is also a glaring difference between *Persuasion* and Austen's other work, and key to the novel's contributions to what I call the conversational outlook. In *Persuasion*, Anne and Wentworth hardly converse directly with one another. The conversations that bring them back together do not constitute the 'form of life' characterised by 'articulate responsiveness, expressiveness' that Cavell argues ratifies marriage in the remarriage genre, and which seems to ratify marriage in Austen's other novels. Instead, Anne and Wentworth relate to one another as *readers*, observing and interpreting each other in conversation with other people.[2] The novel presents a clear remarriage story, and it links conversation to a moral vision encapsulated in Cavell's accounts of acknowledgement and perfectionism, yet the peculiarity of its representation of conversation offers what Cavell might call a 'continuation' of the idea of perfectionism. It invites us to scrutinise something implicit in both Cavell and Austen: the simultaneous correspondences and conflicts between perfectionist conversation and reading.

I make several interrelated arguments in what follows, seeking to extend our understandings of both Austen and the implications of Cavell's moral perfectionism. First, after outlining Cavell's accounts of moral perfectionism and remarriage comedy, I review and expand on his claim that Austen contributes to the perfectionist outlook. Second, I claim that *Persuasion* both confirms and departs from the pattern of perfectionist courtship evident in Austen's earlier novels and the Hollywood films. *Persuasion*'s departure turns on the complex relation Austen sketches between conversation and reading, which crystallises in a series of conversations that occur within the novel's second reunion plot: while she and Wentworth reconnect in Bath, Anne also reconnects with a woman she knew years earlier, Mrs Smith, who is now a destitute widow. I show that Anne's responsiveness to her friend is limited by moral preoccupations she brings to both conversation and reading literature, which cause her to repress aspects of what her impoverished friend says to her. Reading a key exchange between Anne and Mrs Smith as a partially failed perfectionist conversation, I claim, illuminates a new political dimension in Austen's final novel, which in turn helps reframe Cavell's account of the 'conversation of justice', a key phrase in his perfectionist amendment to political liberalism as advocated by John Rawls. Through Anne's responses to Mrs Smith, I argue, Austen subtly registers the limits of values shared by literary culture and the burgeoning liberal culture of Britain. In other words, Austen anticipates historicist literary critics who link the rise of the novel genre to the rise of liberalism, while signalling that the parallels between literary and liberal culture may interfere with something like the 'conversation of justice' by interfering with an individual's responsiveness to others across class lines. This reading builds on the work of Austen scholars who have noted Austen's explicit and implicit evocations of reading as a metaphor for social interactions and love. Drawing attention to the role of reading in the novel's scene of failed perfectionist conversation, I show that *Persuasion* initiates an aversive critique not only of patriarchal Regency society, but also of itself, its complicity as a work of literature in class-based cultural and political exclusion. Revisiting, in dialogue with Cavell, the most ambiguous conversation in *Persuasion* – which is perhaps the most ambiguous conversation in any of Austen's novels – enables a new understanding of the moral and political implications of both *Persuasion* and Cavellian perfectionism, which converge in the ideal of conversation.

### *The Conversation Required to Assess my Life:* Perfectionist Conversation and Acknowledgement in Cavell's Work

As we saw in the introduction, Cavell explicitly avoids defining moral perfectionism. Instead, he undertakes a 'project of reading and thematization', staging in his books a comparative and creative conversation of sorts, drawing together texts 'spanning the range of Western culture' (*CHU*, 4). Each of his readings 'thematizes' the way in which a given text 'contributes to the concept of perfectionism, or confirms, or modifies [it]' (6). In the introduction to *Conditions Handsome and Unhandsome*, he offers a 'list of features of Plato's *Republic*' that could serve 'as candidates for constructing a thematics of perfectionism' (xxx). He does not, in the end, 'construct' anything very systematic. The 'candidate features' he draws from Plato nonetheless offer a good introduction to his understanding of perfectionism: so good, in fact, that he repeats this list as the final chapter of *Cities of Words*. Here is the opening set of 'candidate features' proposed by the *Republic*:

> its ideas of (1) a mode of conversation, (2) between (older and younger) friends, (3) one of whom is intellectually authoritative because (4) his life is somehow exemplary or representative of a life the other(s) are attracted to, and (5) in the attraction of which the self recognizes itself as enchained, fixated, and (6) feels itself removed from reality, whereupon

(7) the self finds that it can turn (convert, revolutionize itself) and (8) a process of education is undertaken, in part through (9) a discussion of education, in which (10) each self is drawn on a journey of ascent to (11) a further state of that self, where (12) the higher is determined not by natural talent but by seeking to know what you are made of and cultivating the thing you are meant to do; it is a transformation of the self which finds expression in (13) the imagination of a transformation of society [. . .]. (6–7)

This list establishes several features that recur across the perfectionist texts Cavell studies: conversation with others enables us to access and grow into our 'further' selves; the further self is not defined as superior by an abstract moral rubric, but, rather, we recognise it as the self we are meant to be; the transformation of the self through conversation is a transformation in vision, in what we perceive of ourselves and our society from our given outlook or position. Cavell plays with the shared etymology of conversion and conversation to capture this aspect of perfectionist transformation: we 'turn' in place, away from our previously fixed point of view, transforming how we perceive ourselves, others and the society in which we live. The conceit of a shared outlook characterises differences between various perfectionist texts as different facets or vistas made visible when we, like the perfectionist conversationalist, 'turn' and look in a new direction.

An important implication of perfectionism is that we are always incomplete, 'partial [. . .] the self is always attained, as well as *to be* attained' (*CHU*, 12). From the standpoint of perfectionism, '"having" "a" self is a process of moving to, and from, nexts' (12). It involves 'my siding with the next or further self, which means siding against my attained perfection (or conformity), sidings which require the recognition of an other – the acknowledgment of a relationship' (31). In the *Republic*, perfectionist development involves a clear hierarchy, and Cavell's account of conversation between oneself and another who exemplifies one's possibilities suggests that hierarchy is integral to perfectionism. But Cavell also stresses that perfectionist education is mutual and dialogic, especially in the remarriage comedies. 'We are educations for one another', he writes (31).³ Moreover, in some of the texts Cavell studies, the person with whom we converse is not straightforwardly attractive: a stranger in whom we recognise our own 'rejected self' can draw us into perfectionist, educative conversation (*Cities*, 174). Conversation teaches us who we want to be when others speak to us in a way that expresses their 'conviction' in our 'moral intelligibility', which 'draws [us] to discover it, to find words and deeds in which to express it' (*CHU*, xxxii). These encounters can feel like a 'crisis', which disrupts us and 'forces an examination of one's life that calls for a transformation or reorienting of it' (*Cities*, 11).

The centrality of conversation to this picture of perfectionism points to one of the key differences between Cavell's understanding of moral perfectionism and the more familiar Christian or otherwise idealistic uses of the term. The latter uphold a model of the perfected self: Christ, for instance, or the ideal citizen in political perfectionisms.[4] Cavell notes that he 'want[s] no part of' the 'metaphysical suggestions' the term might seem to bear, but he defends using the freighted term nonetheless because he finds it important to 'struggle against false or debased perfectionisms' (*CHU*, 13). Perfectionism is debased whenever its representative tells you explicitly how you can live up to your potential (Cavell cites the examples of recruitment ads for the US army and stock trading). According to Cavell's preferred iterations of perfectionism, we transform into better versions of ourselves not by striving to emulate another, nor with the help of a government or corporation that seeks to promote a specific vision of ethics or flourishing, but through striving to meet exemplary others in conversations worthy of them, and worthy of our further selves. There is no model towards which we strive – even the exemplary other is not necessarily a model for anything other than a mode of attunement that elicits the self we wish to be. We discover, through interaction, the further versions of our selves we wish to be, and the transformations or reorientations required to become these versions. The 'false or debased perfectionisms' are dangerous because they lead to moralism or conformity, static judgements or unthinking impositions of norms.[5] The warning against moralism and conformity is strongest in Cavell's readings of Emerson, in which he argues that moralism 'fixates on the presence of ideals in one's culture and promotes them', potentially 'distract[ing] one from the presence of otherwise intolerable injustice' (*CHU*, 13). Moralism, in other words, can be complicit in the perpetuation of injustice. We will find this insight again, or earlier, in *Persuasion*'s gentle satirising of Anne's moralistic literary habits.

Conversation is additionally crucial to the contrast Cavell draws between perfectionism and what he calls 'more academically established dispensations of morality' (*Cities*, 49). He stresses that perfectionism is not an alternative theory of moral judgement, competing with teleological (utilitarian) or deontological (Kantian, Hegelian) moral theories. It does not strive to define what is 'good' or 'right', but rather emphasises a different facet of moral life, 'the worth of a way of life, of my way of life, which has come to a crossroads demanding self-questioning, a pause or crisis' (49). The worth, moreover, is measured by nothing other than conversation: 'The conversation decides', Cavell writes, and 'the state of the relationship' between conversationalists – whether lovers, students and teachers, friends, and so on – 'is itself the measure of the good' (*Cities*, 363). A good relationship is one in which conversation urges each partner onward. In Kantian moral philosophy, the categorical imperative functions as a method for deducing immutable moral law, and utilitarianism proposes a method for calculating practical moral consequences (we might call this the pragmatic or usefulness imperative). Perfectionism, as Cavell describes it, proposes only conversation: 'the conversation required to assess my life', he writes, 'play[s] the role in perfectionism that calculation plays in Utilitarianism or derivation from the moral law plays in Kantianism' (*Cities*, 49).

The comparison between moral perfectionism and other moral philosophy emphasises the continuity between perfectionism and Cavell's other primary ethical theme, acknowledgement. As I discussed in the introduction (and will return to in the next chapter), acknowledgement is Cavell's term for a mode of responding to others in which we accept the incompleteness of intimacy, resisting the allure of melodramatic efforts to overcome the distance between self and other, on the one hand, and the temptation of absolute scepticism and withdrawal, on the other. Conversation is central to both perfectionism and acknowledgement. It is a practice through which, as Cavell writes, 'I must reveal myself' (*Cities*, 49). In the context of his discussions of perfectionism, revealing the self is a matter of discovering and disclosing the further self through conversation. In his discussions of acknowledgement, it means 'allowing ourselves to be seen': 'There is no acknowledgment', he writes, 'unless we put ourselves in [the other's] presence, reveal ourselves to them' (*MWM*, 332–333).

It is largely due to their emphasis on conversation that Cavell devotes so much attention to the films he calls comedies of remarriage. He argues that these films recover the ethical weight of conversation implied in John Milton's *Doctrine and Discipline of Divorce*, which argues that 'in God's intention a meet and happy conversation is the chiefest and noblest end of marriage', and that any legal bond lacking happy conversation is, in God's view, 'no marriage' and should therefore be dissolved.[6] With Milton, the films invite us to understand conversation as a 'form of life' characterised by 'articulate responsiveness, expressiveness' (*Pursuits*, 87). Recall that Cavell describes 'form of life' as encompassing 'routes of interest and feeling, modes of response, senses of humor and of significance and of fulfillment', 'mutual attunement or agreement in our criteria' (*MWM*, 52; *CR*, 168). A conversational form of life, then, is one in which the speakers share not only routes of interest, feeling and criteria – a language in broad terms – but agree that responsiveness is itself a crucial criterion.

As Cavell reads the films, such articulate responsiveness is worldmaking: conversational acknowledgement invents a language or form of life, a world apart from the conformity and drabness of surrounding society. The world created by acknowledgement is one that accepts human separateness and the uncertainty associated with scepticism. Acknowledgement treats separateness as 'a reasonable condition for a ceremony of union', rather than a barrier to overcome (*CT*, 22). To acknowledge another is to see that 'separateness' is simply 'the logic of human intimacy' (*CT*, 221). Accepting this 'logic' allows us to enter 'the field of serious and playful conversation', in which our task is not to 'know' the other, but rather, to articulately respond to them (*CT*, 221).

Although Cavell does not initially read the remarriage films as perfectionist texts, he eventually recognises them as indicating that perfectionism entails a specific mode of acknowledgement. As he comments, the 'conversation resumes' in the remarriage comedies 'when the man shows himself anew [. . .] to be the one with whom for her the intelligible world is opened, her further self sought and acknowledged' (*CHU*, 117). By emphasising recommitment, the remarriage comedies formally enact the ongoing-ness of perfectionism, the way in which it represents moral life as self-questioning and ceaseless movement from one attained self to the next. As Cavell reads them, the films suggest that the best marriages – and more generally, the best relationships – are those in which the partners remain 'educations for one another', day after day, prompting each other to turn in endlessly new directions. The 'articulate responsiveness' of acknowledgement becomes a matter of discovering the voice of one's 'further self' and speaking to the other's further self. In his earlier formulations, Cavell describes acknowledgement as requiring humility akin to the 'humbling of the intellect' required to 'accept' the existence of the world, despite the sceptic's demonstration that we cannot be certain about the evidence of our senses. His work on perfectionism suggest that perfectionist acknowledgement requires the additional humility of recognising that our own selves are always partial, always capable of further development through ongoing conversation with others. Others remain at once separate and integral to our further selves. A perfectionist conversation entails acknowledgement of each other's separateness, combined in a not quite paradoxical way with the recognition that our further selves are interdependent.

A second source of Cavell's interest in the genre of remarriage – as it is developed in Hollywood films and as it is anticipated in literary 'precursors' or 'relatives' of the films, from works by Shakespeare through Austen and George Eliot – is his sense that marriage bears a heavy symbolic burden in Western culture. Marriage is 'the name of our only present alternative to the desert-sea of skepticism', he claims, and 'the splitting or pairing contracted in marriage' stands for intimacy as such in a cultural landscape that denies institutional and imaginative support for alternative forms of intimacy (*IQO*, 65, 64). In much Western literature and film, he argues, marriage functions as 'an image of the ordinary in human existence', which is 'under attack in philosophy's tendency to skepticism' (*Cities*, 422). Yet because marriage is our culture's 'only present alternative to the desert sea of skepticism', it 'cannot be celebrated, or sanctified; there is no outside to it' (*IQO*, 65). If marriage is essentially compulsory, there is no reason to have faith that it can bear the burden of reassuring us we are not isolated or deceived in our experiences of the world, and that others are at once separate and present, demanding our responsiveness.

The remarriage trope offers a partial 'outside' to marriage, just as Milton's 'defence of divorce' doubles as a visionary 'defence of marriage': we can only affirm marriage, Milton and the films imply, by establishing the possibility of choosing a life 'outside' the institution (*Pursuits*, 87). The 'comedies of remarriage', Cavell claims, propose that 'nothing legitimizes or ratifies marriage – not state, or church, or sex, or gender, or children – apart from the willingness for reaffirmation, which is to say, remarriage' (*PDAT*, 121). Marriage must be affirmed as chosen, again and again, rather than lapsing into a dull default. In an echo of Kierkegaard and others, Cavell suggests that one important lesson of the remarriage genre is that conscientious repetition is the ethical foundation of marriage. Here, too, conversation encapsulates the underlying ideal: 'What makes marriage worth reaffirming is a diurnal devotedness that involves friendship, play, surprise, and mutual education, all manifested in the pair's mode of conversing with each other (not just in words)' (*PDAT*, 121–122).

## Cavell's Austen

In his brief discussion of Austen in *Philosophy the Day After Tomorrow*, Cavell draws attention to *Pride and Prejudice*, *Emma* and *Mansfield Park*, arguing that the first two spotlight the risk (to the further self) of intellectual isolation, and the latter darkly situates the perfectionist craving for 'life's higher moments' against the backdrop of a social order built through slavery.[7] Although he does not elaborate on his naming of Austen's novels as precursors to the remarriage films, commonalities are easy to perceive: Austen's novels express a Miltonic view of 'happy conversation' as the 'chiefest and the noblest end of marriage', their central couples typically reunite after a separation, and their (off-page) weddings are ratified, according to the logic of the novels, by their conversations' demonstrations that they share a form of life characterised by articulate responsiveness. As in the remarriage films, Austen's central couples typically share – or invent – a form of life somewhat apart from the provincial, shallow and/or obtuse forms of life surrounding them.

As Cavell observes, Austen's works express a perfectionist attunement to encounters that draw forth the further selves of participants. He spotlights a moment in *Pride and Prejudice*, for instance, after Elizabeth reads Darcy's letter disclosing the true backstory between him and George Wickham. The letter prompts her to reflect, 'Till this moment, I never knew myself.'[8] In Cavell's gloss, Elizabeth 'reinterprets her character and goes on to attribute her folly, let's say, to vanity and bias' (*PDAT*, 127). This reinterpretation encompasses more than an awakened desire for moral reform. Reviewing other key exchanges between Elizabeth and Darcy, Cavell suggests that 'what she feels as an initial onset of self-knowledge, is the reality for the first time of *being* known, being acknowledged in her difference, as if until then her existence had been denied' (127–128). Darcy's letter prompts Elizabeth to reassess their earlier interactions, including those in which he offended her by criticising her friends and family. Now, Cavell suggests, she begins to realise that however rude he is on the surface, Darcy acknowledges 'her difference' from those around her, and he also acknowledges her potential, further self. She sees, with the help of his promptings, that her 'powers for amusement and for study' are currently 'confined to the point of paralysis' (128). Without a significant change in society, she understands, she will not move onward to her next, unattained self. Cavell argues that her growing relationship with Darcy makes her realise the risk that 'her consciousness [. . .] is] unshareable', at least if she remains in the same narrow circle (128).

Cavell does not discuss Darcy's education, but it too exhibits the dynamics he associates with perfectionism and affirms conversation as essential to moral life. Early in the novel, Darcy is proud and reserved, hardly speaking to anyone. He defends his lack of 'the talent which some people possess [. . .] of conversing easily with those [they] have never seen before', as though his dour reserve is a sign of authenticity.[9] Perhaps this is true in some cases: as Elizabeth must learn, Wickham's 'happy readiness for conversation' is no sign of ethical responsiveness to others (*PP*, 97). Darcy learns, in turn, that he has been 'selfish and overbearing', too inclined to 'think meanly of all the rest of the world; to wish at least to think meanly of their sense and worth compared with my own' (460). Significantly, he tells Elizabeth that she 'taught [him] a lesson' about his 'insufficien[cy]', and that he fell in love with her because of her 'liveliness' (460). This is the same word that Elizabeth and her aunt use when reflecting that he needs 'a little more liveliness' in his conversational manners, which, 'if he marry *prudently*, his wife may teach him' (404). Darcy's use of the word suggests that he has been converted, in perfectionist terms, to a desire for a new, more responsive mode of living, more alive to the rest of the world.

Cavell's discussion of *Emma* focuses on the novel's opening rumination about Emma's risk of intellectual loneliness following her governess's marriage. We are told in the first few pages that Emma's 'father could not meet her in conversation, rational or playful'.[10] Austen's fiction is in fact populated by fathers drained of 'taste or energy for the world', Cavell notes: the novels depict a thoroughly 'patriarchal' world in which 'there are no patriarchs', a subtlety that underscores the novels' criticisms of the restrictions on women (and men) (*PDAT*, 125). As Cavell observes, in Austen's day, 'a refusal to marry is apt to mean economic and social destitution and the acceptance of a bad marriage will mean the suffocation of the expression of rationality and playfulness' (125). Marriage in Austen's world is the primary, yet far from guaranteed, opportunity for women to experience perfectionist conversation, their main provision for a life of articulate responsiveness that draws forth their further selves.[11]

Cavell's discussion of *Emma* ends there, but Emma's awakening love for Mr Knightley follows perfectionist patterns. Knightley, Emma's older family friend, has served as a kind of disciplinary mentor to Emma her entire life, but his lessons are less moralistic than perfectionist. When he chastises Emma for her cruelty towards Miss Bates, for instance, he tells her, 'I had not thought [such behaviour by you] possible' (*Emma*, 295). Emma responds, unconvincingly, that Miss Bates could not have understood the 'full meaning' of her mocking words, which Knightley quickly dismisses. The exchange can be glossed with a sentence Cavell uses when describing an exchange between the pair who remarry in *The Philadelphia Story*: 'he is not accusing her of some misdeed (as lying, stealing, treachery of some kind) but rather describing her as being unworthy of herself, of what she could be' (*Cities*, 12). In other words, Knightley addresses a different Emma than the Emma of the novel's opening pages, the self-assuredly 'handsome, clever, and rich' protagonist (*Emma*, 19). Knightley speaks, instead, to a further self within Emma, a self that is less self-involved, less motivated by private amusements and snobbery (as her match-making efforts display) and more alert to the effects of her words and acts on others. The moment reads as a perfectionist crisis for Emma, a crossroads prompting her into a new understanding of herself and a desire to be worthier of the self that Knightley perceives.

Cavell's readings hint at a further continuity between Austen's novels and the remarriage films: they offer a subtle 'rebuke' to their societies, while sketching hopes for their societies' further possibilities. According to Cavell, the remarriage films are 'in conversation with their culture, [a conversation] of the kind they depict, an aversive conversation which is yet meet and happy' (*CHU*, 124). He argues that, by emphasising their couples' separateness and the uniqueness of their forms of life, the films prompt us to recognise 'unfinished business' in our own world, the distance between 'our lives as constituted' and the lives we might wish (126). Our world – the film viewer's world – is not yet hospitable to couples like those depicted in the films, hence their creation of a distinct form of life. Austen's novels rebuke their society by similarly stressing the exceptionality and vulnerability of the conversational forms of life shared by their central couples. Not only are the couples uniquely responsive to one another, but their mutual responsiveness is contextualised by widows and desperate mothers, a dearth of deserving patriarchs, vapid chatter and passages of explicit criticism, such as Charlotte Lucas's dry observation in *Pride and Prejudice* that marriage is 'the only honourable provision for well-educated women of small fortune, and however uncertain of giving happiness, [it] must be their pleasantest preservative from want' (161–162). The novels, to draw on Cavell's description of Emerson, 'show [their] disdain for, [their] refusal to participate fully in, the shameful state of current society, or rather [. . .] participate by showing society its shame' (*CHU*, 7). 'Aversive conversation' is Cavell's phrase for such participatory critique, initiated by texts that rebuke society by representing an unattained alternative, possible only if society transforms. Cavell's account of aversive conversation again taps into the roots shared by conversation, conversion and now also aversion: aversive texts engage society in 'an unending turning away from one another, but for that exact reason a constant keeping in mind of one another, hence endlessly a turning *toward* one another' (*CHU*, 138).

Here we can begin to discern the political implications Cavell draws from his perfectionist outlook. There is no 'end' to the conversations or the transformations he associates with perfectionism, but there is nonetheless a direction, a tendency towards social critique. We will return to this facet of perfectionism near the end of the chapter, as *Persuasion* advances a further criticism of Austen's society by raising sharp yet subtle questions about the mutual attunement, or agreement in criteria, shared by novels and a liberalising Britain.

### 'The happiness of being listened to': *Persuasion*'s Readerly Conversations

*Persuasion* tells the story of a woman coming back to life, regaining her 'bloom' and ascending towards a further state of herself in part because she is acknowledged once again by the man she has loved.[12] As Cavell writes of the remarriage genre, Anne and Frederick's reunion is a matter not 'of overcoming external obstacles to their union, but one of overcoming internal obstacles' (*Cities*, 421). Both must experience an inner conversion, a 'transfiguration of their way of life' (*Cities*, 421). Anne's transformation is especially evocative of Cavell's conversational ethics insofar as she must, above all else, recover both agency and voice, assuming a new degree of responsibility for her words that allows her to more fully acknowledge others. Just as 'revealing oneself' is essential in both perfectionism and acknowledgement, Anne's development entails recognising that she has a part to play in the social world she initially regards passively, from a distance. Her blossoming is not completed until she is ready to respond, articulately, to Wentworth and her world.

The transformation Anne must undergo may be analogised to a shift from *reading* her society to *participating* in its conversations. When the novel opens, Anne is living, or lingering, in a state of loss. Now in her late twenties, she continues to regret her refusal of Wentworth eight years earlier. Her family is losing its social standing, forced by debts to lease out their home. And most pointedly to my interests, Anne is conversationally at a loss. Refusing Wentworth meant that she lost the chance for meet and happy conversation, as the narrator stresses by referring to their first courtship as the 'one short period of her life' during which Anne experienced 'the happiness of being listened to'.[13] Anne is 'nobody with either father or sister: her word had no weight' (5). She is depicted as practically silent throughout the first section of the novel, and when she speaks, she does so as a sort of handmaiden to the interests of a social world that otherwise excludes her. In scene after scene, she 'do[es] little more than listen patiently, soften every grievance, and excuse each [family member] to the other; give them all hints of the forbearance necessary' (35). She treats her conversations with her remarkably self-absorbed and peevish relatives as chances to practise 'the art of knowing our own nothingness' (31). When she speaks, her utterances are often glossed in summary rather than quoted, the free indirect style infused with her sense of her own insignificance.

Anne's silence intensifies when Wentworth first reappears in her life, visiting his sister and brother-in-law, who happen to rent Anne's family home. The two are so constrained by uncertainty, regret and bitterness that they have 'no conversation together, no intercourse but what the commonest civility required' – a painful contrast to that earlier period when 'they would have found it most difficult to cease to speak to one another' (*Persuasion*, 48). Instead of articulate responsiveness, the novel stresses, their rapport is that of detachment and interpretation, a readerly process that prepares each to trust the other and their own sentiment enough to resume conversation. Before the conversation can be resumed, we might say, each must show (and discern) a readiness to hear and respond to the other. During the first stage of their reunion, Anne sits 'listening and thinking' as Wentworth talks with others, particularly alert to his conversations with the Musgrove sisters, her flirtatious in-laws. She repeatedly finds herself with 'opportunities of making her observations', telling herself (as the free indirect style hovers at a small remove from Anne's inner narration) that 'it was not possible that when within reach of Captain Wentworth's conversation with either of the Miss Musgroves, she should not try to hear it' (63–64). She 'judge[s] from memory and experience', interpreting Wentworth's responses to the Musgroves by comparing them to his earlier responses to herself.

Although the novel does not explicitly offer the analogy of reading, here, the patterns Anne establishes in her manner of listening, observing and judging are suggestively similar to her references to reading in two conversations I will turn to shortly, with Captain Benwick and Mrs Smith. First, I want to draw attention to Anne and Wentworth's reversal of positions after the visit to Lyme, a reversal in which the reading analogy is overt. The famous scene that seals their reunion makes the convergence of conversation, reading and romance explicit, even to the point of hyperbole. Wentworth listens as Anne tells their friend, Captain Harville, that contrary to literary representations that suggest otherwise, a woman's love lingers long after an affair has ended. While she and Harville talk, Wentworth writes Anne a letter in which he describes his effort to 'read [Anne's] feelings' from the conversation, which is itself, of course, partly about reading (*Persuasion*, 186). He frames the letter as an attempt to 'speak to you by such means as are within my reach' (186). Shortly after this scene, Anne and Wentworth vocalise their feelings in an unrepresented conversation, a private exchange in which 'the power of conversation would make the present hour a blessing indeed' (189). Wentworth's writing about overhearing a conversation about (among other things) literature is figured as speaking, and the letter describes a reading of a conversation about reading. This manifold convergence of reading, writing and speaking reopens the possibility of uninhibited face-to-face conversation, which in *Persuasion* as elsewhere in Austen signifies the aptness of their bond.

The scene is a powerful example of an analogy between loving and reading that Deidre Lynch has identified throughout Austen's work, which she argues frequently 'associates love with the processes of interpreting a text'.[14] As Lynch notes, building on Adela Pinch's similar reading of the novel, the scene underscores Austen's persistent analogies between Anne and the reader of *Persuasion*.[15] We read 'with' Anne as she reads Wentworth's letter, the third person narrator temporarily standing to the side. The novel has already established similarities between the bookish heroine and its reader, including Anne's tendency to interpret others' conversations from a distance, as though she is uninvolved. Pinch proposes that Anne's repeated withdrawals from company in order to reflect on her memories parallel private reading (and rereading). Lynch observes that the letter Wentworth writes 'is annotating Anne's text', that is, her speech in conversation: 'The stops and starts in his prose testify to how closely structured on Anne's conversation with Harville his composition is' (*Economy*, 245). The conversation that seals Anne and Wentworth's reunion, mostly withheld from readers, continues a pattern Lynch notes in other Austen novels: near the end of Austen's novels we typically find a 'vaguely giggly conversation between the newly engaged couple in which [. . .] [they] rea[d] their own story and repea[t] passages from it' (218). In *Persuasion*, the conversation between the reunited lovers is described as a chance to 'indulge in those retrospections and acknowledgements, and especially in those explanations of what had directly preceded the present moment [. . .] All the little variations of the last week were gone through; and of yesterday and to-day there could scarcely be an end' (189–190). That is, the conversation they experience as 'a blessing indeed' blends interpretive, readerly activity with generative, storytelling activity. Not only has Anne ceased to be a passive 'reader' of others' conversations, she has also become, with Wentworth, an active creator. Their collaborative storytelling becomes indistinguishable from what Lynch calls their 'reading' of the story; their talk produces the text through which they come to re-understand – and thus inhabit together – the shared world of their love. In other words, their interpretive conversation is worldmaking.

According to Lynch, Austen's emphasis on interpretation reflects a Romantic preoccupation with valorising literature as a particular kind of private experience that cultivates 'taste' and 'cultural competence' (*Economy*, 127). In scenes of interpretation, characters model the self-fashioning by which readers can transform themselves into the right kind of individuals with 'interior resources of sensibility' (126). The analogies between the characters' activities and reading serve to provide 'instructions in fashioning an individualized interiority', which, crucially, distinguishes sensitive readers from the mass consumers of the expanding print market (131). Lynch proposes that Austen's novels promise her readers 'the opportunity to certify their powers of taste, mental discipline, and sympathetic identification', to 'affirm their *individual* distinction' (131). The argument appears especially well-suited to *Persuasion*, whose heroine is bookish and one of the most disciplined and inward characters in all of Austen's work.

Moreover, Anne discusses reading as though it were indeed an activity through which we gain moral instruction, fashioning – and taking individual responsibility for – our interiority. In the previously mentioned conversation with Captain Benwick, whose fiancée has died and who indulges his grief by reading Romantic poetry, Anne advises a shift in reading habits that at first glance sounds like the recommendation of a perfectionist curriculum. She warns Benwick that poetry is risky, that it might over-exercise what Lynch calls a person's 'interior resources of sensibility': 'she ventured to hope he did not always read only poetry, and to say, that she thought it was the misfortune of poetry to be seldom safely enjoyed by those who enjoyed it completely; and that the strong feelings which alone could estimate it truly were the very feelings which ought to taste it but sparingly' (78). She urges Benwick to supplement his poetry diet with 'such works of our best moralists, such collections of the finest letters, such memoirs of characters of worth and suffering', which 'occurred to her at the moment as calculated to rouse and fortify the mind by the highest precepts and the strongest examples of moral and religious endurances' (78). The phrasing echoes the perfectionist idea that examples might 'rouse' possibilities already internal to the self, as well as Cavell's notion that reading can unfold like a perfectionist conversation, drawing forth one's further self. Notable, too, is Anne's vision of feelings – interior resources – as both an aid to interpretation and a facet of the self that can be overdeveloped. We must choose our literary interlocutors carefully, and in balance, because to read well requires reading with the facet of the self that is addressed by the text. A perfectionist outlook clarifies why reading attains this halo of opportunity and risk.

Yet Anne's advice to Benwick diverges from Cavellian perfectionism in its preconception of the kind of improvement a person, or at least the grieving Benwick, needs: discipline, endurance, and fortification against too much sensibility. Anne's lecture on virtuous reading presupposes a vision of virtue, complementary to the sense of virtue Anne conceives in her self-effacing conversational style, 'the art', or morality, 'of knowing our own nothingness'. By contrast, as we saw, perfectionism unfolds without any preconception of 'the good', and it is opposed to moralism. For

Cavell's moral perfectionists, 'the conversation decides'. Anne's approach to reading thus recalls the 'debased perfectionism' Cavell criticises, an approach to personal growth (or reading) that forecloses the genuine responsiveness of conversation. Her advice to Benwick also suggests that there are limits to the openness of conversation: even if a given 'conversation decides' how worthy a relationship or reading is, we have already decided something when choosing our interlocutors. Should Benwick manage to read in the open frame of mind implied by Cavell's conversational ethos, this is precisely why, according to Anne, he ought to carefully choose what he reads, which voices he responds to by turning anew towards his life and world. This, as we'll see repeatedly, is a constitutive hitch in the conversational ideal, which in *Persuasion* as elsewhere oscillates between openness and conventionality.

As the famous exchange between Anne and Harville about literary representations of faithfulness in love drives home, Austen is alert to the limitations of literary examples. But the critique initiated by *Persuasion* encompasses more than the genre and represented contents of literary works. It encompasses the patterns of perception – routes of interest and feeling – that crystallise in the orientation towards reading that Anne expresses. This extension of *Persuasion*'s critique is most legible in the novel's second reunion plot, Anne's rekindled relationship with her old friend Mrs Smith.

### Reading vs Acknowledging

Mrs Smith's moral position in *Persuasion* is ambiguous, and readers have been divided about how to interpret her significance. When she and Anne reunite, Mrs Smith is a disabled widow living in poverty because of her late husband's debts, exiled from the higher society she once enjoyed alongside Anne. By most reckonings, she is not an especially *good* friend to Anne, nor a particularly good person. When gossip reaches her that Anne is likely to marry her selfish and dishonest cousin Mr Elliot – a man who has repeatedly insulted Anne's family, whose influence led the Smiths into debt, and who has contributed to Mrs Smith's impoverishment by neglecting his duties as executor of Mr Smith's will – Mrs Smith is prepared to encourage the marriage because she senses an advantage to herself. She reckons that Anne might persuade her husband to help the widow recover property in the West Indies that would make her 'comparatively rich'. Some have called Mrs Smith a 'mercenary' for this willingness to sacrifice Anne to a bad marriage, as well as for a scheme she describes to Anne, in which she and a nurse exploit Anne's 'fashionable' peers.[16]

Others have attempted to draft Mrs Smith into readings of Austen as a progressive, subversive writer, suggesting that the widow's eventual recovery of the West Indian estate (thanks to Wentworth) is a victory for the oppressed she partly represents, or noting that her situation is a subtle rebuke to the fantasy (nourished, perhaps, by other Austen novels) that marriage itself is a happy ending.[17] Twelve years before their reunion in Bath, Anne saw her friend leave 'as many heroines depart from Austen's novels', Laura Brodie observes, drawing another parallel between Anne and Austen's readers.[18] 'Anne witnesses one sequel to the marriage plot', Brodie writes, and 'widowhood becomes a tangible possibility for a young woman's future'.[19] For Eric Walker, the most notable feature of the novel's treatment of this character is simply the amount of attention it gives her in the final section, particularly in the closing paragraphs. Recounting her recovery of colonial property and her frequent visits with the newlywed Wentworths, these paragraphs elaborate at greater length on her restored health and improved circumstances than on Anne's.[20] Walker proposes that the curious amount of attention devoted to a minor character's fate registers a subtle critique of the cloistered associations of marriage: 'marriage and friendship resist easy balance', just as the narrator's interest wavers, unbalanced, between the newlyweds and their friend.[21]

For me, Mrs Smith's most provocative narrative function is to introduce an otherwise superfluous, unresolved class tension to the novel's social world. Part of the reason this tension is not resolved – indeed, cannot be resolved – is that Anne resolutely folds their conversations into the instrumental moralism she advocates as a method for reading literature. In Mrs Smith, Anne thinks she has found a compelling 'example of moral and religious endurances', as she counselled Benwick to seek in literature. Mrs Smith has much to endure – widowhood, poverty, illness – but she appears to have 'moments only of languor and depression [compared] to hours of occupation and enjoyment' (119). Anne is struck by the woman's 'disposition to converse and be cheerful beyond her expectation', and she strives to derive guidance by studying the woman's example (118). Anne 'watched – observed – reflected – and finally determined that this was not a case of fortitude or of resignation only', that Mrs Smith possesses a 'power of turning readily from evil to good, and of finding employment which carried her out of herself, which was from nature alone' (119). Once again, Anne is in a position similar to that of a reader, taking in and interpreting information, although her conclusion that Mrs Smith's optimism is 'from nature alone' implies it might not be easy to learn by example. This points to another reason to let go of the 'debased perfectionism' that strives to mimic, rather than converse with, an exemplar: if I discover I cannot emulate an admired friend, a debased perfectionist attitude might lead me to despair of ever changing, whereas Cavellian perfectionism would prompt me to discover my own further self, through conversation with the friend.

Anne nonetheless persists in seeking moral lessons in her conversation with Mrs Smith, even as the latter begins relating things difficult to reconcile with Anne's understanding of morality. Mrs Smith credits her good spirits to her friendship with the sister of her landlady, nurse Rooke.[22] During one of Anne's visits, she describes the scheme I mentioned above, in which Mrs Smith makes trinkets that the nurse sells to her high-society patients, choosing moments when the women are especially vulnerable or grateful. 'She always takes the right time for applying', Mrs Smith explains. 'Every body's heart is open, you know, when they have recently escaped from severe pain, or are recovering the blessing of health' (119–120). Mrs Smith redistributes the proceeds from this shadow market among 'one or two very poor families in the neighbourhood', a moral twist that does not so much redeem the exploitation as align it more squarely with class (119). Mrs Smith caps her account by describing the pleasure of gossiping about patients with nurse Rooke:

> 'She is a shrewd, intelligent, sensible woman. Hers is a line for seeing human nature; and [. . .] as a companion [. . .] [she is] infinitely superior to thousands of those who, having only received "the best education in the world" know nothing worth attending to. Call it gossip if you will; but when nurse Rooke has half an hour's leisure to bestow on me, she is sure to have something to relate that is entertaining and profitable, something that makes one know one's species better [. . .] the newest modes of being trifling and silly'. (120)

Anne's response to this extraordinary disclosure of contempt and exploitation is just as extraordinary: she quickly, and implausibly, draws nurse Rooke into the circle of moralising readers. She tells Mrs Smith:

> 'I can easily believe it. Women of that class have great opportunities, and if they are intelligent may be well worth listening to. Such varieties of human nature as they are in the habit of witnessing! And it is not merely in its follies that they are *well read*; for they see it occasionally under every circumstance that can be most interesting or affecting. What instances must pass before them of *ardent, disinterested, self-denying attachment, of heroism, fortitude, patience, resignation* – of all the conflicts and all the sacrifices that ennoble us most. A sick-chamber may often furnish the worth of *volumes*'. (120, my emphasis)

Instead of objecting to the characterisation of her peers as silly and trifling, or to exploitation of convalescing women, or even to the implicit dismissal of her own 'best education in the world', Anne offers a strained attempt to draft the scenario into the framework of literary, moral education. She is back on her 'fortitude and resignation' hobbyhorse, implying an equivalence between the sick chamber and the 'volumes' she has earlier endorsed.[23] Not only does she treat her conversations with Mrs Smith similarly to how she advocates treating reading, but she generalises this conflation of social and literary experience.

It is difficult to square Anne's interpretation with the practices Mrs Smith has described. Nothing her friend has said supports Anne's assertion that nurses are 'well read' in more than the 'follies' of human nature. Mrs Smith attempts to correct her, saying 'generally speaking, it is its weakness and not its strength that appears in a sick chamber: it is selfishness and impatience rather than generosity and fortitude, that one hears of' (120). Anne dismisses this response as the consequence of her friend's misfortune in marriage, which placed her 'among that part of mankind which made her think worse of the world' (120).

The scene offers a powerful example of the evasion of knowledge, as Anne resists the possibility that her friend is less morally exemplary than she wants to believe. When read by the lights of Cavell's moral perfectionism, the scene also reveals Anne resisting a new perspective on her world suggested by an outsider's view. She represses or dismisses evidence that conflicts with her preferred interpretive framework, erasing not only the negative judgements expressed by Mrs Smith (and by implication, nurse Rooke), but also the labour and class dynamics captured in the vignette. Anne's valorisation of 'women of that class' works because she translates the nurse's labour into her own preferred activity of reading: the labourer becomes a reader, and the value she contributes is thus measured in terms of her interior, sensitive subjectivity. Anne projects her own story as a reader, in which she derives instructions in self-denying attachment from readerly encounters with people and texts, onto the actions of a woman she is unable to acknowledge in the Cavellian sense.

I will put the stakes of this encounter in even sharper, Cavellian terms. If Anne's 'further self' would, for instance, be critical of the inequality and injustice hinted in the stratification between frivolous society women and nurses, widows and 'very poor families', she holds back this further self by doubling down on her readerly self. The sequence shows how the denial of acknowledgement can double as the refusal of a perfectionist moment. Anne's refusal to acknowledge the perspective associated with Mrs Smith and nurse Rooke is also a refusal of self-knowledge, as Cavell argues the evasion of acknowledgement so often is. Anne's projection of a literary analogy shuts down the possibility for the kind of conversation characterised by articulate responsiveness, the kind of conversation that can create a form of life that elaborates its own criteria of worthiness.

It is worth pausing to appreciate the unusual nature of these references to nurse Rooke and the perspective she represents. Rooke is not the only gossiping working-class figure in *Persuasion*. When Anne visits Mrs Smith the morning after a memorable music concert, the latter is unsatisfied by Anne's report, which adds little to what she already knows 'through the short cut of a laundress and a waiter' (150). Such references to workers are unique in Austen's fiction, and they remind us of vibrant social worlds beyond or beneath the novel's vision. Even more unique is the fact that *Persuasion* draws attention to its exclusion of nurse Rooke from direct narrative representation. During one of Anne's visits, Mrs Smith asks her friend if she 'observe[d] the woman who opened the door to you, when you called yesterday?' (155). Anne's response – 'No. Was not it Mrs Speed, as usual, or the maid? I observed no one in particular' – betrays a thorough indifference to those who open doors, underscoring her incapacity to acknowledge nurse Rooke (155). The indifference is one-sided. 'Nurse Rooke', Mrs Smith tells Anne, 'had a great curiosity to see you, and was delighted to be in the way to let you in' (155). The nurse is invisible as she gazes upon the oblivious Anne, just as she is invisible while collecting gossip among the 'silly and frivolous' women of Anne's class. Anne's failure to notice the people who open doors parallels her lofty, readerly gloss on Rooke's labour, in the sense that both erase her. It also ensures that the reader of *Persuasion* never 'observes' nurse Rooke directly, as the narration remains tethered to Anne's attention.

There is no need, within the terms of *Persuasion*, for Austen to draw attention in this way to Anne's failure to notice the person who opens the door for her. Indeed, in this superfluous reference, *Persuasion* gestures to the limits of its terms, which are also the limits of the wider literary culture in which it participates. Anne imagines the nurse's perspective to be a duplicate of her own perspective – rather than, say, a perspective informed by class, labour and associated experience. We might further say that Anne imagines the nurse's perspective to be a duplicate of Austen's reader's perspective: reading *Persuasion*, we are following an educated, literate heroine insistent on her own ardent, self-denying attachment, fortitude and resignation. Anne is her own favourite type of character, or at least she tries hard to be. Through the filters of such subjectivity, Anne – and the novel's reader – cannot perceive the nurse in her otherness as inhabiting the same world. Insofar as literary fiction is an act of worldmaking, the sequence suggests that its creative and interpretive norms (thus far) do not welcome the nurse into literature's made worlds. Conversations that project these norms might, moreover, foreclose the possibility of epistemologically sharing the world. While Anne is 'nobody with either father or sister', her word holding no weight in such circles, nurse Rooke is 'no one in particular' with Anne, and her words so weightless they do not even land on the balance of Anne's, and possibly the reader's, interests and feelings.

Or perhaps things are not so straightforward.

## Literary Examples and the Conversation of Justice

Anne, of course, reverses her stance on the power of literary examples in her famous disagreement with Captain Harville about women's constancy, the conversation Wentworth 'reads' while writing Anne the fateful letter. To support his argument that men are more faithful in love than women, Harville reminds Anne that 'all histories are against you – all stories, prose and verse [. . .] talk of woman's fickleness', before ruefully anticipating that she 'will say, these were all written by men'. 'Perhaps I shall', Anne responds, then warms to what will become the central claim of early feminist literary criticism: 'Yes, yes, if you please, no reference to examples in books. Men have had every advantage of us in telling their own story. Education has been theirs in so much higher a degree; the pen has been in their hands. I will not allow books to prove anything' (184). Just before this turn in the discussion, Wentworth drops his pen, evidently moved by Anne's 'faltering voice' and insistence that women's feelings remain stronger than men's, long after a love affair has ended. Readers are invited to take this moment as Austen's playful allusion to the fact that the pen is now, at least sometimes, in a woman's hands. Women, the scene announces, are beginning to tell their own stories.

Yet if we keep in mind Anne's attempt to rewrite the nurse's experiences in terms of her own moral and literary preconceptions, we must acknowledge that women of Anne's class now have 'every advantage' in comparison to women (and many others) from lower classes. The pen directing *Persuasion* is in the hand of 'a Lady', and, as the novel makes a point of noting, it does not represent the experiences of servants and nurses, except obliquely, with a conspicuously strained analogy to its own story about reading, fortitude and moral courage. The present story may not 'prove' much beyond a narrow scope of experience. Crucially, *Persuasion* suggests that literature fails as the source of information about others' emotional and moral lives – all women, historically; nurses, now – not only because of an author's biases, but also because of bias built into the very premise of reading for such guidance. What attitude should the reader take, then, to the 'examples' in *this* book – examples of patience and resignation, but also of inattentiveness because of an attachment to an understanding of moral exemplarity associated with books? A compelling answer to this question becomes available if we reconceive reading, along with moral development, in terms of Cavellian perfectionist conversation.

*Persuasion*, I suggest, opens itself to such an approach through its reservations about Anne's readerly moralism, as well as its reflexive attention to the interconnections between social order, knowledge and literary form. Beginning with its first chapter's portrait of the waning illiberal world via a description of the reading habits of Anne's father, the novel infers many of the correspondences between literary form and social order that contemporary literary historians have since debated. Sir Walter Elliot, we read in the first sentence, 'was a man who, for his own amusement, never took up any book but the Baronetage', a dry record of the hereditary ruling class in which he likes to read about his ancestors (3). Sir Walter is thus by definition unlike the reader of *Persuasion*, and his reading prejudices find a parallel in his social conservativism. He abhors the recognisably liberal values associated with the Royal Navy, such as hard work, mobile rather than proprietary relations to land, and social advancement through individual effort. Novels have often been described in the same terms he uses to denounce the Navy: in contrast to earlier literary forms such as chivalric romances or historical dramas, and in contrast to the Baronetage, the novel genre joins the Navy in 'bringing persons of obscure birth into undue distinction, and raising men to honours which their fathers and grandfathers never dreamt of' (15). Coming from a vain, irresponsible and selfish man without a direct heir, Sir Walter's complaint about the Navy doubles as an endorsement of both the Navy and the novel, two media of the transitioning social order.[24]

In other words, the opening of *Persuasion* presents a condensed version of a familiar narrative in historicist literary studies, according to which the novel and liberal modernity are deeply interwoven. As I noted in the introduction, many have cast the novel as playing a key role in the development of liberal modernity, 'the great disembedding', in Charles Taylor's words, of the individual from the collective.[25] Especially in its nineteenth-century realist apogee, the story goes, the novel helped to form (or reinforce) the modern individual through its modes of characterisation – its focus on 'persons of obscure birth' and private experience, agency, feelings, subjective individuality, and so forth – and also through the privatisation of reading and interpreting, facilitated by the expansion of literacy and print culture. Some versions of this literary historical narrative stress the correspondence between novels and bourgeois subjectivity or individual judgement, others emphasise how novels helped map social and national ties to complement the emergence of modern nation-states, and still others direct attention to the moral function of literature and the arts generally, insofar as art trains us to sympathise or empathise with others in terms beneficial to liberal democracy.

*Persuasion*, I suggest, anticipates this narrative about its genre's relation to liberal modernity. Moreover, the character of Anne Elliot can be seen as a transitional figure, representing both the self-fashioning of Romantic readers described by Deidre Lynch and the austere self-government Elaine Hadley has termed 'liberal cognition': 'disinterestedness, objectivity, reticence, conviction, impersonality, and sincerity, all of which carried with them a moral valence'.[26] Anne is at once a reader of Romantic poetry, arguing that sentiment aids in interpretation, and the advocate of a 'severe degree of self-denial' in the face of debts the family has incurred, as well as in her romantic and social life (*Persuasion*, 10). Anne and Wentworth's (re)marriage is itself an affirmation of impersonal, reflective judgement, described by the narrator as 'more justified' than it would have been had they married eight years earlier, before they had gained 'fixed [. . .] knowledge of each other's character, truth, and attachment' – knowledge they have gained through observation rendered disinterested by their lack of hope (189). Indeed, variations on the remarriage trope across Austen's novels formally articulate the modestly liberal view that women have the cognitive if not always material capacity to enter rationally into the main legal contract of their lives.[27] Framed on one end by a youthful, misjudged susceptibility to persuasion (by another representative of the waning aristocratic order, Lady Russell), and on the other by the correction of this misjudgement through a 'justified' marriage, *Persuasion* makes a strong case for independent and rational judgement when deciding to marry. It moreover shows Anne and Wentworth coming to their decision to marry through a process of interpreting one another's conversations: an activity evocative of reading prepares them to freely enter into a contract with one another.

If the parallel between the realist novel and the Royal Navy posits a link between liberalism and conventions associated with novels, Anne's criticism of men's 'advantage of [. . .] telling their own story' proposes a further stage of literary liberalisation. Picking up Wentworth's temporarily dropped pen, women, at least of Anne's and Austen's class, begin to expand the representational field. All of this suggests that *Persuasion* reflexively advocates liberalisation through literature, a step ahead of liberalisation through societal change. We can easily read the scene of the dropped pen as a variety of perfectionist conversation within literary culture, an aversive, yet meet and happy, dialogue between Anne's speech and the pen's fall that solicits a further, less patriarchal literary culture. Yet there is still the lingering, absent presence of the nurse, her critical perspective on this liberalising world neither condemned nor resolved. Not only does the novel not propose handing the pen over to nurse Rooke or her gossiping colleagues, it suggests that the governing conceptualisation of reading is somehow at odds with the livelihood of these gossiping working-class figures.

How should we make sense of this dangling plot thread, and the caveat it appears to add to the novel's otherwise optimistic (albeit still critical) outlook on liberalisation in society and literature? One answer to this question becomes available if we return to Cavell's account of aversive, perfectionist conversation: Austen, I propose, initiates a particularly challenging 'conversation', in Cavell's metaphoric sense, which cannot continue within the novel's own language, or form of life. The critique *Persuasion* initiates with its allusions to nurse Rooke and Anne's suppression of her perspective resonates with what Cavell calls the 'conversation of justice', a further stage of perfectionist education, while simultaneously spotlighting the paradox of envisioning justice advancing through conversation, which presupposes (while refashioning) shared forms of life.

The phrase 'conversation of justice' appears in Cavell's discussions of John Rawls, where it serves to distinguish the political dimension of his perfectionism from more conventional accounts of the procedures that support liberal politics. Before turning to Cavell's remarks, let's recall that Rawls's aim in his classic work of liberal political thought, *A Theory of Justice*, is to outline the principles and procedures that would promote justice in an ideal society. At the centre of *A Theory of Justice* are two principles: civil liberties ought to be equal among members of a society and as far-reaching as possible, without infringing on the liberties of others; and society ought to be arranged 'to the greatest benefit of the least advantaged'.[28] Inequality is justifiable as long as those with the least advantage are better off in the unequal society than they would be in any alternative society that does not also infringe on civil liberty. A 'general conception' draws these principles together: 'All social values – liberty and opportunity, income and wealth, and the social bases of self-respect – are to be distributed equally unless an unequal distribution of any, or all, of these values is to everyone's advantage' (54). Rawls calls this the conception of 'justice as fairness'. He proposes arranging society to fulfil this conception of justice by undertaking a thought experiment, in which we imagine how we would organise social institutions if we had no idea what specific position within society we would occupy. 'The principles of justice are chosen behind a veil of ignorance', he writes. In this imagined 'original position' behind the veil of ignorance, 'no one is able to design principles to favour his particular condition, [so] the principles of justice are the result of a fair agreement or bargain' (11). According to this ideal scenario, deliberation about how to justly organise society unfolds unencumbered by selfishness or grievance.

A second preface before turning to Cavell: his criticisms of Rawls do not carefully distinguish between Rawls's 'ideal theory' and Cavell's own orientation towards political life, which is characteristically rooted in the realm of the ordinary, rather than the ideal. My aim here is not to assess Cavell's reading of Rawls, which I find occasionally off the mark yet clarifying. It is off the mark not only when it suggests Rawls falls short of a task he does not undertake (that is, Rawls does not aim to delineate principles immediately useful in our unjust, actual society), but also because Rawls's theoretical project is more powerfully criticised for its explicitly idealistic aims. Charles W. Mills, for instance – one of Rawls's most compelling critics (whose work is itself aversively perfectionist, seeking a 'further self' of liberalism rather than a more radical political model) – forcefully argues that ideal theory is complicit in, or even responsible for, political theory's historic neglect of 'the hard facts of class, gender, and racial oppression'.[29] By constructing thought experiments that would help us develop an ideal society, Rawlsian ideal theory postpones indefinitely the theorisation of how to progress in our far-from-ideal world.[30] Theoretical neglect supports political stasis, and thus persistent injustice, according to this line of criticism of ideal theory.

Cavell's adjustments to Rawls yield insights useful to our non-ideal political projects, beginning with the difference from ideal theory that he marks by emphasising conversation. Cavell claims that *A Theory of Justice* contains an implicit association with conversation, that 'there is threading throughout that text the thing I call the conversation of justice' (*CHU*, 102). He anchors this claim on Rawls's consistent communicative framing, his repeated references to what a person 'can say' to another, such as in this summation by Rawls of his book's vision: 'whenever social institutions satisfy these principles [agreed upon from the original position] those engaged in them *can say to one another* that they are cooperating on terms to which they would agree' (*ToJ*, 12, my emphasis). From such allusions to what we 'can say to one another', Cavell draws the implication that the pursuit and testing of justice is an ongoing conversation, that every challenge to the present organisation of society is a test of whether we can say to one another that our society is fair. Yet as the following passage from *Cities of Words* shows, he argues that Rawls's theory of justice is in fact insufficiently informed by conversation:

> [M]y invocation of conversation, while it means talk, means at the same time a way of life together. 'Conversation' is taken by me to represent perhaps a different goal or ideal, or a different inflection of the goal from that of 'cooperation', as Rawls puts the context of justice [. . .] 'Cooperation', as a general state of social interaction, suggests the idea of society as a whole either as having a project or, at the other extreme, as being a neutral field in which each can pursue his or her own projects. [. . .]
> 
> The idea of 'conversation', in contrast, emphasizes neither a given social project nor a field of fairness for individual projects. (Nor, as I have insisted, does it deny the importance of these ideas.) What it emphasizes is, I might say, the opacity, or non-transparence, of the present state of our interactions, cooperative or antagonistic – the present seen as the outcome of our history as the realization of attempts to reform ourselves in the direction of compliance with the principles of justice. The virtues most in request here are those of listening, the responsiveness to difference, the willingness for change. The issue is not whether there is a choice between the virtues of cooperation and of conversation. God forbid. The issue is what their relation is, whether one of them discourages the other. The imperative to conversation is meant to capture the sense that, even when the veil of ignorance is lifted, we still do not know what 'position' we occupy in society, who we have turned out to be, what our stance is toward whatever degree of compliance with justice we have reached. To know such things is to have a perspective on our lives, on the way we live, and this is precisely the province of what I call, of what interests me in, moral perfectionism. The idea of conversation expresses my sense that one cannot achieve this perspective alone, but only in the mirroring or confrontation of what Aristotle calls the friend (what Nietzsche calls my enemy, namely one who is, on my behalf, opposed to my present, unnecessary stance), what Emerson calls the true man, the neutral youth, my further, rejected self. (173–174)

Although he largely praises Rawls, Cavell, like others, finds that his theory of justice presumes too much agreement prior to political deliberations and judgements, despite the thought experiment of the veil of ignorance. In fact, Cavell's perfectionist outlook suggests that the veil of ignorance veils precisely what we *need to know* if we are to pursue justice. Like many of Rawls's more severe critics, Cavell challenges the premise of ideal theory itself. Cavellian perfectionism tells us that any pursuit of an ideal society must begin with scrutiny not only of actual society, but also of our own position or stance towards the failures and possibilities of our society. Idealised disinterestedness, or ignorance, is contrary to the perfectionist route towards justice.

Framed as a conversation in Cavell's sense, the pursuit of justice transpires without the mediation of a concept of 'justice': 'the conversation decides', but never with finality. If and as it continues, it continues to revise our visions of personal and collective further states. These points anticipate Chapter 4's elaboration of the theoretical resources and limits of the ideal of 'conversation' in democratic theory, but, for the moment, note that this invocation of conversation leaves the discursive and cognitive norms associated with liberalism or any political system to one side, suggesting that the first task of political life is to discover where we stand, as individuals and society, in relation to ideals of justice that are themselves discerned and developed in conversation. Cooperation and conversation can generally coexist, Cavell writes, but he stresses that conversation should be the *foundation* of collective life. Insisting on cooperation can shut down conversation, whereas insisting on conversation makes cooperation – and its aims – subject to continuous self-questioning. Choosing conversation, here, is a matter of choosing an outlook, rather than choosing a direction in which to send our gazes: an outlook in which we, and our societies, are always partial, incomplete and requiring the conversation of others in order to repeatedly discover new perspectives on our lives. This outlook is simultaneously individualising and collectivist, moral and political. A 'democracy', for Cavell, is a society that affords perfectionist conversation at both individual and institutional scales, as people and groups confront the unnecessary states of existing political arrangements and our own 'compliances' therewith.

Although our visions of justice are in this view continuously transforming in the living and unpredictable exchange Cavell calls conversation, his conversational ideal nonetheless requires shared conventions and investments in openness, and this catch – the fact that we must already be mutually attuned to at least some degree if we are to converse – returns us to *Persuasion*. We can now formulate and approach a key question regarding the novel: What does it achieve by including – yet also markedly excluding – a position critical of its characters, which moreover marks the limits of literary examples the novel otherwise reflexively expands? We might read the passages of conversation between Anne and Mrs Smith as a minimal acknowledgement of 'compliance' – by both Anne and *Persuasion* – with an imperfect society and its imperfect yet progressive aims. By this reading, Mrs Smith and nurse Rooke serve as the friends, enemies or rejected selves, whose words could throw Anne's perception of her own values into question. Importantly, *Persuasion* invites readers to subversively enjoy the scenario Mrs Smith describes. Austen has satirised Anne's frivolous peers, showing that there is no morally legitimate reason they should have wealth and ease, while Mrs Smith suffers and vaguely described 'very poor families' are so very poor. The infirm, indebted widow siphons a bit of money from a class that dropped her once she was in need, and she redistributes it to those poorer than herself. Why should Anne, or we, censure such redistributive measures? To hesitate before censuring them, however, is to glimpse a new perspective on the present distribution of resources. It is also to consider moral questions from a perfectionist rather than categorically imperative or strictly utilitarian outlook: continuing this line of response to the scene between Anne and Mrs Smith is not ensured by the passage, but its ambiguities do, I think, call for hesitation.

### Consent and Cities of Words

In one of his discussions of the 'conversation of justice', Cavell describes a situation rather like the situation Anne faces in her conversations with Mrs Smith: one person is 'society's moral representative', and when challenged by another to justify the present state of society, she finds that 'reasons suddenly, embarrassingly, run out' (*CHU*, 112). This challenge might arise through a direct confrontation, or it might arise indirectly, for instance through the other's expression of resentment. Here Cavell takes issue with Rawls's discussion of resentment, in which he stipulates that the person who resents society 'must be prepared to show why certain institutions are unjust or how others have injured them' (*ToJ*, 533).

Cavell turns the situation on its head: whereas Rawls emphasises the obligations of the individual expressing resentment, Cavell considers what kind of responsiveness ought to be offered by the person to whom resentment is expressed. It is 'overwhelmingly likely', he observes, that society's moral representative will 'continue to consent to the way things are', despite the altered perspective prompted by the other's resentment (*CHU*, 112). But if the conversation – and their own perfectionist work – is to continue, they must still respond, not by offering reasons after reasons run out, but by showing something:

> what must be shown, acknowledged, is that my consent [. . .] compromises me; that I know change is called for and to be striven for, beginning with myself. But then I must also show, on pain of self-corruption worse than compromise, that I continue to consent to the way things are, without reason, with only my intuition that our collective distance from

perfect justice is, though in moments painful to the point of intolerable, still habitable. (*CHU*, 112)[31]

Consent 'from above' – that is, by people relatively advantaged within the unjust dispensation of their society – is not acquiescence to society's current state.[32] It is a commitment to struggle onward with society, recognising your fate and society's to be intertwined and furthered by turning aversively towards and away from one another. A perfectionist society (which for Cavell means a democracy) never reaches a state of perfect fulfilment of its principles, just as a self is always a work in progress.[33] The perfectionist, democratic society is for Cavell a conversation premised on consent and aversive critique. Acknowledging that I consent to the present state of society, and that I understand this consent to be 'compromising', 'means holding [myself] in knowledge of the need for change' and showing myself 'prepared to recognize others' as belonging, with me, in a society that would not compromise us (125).

*Persuasion*, by my reading, acknowledges that as a novel it consents to – even endorses and contributes to – a modest, slow liberalisation that does not yet register the voices of vast portions of society, even as it begins to register the voices of women like Anne. Anne's recovery of voice, by this light, is all the more poignant in comparison to the persistent denial of voice to a character like nurse Rooke. If Anne is compromised, so are *Persuasion*'s readers. The novel's acknowledgement of its compromised state provides no immediate help to the very poor families of Bath, of course, nor does it illuminate how readers might begin to share a language with labouring nurses and waiters. The nurse Rooke subplot nonetheless holds the novel and the reader 'in knowledge of the need for change' – insisting that the happiness of Anne's (re)marriage and reawakening to her life includes at least a minimal awakening to the existence of those whose happiness must be found and made elsewhere, but who we readers might begin to 'prepare to recognize' as parts of our own further selves.[34]

Here *Persuasion* at once invites the reader into a Cavellian, perfectionist conversation, and prompts what Cavell might call an aversive continuation of his work on perfectionism: the novel calls into question both the limitations of conversation as a metaphor for political change, and the value and limits of literature as a 'voice' in our collective, perfectionist conversations. Throughout his readings of literature and film, Cavell both implicitly and explicitly frames textual interpretation as an occasion for the aversive, self-questioning exchanges that cause us to reassess our lives and our societies. The second to last item in his list of 'candidate features' for a thematics of perfectionism, for instance, proposes that in addition to representing conversational education, perfectionist texts draw their societies into a widening conversation:

> the burdens placed on writing in composing this conversation may be said to be the achieving of an expression public enough to show its disdain for, its refusal to participate fully in, the shameful state of current society, or rather to participate by showing society its shame, and at the same time the achieving of a promise of expression that can attract the good stranger to enter the precincts of its city of words. (*CHU*, 7)

A text's demonstration of society's shameful state – and its acknowledgement of its own consent to, or partial participation in, this compromised state – functions as an appeal, a *promise*, to the stranger (friend, enemy, and so on) who would bring a new, critical perspective: a promise that it, and society, might become capable of responding to the good stranger in some as-yet-unarticulated expression. The text is a self-questioning interlocutor for society, and a compromised, but inviting, representative of that society, trying to attract the reader/writer/stranger whose responsiveness might draw the society forwards.[35] It is telling that Cavell blurs the distinction between a text as a 'city of words' and democratic society as comprised of cities of words, that he treats writing and reading as synecdochic of democratic perfectionism, both enacting and modelling a key component of the conversation of justice.

*Persuasion* in turn wonders about cases when the 'promise of expression' is offered in an exclusionary language – not only cases when the promise fails to be attractive, but when its underwriting conventions pre-emptively negate the voice of the 'good stranger'. The nurse's entrance would require, or effect, transforming not only a society's perception of itself and its imperfections, but also the language or form of life in which its conversations take place. The novel does not dispute Cavell's understanding of textual interpretation as an occasion for perfectionist conversation: by my reading, it invites or provokes this kind of aversive, conversational reading. But it also thematises textual interpretation as an activity whose 'language' we might need to critically reassess and possibly transfigure, a thematisation through which *Persuasion* also raises questions about the conversational outlook on moral and political development. It stresses the relay between the form of life a reader already shares with a text – in order to read at all – and the form of life in which the text instructs or initiates the reader. If conversation is our route to justice, what do we do when we find that our language cannot register certain voices or outlooks? What do we do when our consent compromises not only us, but the premises of perfectionist conversation? As David Rudrum, Aletta Norval and other readers of Cavell have noted, Cavell's commitment to conversation seems to foreclose the kind of critique suggested by a figure like nurse Rooke, or, in Rudrum's reading, Nora in Ibsen's play: 'a consent-based conversation of democracy as Cavell describes it', Rudrum writes, 'is founded on the silencing of certain voices, namely, those voices that cannot consent to the terms on which the conversation is held'.[36]

This is the main contribution I suggest *Persuasion* can offer to the conversational outlook: its ambivalent awareness and negotiation of the limitations constitutive of any 'conversation' of justice or morality. Conversation presupposes a shared form of life, and thus, perhaps inevitably, presupposes criteria that some 'strangers' may lack or refuse to share. Moreover, it tells us that our responsiveness in conversation might be cultivated by – or an extension of – the forms of life we practise when reading, particularly if we, like Cavell, understand reading in perfectionist terms. Reading, for *Persuasion*, extends and refines the criteria of a form of life, and thus routes our interests and feelings outside of our encounters with texts. This is a source of literature's power – a reason to cheer the migration of the pen into a Lady's hands – and a source of its responsibility. *Persuasion* does not repudiate literature or reading, but it turns aversively on itself and on the social and interpretive norms it understands itself to 'comply' with. In this aversive turning away from and towards literature (specifically the novel genre, as the parallels between the Navy and the novel suggest), *Persuasion* also turns towards and away from its readers, challenging us to acknowledge how our own forms of life might alter our perceptiveness and hence worldmaking responsiveness to others. The novel becomes the good stranger with whom we converse and thereby assess our lives, the cities we build with words. But the nurse remains outside its precincts – conspicuously, constitutively, so.

We can frame these insights in terms of scepticism, the implicit backdrop to the world-disclosing work associated with conversation in Cavell's conversational outlook. Austen indicates that one reason we do not see the same world that some of our neighbours see is that we do not inhabit the same forms of life, that our attunements conflict with acknowledging the presence and thus voice of certain 'strangers'. *Persuasion* draws the reader into a conversation of justice, prompting us to assume a new critical outlook towards our criteria, including the perceptual and meaning-making criteria we refine in reading novels like *Persuasion*. Yet, it also refuses to celebrate this conversation. It spotlights its borders, and thus the possibility of a change more radical than the 'turning away' of aversive conversation. *Persuasion* does not launch a radical break, and, indeed, it performs the impossibility of doing so within its own form of life, reminding us that novels, at least in its age, imply consent from above. But it also holds itself and us 'in knowledge of the need' for change, possibly not only *in* language but also *of* language. Acknowledging as much also entails acknowledging that the ideal of conversation, as a model and technique in justice and morality, is itself subject to transformation. This is an implicit premise of each of my ensuing chapters, beginning with *The Egoist*'s interrogation of promising: the speech act on which turn many conventional ideas of worlds made through words.

Chapter 2

# Performative Conversation and Acknowledgement: Meredith, Austin and Cavell

If conversation ideally involves something like the free play of the imagination and an inner purposiveness, unsubordinated to external purposes, its discursive opposite would seem to be the performative speech act, the utterance that alters the social or legal structures of the world. Performative speech acts, also known as illocutions or illocutionary acts – like the emblematic 'I do' of wedding vows, promises, official nominations, and so on – do not describe separate acts or feelings: they *perform* what they assert. As J. L. Austin explains in his pathbreaking lectures on speech performativity, delivered in 1954–1955 and published in 1962 as *How to Do Things With Words*, 'When I say, before the registrar or altar, &c., "I do", I am not reporting on a marriage: I am indulging in it.'[1] One of the tasks Austin undertakes in the lectures is to clear up 'traditional philosophical perplexities' caused by a lingering tendency to assess utterances as either true or false descriptions of the world (ibid., 3). Performative utterances, in Austin's terms, are either felicitous (successful) or infelicitous (failed, misfired), rather than true or false.

As far as I can tell, Cavell does not directly note the suggestive friction between the 'happy conversations' signifying good marriage that he tracks from Milton through remarriage films, and the 'felicitous' wedding scene that recurs repeatedly in *How To Do Things With Words*, despite referring often to Austin as a singular teacher and influence. Speech can hardly get more instrumental than the 'I do' of the marriage vow, yet the conversations that emblematise good marriages for Cavell have no instrumental purpose other than the endless re-establishment of a shared form of life characterised by 'articulate responsiveness, expressiveness': repeated acts of acknowledgement, mutual education, and quests for the further self. As Cavell observes, illocutionary acts invoke 'the order of law', rather than the 'disorders of desire' (*PDAT*, 19).² The friction between the figurative uses of marriage by Cavell and Austin is suggestive because, as Cavell of course knows, there are no clear boundaries between orders of speech, just as law and desire are not tidily opposed compartments in a life. Likewise, as many of Austin's readers have noted, his lectures begin by announcing the existence of a class of utterance hitherto unstudied in philosophy, but by their end, he has moved from identifying 'the performative' as a class of utterance to demonstrating that performativity is an aspect of speech, that all speech has performative force. In the final lecture, Austin declares the dissolution of 'the dichotomy of performatives and constatives [. . .] in favour of more general *families* of related and overlapping speech acts' (*How to Do*, 149). Austin's lectures tell us, in other words, that even our happiest conversations are touched by the 'order of law', and that there is continuity between conversation and contract.

If we are to talk *at all* – in happy, disorderly improvisation or backed by legal conventions – we must share a language, routes of interest and feeling, 'mutual attunement or agreement in our criteria'. Indeed, in Cavell's work, 'meet and happy conversation' requires accepting that our capacity to communicate relies on such public, shared conventions, rather than nursing scepticism about 'other minds' by fixating on the imperfections of language as a medium for communication. The sceptic must accept that our most intimate expressions of desire, our most playful improvisations, work both through and against convention. These observations point not only to a tension constitutive of the conversational outlook – between openness, experiment and play, on the one hand, and conventions, norms and worldly materials, on the other: a tension that of course is central to ethical and political thought writ large – but also to a charge occasionally made against ordinary language philosophy, that its appeal to ordinary language is conservative. As we saw in the previous chapter, our prior attunements might constrain our responses to the specific people or situations before us. Ordinary language, like literature, cannot be disentangled from power.

The present chapter investigates these tensions by turning to George Meredith's *The Egoist* (1879), a novel whose plot may be summarised as a struggle between conversational acknowledgement and the normativity exemplified in performative speech. Clara Middleton promises to marry Sir Willoughby Patterne near the book's beginning, then spends most of the ensuing chapters trying to disengage herself, straining against the power of her verbal bond.³ The novel shares with Cavell the sense that marriage ought to be founded on a 'meet and happy conversation', or what Clara calls 'comradeship, a living and frank exchange of the best in both'.⁴ It also shares the perception that scepticism interferes with what Cavell calls acknowledgement: Willoughby fears Clara's separateness, which reminds him of the limits of his knowledge and power, and he tries to overcome this separateness by invoking performative speech. Yet the novel's critique of the patriarchy underpinning its Victorian form of life, which it links to Clara's restricted capacity for self-expression in language, courts a different, more historically specific, variety of scepticism. In its depictions of the central pair's conversations, then, *The Egoist* throws into doubt the possibility that any 'happy' conversation can take place in a language that reflects and perpetuates the injustices of a specific form of life.

I am far from the first reader to note the philosophical register of *The Egoist*'s representation of conversation. One of the first important readings along these lines was made by no less influential a figure than Sigmund Freud, who cites a passage of *The Egoist* in his account of the self-betraying 'slips' of the tongue that would come to bear his name.⁵ More recently, and more closely reflecting my interests in this chapter and book, Randall Craig has outlined the novel's critique of a 'system of rhetorical norms' that 'restricts women's voices to ornamental accompaniment, or to silence'.⁶ Anne Toner has argued that Meredith is fascinated by 'the land- or sound-scape of conversation', and that his proto-modernist permeation of dialogue with 'pauses, stammerings, wanderings, and false starts' represents his sense of the deficits of everyday talk as well as a kind of mimesis between broken speech and muddled thought.⁷ And Daniel Wright has drawn forth the significance of Willoughby's 'bad logic' in treating Clara's promise tautologically: a promise is a promise.⁸

Reading the novel in a sustained conversation with ordinary language philosophy allows us to develop its enquiry further, focusing on what it reveals about the constitutive friction between conversation and convention. In what follows, I outline the correspondences between *The Egoist*'s picture of language use and the account of performative speech developed decades later by Austin. I show that through its prescient analysis of performativity, the novel makes explicit the ways in which language conventions might become the focus of scepticism about our capacity to know 'other minds'. The conversations between Meredith's characters manifest what Cavell calls 'struggles for acknowledgment', encapsulating the challenge of coming to terms with – and building happily upon – our ineluctable separateness and the limits of the intimacy we can forge with the public material of language. Yet, by insisting on the political baggage of this material via its emphasis on Clara's restricted agency as a woman, the novel's critique of language use anticipates some of the thorniest questions suggested by, and of, ordinary language philosophy about the relationship between conversation, acknowledgement and (oppressive) normativity.

The climax of the novel – and this chapter – takes the enquiry a step further, anticipating the more explicitly political turn of scepticism we'll take up in a concerted way in this book's final chapters. The novel culminates in a conversation in which Willoughby turns performativity inside out: his language performs *nothing*, or rather, performatively strips an entire community of its common sense of reality, in order to protect his 'tender infant Self' from the community's judgements (*Egoist*, 346). The anxious, unethical sceptic exploits the conventions that give language meaning in a way that erodes confidence in meaning as such. As *The Egoist* helps us see, this worldlessness is a possibility always latent in the forms of life we share, and make, in conversation.

### Binding Ceremonials: Commissive Speech in Austin and Meredith

Promises belong to the family of utterances Austin calls 'commissive' illocutions, which commit us to doing some further act. Commissives have less immediate, absolute illocutionary force than 'verdictives' (the utterances of a jury, for instance) and 'exercitives' (such as appointing someone to a position or naming a ship). Like other illocutionary acts, they involve ritual formulas of speech, and to be effective they must be uttered by appropriate people in appropriate circumstances. A child can promise her parents to make her bed, but she cannot effectively promise a bank to repay a loan. A promise performs something immediately – when I say 'I promise', I am doing the act of promising – but its performativity also relates in a more ambiguous way to the future act it anticipates. As Judith Butler has noted, a commissive utterance 'begins a temporal horizon', stretching between the utterance and the fulfilment or derailment of what it portends.[9] This is the insight that structures *The Egoist*: when their lease expires prior to Clara's marriage, she and her father move to Willoughby's ancestral home of Patterne Hall, which gives her a unique (for the era) chance to learn how incompatible she and Willoughby are within the temporal horizon between her engagement promise and the moment that will prove its status as felicitous or infelicitous. Promises launch plots, as *The Egoist*'s narrative form underscores.

The plot of *The Egoist* unfolds primarily through conversation, or what Margaret Oliphant unflatteringly described as the novel's 'weak, washy, everlasting flood of talk'.[10] Talk indexes how badly suited Clara and Willoughby are, and how much better matched she is with Vernon Whitford, Willoughby's widower cousin who serves as his estate secretary. As Erik Gray observes, Clara and Vernon elaborate one another's metaphors in conversation, as though compatibility in speech habits signals compatibility in other ways relevant to marriage.[11] Whereas Willoughby proves to be pathologically incapable of acknowledging Clara, or indeed anyone, Vernon grows out of his initial view of her as a 'Mountain Echo' – a metaphor suggesting subservience to the speech of her partner – and comes to see her as possessing 'natural wit' making her 'fit [. . .] for the best of comrades anywhere' (159). Resonating with Clara's own desire for 'comradeship' linked to conversation, 'the living and frank exchange of the best in both', Vernon's transformation powerfully endorses their coupling and confirms the novel's affinity with the conversational ethos Cavell identifies in Milton. Just as Milton advocates divorce where happy conversation is impossible, the novel invites its readers to root for the derailing of Clara's promise in order to enable her a lifelong conversation with Vernon. But *The Egoist* is principally about performativity, and its flood of talk charts the tension between ethical acknowledgement and speech that *acts* according to convention.

We first learn about Clara's promise to marry Willoughby through gossip, 'hints [. . .] dropping about the neighborhood' (65). The presiding neighbourhood gossip, Mrs Mountstuart Jenkinson, blends sentimental cliché and material concern in her account: 'Both were struck at the same moment', she says, before explaining that the Middletons have 'money' but 'no land', and that Clara is 'eighteen, perfect manners; you need not ask if a beauty' (ibid.). It is appropriate that Meredith introduces readers to the engagement in this secondhand manner. A more detailed account of the couples' engagement follows in the next chapter and establishes that Willoughby's pursuit of Clara is motivated by an eagerness to prove to 'the world' that he is the 'best man': he throws himself into courting her 'while yet he knew no more of her than that he was competing for a prize' (71–72). That we first encounter Clara through gossip foreshadows the powerful role that the 'world' and its conventions play in the novel: not only does his concern about the 'world' drive Willoughby's obsession with marrying Clara at all costs, even after she begins to express her wish to be released from her promise, but as we'll see most clearly in the novel's climax, the 'world' of the gossips stands ambivalently for the language community whose form of life stabilises meaning.

Our direct introduction to Clara tells a different story than Mrs Mountstuart. Hardly 'struck at the same moment' as Willoughby, Clara evidently commits herself only after a great deal of hedging and delay, in an exchange notably filled with performative utterances:

> She begged for time; Willoughby could barely wait. She unhesitatingly owned that she liked no one better, and he consented. A calm examination of his position told him that it was unfair so long as he stood engaged, and she did not. She pleaded a desire to see a little of the world before she plighted herself. She alarmed him; he assumed the amazing god of love under the subtlest guise of the divinity [. . .] The plea of urgency was reasonable. Dr Middleton thought it reasonable, supposing his daughter to have an inclination. She had no disinclination, though she had a maidenly desire to see a little of the world – grace for one year, she said. Willoughby reduced the year to six months, and granted that term, for which, in gratitude, she submitted to stand engaged; and that was no light whispering of a word. She was implored to enter the state of captivity by the pronunciation of vows – a private but a binding ceremonial. She had health and beauty, and money to gild these gifts; not that he stipulated for money with his bride, but it adds a lustre to dazzle the world; and, moreover, the pack of rival pursuers hung close behind, yelping and raising their dolorous throats to the moon. Captive she must be. (72–73)

As the scene of their engagement continues, Willoughby's demands on Clara's speech become increasingly extreme. 'He made her engagement no light whispering matter', the narrator notes. 'It was a solemn plighting of a troth [. . .] Having said, I am yours, she could say, I am wholly yours, I am yours forever, I swear it, I will never swerve from it, I am your wife in heart, yours utterly; our engagement is written above' (73). Willoughby was 'jilted' once before, by the ironically named Constantia, and his fears of a second jilting prompt these relentless and escalating demands on Clara.

The central illocutions in the scene are commissives: the 'binding ceremonial' that draws Clara into 'the state of captivity' and her vows of unswerving future fidelity. But nearly every other utterance mentioned in the scene is also a form of speech act. Clara 'pleads' rather than states a desire for more experience before plighting herself, for instance; pleading, begging and imploring are all examples of what Austin calls exercitive utterances, which include advocating 'in favour of or against a certain course of action' (*How to Do*, 154). Clara's 'owning' that she likes no one better is an 'expositive', an act 'of exposition involving the expounding of views' (ibid., 160). That Willoughby 'consents' to this expositive is comical and jarring because 'consent' is also a commissive, one that implies the other has made a proposition, not an exposition of their feelings. Austin's terminology helps to highlight Meredith's interest in the misalliance of speech acts, one of the primary strategies through which Willoughby will try to manipulate Clara and others in conversation throughout the novel: he treats utterances as though they are different kinds of utterance than they are, as though they express commitments and carry obligations they do not.[12] In short, Meredith represents the conversation that results in their engagement as a struggle that plays out in speech acts.

Such exchanges underscore an insight expressed in the novel's plot, as well: there is a gap between a performative utterance's effect and the speaker's intentions. The central drama turns on Clara's discovery that illocutionary speech can hijack a person, committing her to a future she could not have intended. The text makes the point sharply in an early conversation between Clara and Vernon, whose help she seeks as she begins to understand her situation. Vernon reminds her that she is 'in a position of [her] own choosing', and she responds by shifting emphasis to the speech act she performed, away from the 'choice', or inner resolution, supposedly behind it: 'Not my choosing; do not say choosing, Mr Whitford. I did not choose. I was incapable of really choosing. I consented' (196). Consent, again, is a commissive, and Clara's response insists on the difference between the act she performed and the intention supposedly behind it. Vernon's retort is also true: 'it's the same in fact', he says (ibid.). This aspect of speech performativity is key to the power of promises: we could not promise if our promises might be rendered void by each other's unknowable inner lives. As Austin notes, a promise given without the appropriate or implied intention is less likely to prove 'felicitous', but it is still a promise. Even a promise that a person intends to break 'is not even *void*', he remarks, lingering on a source of social and moral difficulty: 'it is given in *bad faith*. [It] is perhaps misleading, probably deceitful and doubtless wrong, but it is not a lie or a misstatement' (11). Clara's situation is one in which she has not deliberately deceived Willoughby, but rather has spoken without knowing everything she ought to know about either herself or the man she is to marry. 'Be sure of what you wish', Vernon lectures (196). Of course, readers know that she tried, but was bullied and confused until she spoke herself into her present 'state of captivity'.

The gap between utterance and intention highlighted by Clara's qualification has been crucial to the uses of Austin's work in literary studies, primarily via its radicalisation by theorists associated with deconstruction and poststructuralism. In 'Signature Event Context', Jacques Derrida proposes that the performative force of language exemplifies the 'citationality' or 'iterability' of all speech, the dependence of speech on pre-existing scripts, which means that 'the intention animating the utterance will never be through and through present to itself and to its content'.[13] Derrida further claims that Austin does not acknowledge the radicalism of his own view of language, and even reproduces metaphysical fantasies of presence and intention in voice. In Austin's work, Derrida writes, 'performative communication becomes once more the communication of an intentional meaning, even if that meaning has no referent in the form of a thing or of a prior or exterior state of things'.[14] In sum, Derrida charges Austin with giving a falsifying 'rigor' and 'purity' to his account of language. But as noted by Cavell and other readers of Austin – including John Searle, in a notorious dispute with Derrida that is outside my scope here – Austin's project was never to 'rigorously' theorise a totalising principle about speech or language as a 'pure' system: his project was to describe, not theorise, how we often do things with words, when our speech doesn't misfire and also when it (frequently) does.[15]

The deconstructive concern with 'iterability' and intentionality is not alien to ordinary language philosophy, however. Cavell's phrase for the mismatch between Austin and Derrida – a 'systematic turning' – aptly captures the geometry: they see similar issues as problems, but from different outlooks, and they never quite meet in conversation as they turn towards their interests (*Pitch*, 63). For ordinary language philosophers, the problem posed by 'iterability' is primarily ethical and ordinary, rather than abstract or metaphysical. Austin distinguishes between a promise that 'misfires' because of accidents or mistakes, and a promise that fails because its initial utterance was an 'abuse' of the institution. It is a 'misfire', for instance, if I promise to meet someone at a specific time but get a flat tyre on my way. It is an 'abuse' if I promise to meet at a specific time with the intention of showing up late, perhaps to increase my allure or the other's exploitable anxiety. I can also make a promise with conflicting or ambivalent intentions, of course, which changes but does not negate the relevant ethical questions. Such possibilities are indeed internal to the structure of the utterance, but whereas a poststructuralist might maintain, as Jonathan Culler has written, that 'in principle [. . .] the performative breaks the link between meaning and the intention of the speaker', for Austin performative utterances *trouble* rather than fully break the link between meaning and intention.[16] Intention is not essential to the social meaning of the initial performance, if its meaning is its immediate effect, but it matters both ethically and practically to the utterance's 'felicity'. At the same time, our knowledge of intentions – in ourselves and others – is, like all knowledge, lacking in guarantees.

Like an ordinary language philosopher, *The Egoist* trains our view on the ethical abuses of the conventions of promising, linking these abuses to anxieties about the source and extent of language's power. The gap between a performative act and a conscious intention troubles Willoughby, and his verbal struggles with Clara point to an additional force that Austin identifies in speech, the 'perlocutionary' power of our words to 'produce certain consequential effects upon the feelings, thoughts, or actions of the audience, or of the speaker, or of other persons' (*How to Do*, 101). Perlocution, Austin elaborates, is the psychological effect 'we bring about or achieve by saying something, such as convincing, persuading, deterring, and even, say, surprising or misleading' (ibid., 108). He quickly explains that perlocutions are not a separate, discrete family of speech acts. The same utterance can be an illocution and a perlocution, and everything we say likely elicits a 'perlocutionary sequel' (103, 117). In the engagement scene, Meredith shows how an illocution's perlocutionary sequel can in fact contradict its implied intentions. As the scene proceeds, Clara qualifies her vows with the 'somewhat chilling generosity' of the phrase, 'as far as I am concerned' (*Egoist*, 73). The addendum is chilling not only because it suggests she is open to separation if Willoughby changes his mind, but also because it contradicts Willoughby's demand that she idealise their engagement as 'written above'. The remark gives her words a perlocutionary, 'chilling' effect by referencing the fact that language binds us because we agree to its binding power, not because of a transcendent, divine force underwriting our conversations. It also references the separation between words and intentions, precisely by affirming Clara's intentions to keep her word.

Willoughby, alarmed by Clara's 'generosity', immediately 'forced her to pass him through love's catechism in turn, and came out with fervent answers that bound him to her too indissolubly to let her doubt of her being loved' (*Egoist*, 73). Austin's account of perlocution helps clarify what Willoughby misperceives when making his 'fervent answers'. The narrator implies that he hopes to reassure Clara of his love – and perhaps to reassure himself that what she needs is this reassurance. But perlocution depends at least as much on the listener as on the speaker. There is no perlocutionary equivalent to 'the performative formula' that guarantees a person we address will feel persuaded, alarmed or loved. 'Thus', explains Austin, 'we can say "I argue that" or "I warn you that" but we cannot say "I convince you that" or "I alarm you that"' (*How to Do*, 103). This distinction between illocution and perlocution reflects the different role of intentions and feelings in each type of force performed in speech. Because illocution does not depend on the uncertain feelings of others, or on one's own uncertain feelings, one need only recite the performative formula in the appropriate circumstances to guarantee that speech has acted (at least initially: commissives, again, are complicated by the 'temporal horizon' between the initial, felicitous performance and what we might call its illocutionary sequel). By contrast, the 'perlocutionary sequel' that follows most (if not all) illocutions and locutions is unpredictable. 'Illocutionary acts are conventional acts', Austin summarises, and 'perlocutionary acts are not conventional' (ibid., 120). We can never control the affective effects of our words on others.

Cavell picks up the thread of perlocution in an important late essay devoted to what he calls 'passionate utterances', utterances made with an express perlocutionary aim. Speech, he notes, is 'designed to work on the feelings, thoughts, and actions of others', at least as much as it is designed for establishing contracts or 'revealing our desires to others and to ourselves' (*PDAT*, 186). Austin's emphasis on performance over perlocution means his theory requires an 'extension', which Cavell proposes to offer while 'remaining in the spirit of his theory', extending to himself an 'invitation' to 'open the door' closed by Austin's swift movement past perlocution (ibid., 160). (I linger with Cavell's preamble to continue tracking his writing's consistent performance of the ethical responsiveness he associates with conversation.) When I express a passionate utterance, Cavell claims, I 'acknowledg[e] my desire', I 'declare my standing with you and single you out, demanding a response in kind from you' (185). Passionate utterances make us 'vulnerable to [the other's] rebuke, thus staking our future' (185). For Cavell, the vulnerability made conspicuous in passionate utterances highlights an aspect shared by all speech, allowing us to recognise 'speech as confrontation, as demanding, as owed' (187). Even 'when it proceeds out of sincere cooperation, as in [the pragmatic language philosopher] Paul Grice's study of rational conversation', talk also proceeds out of desire, reaching outwards across the distance separating us, implicitly communicating a need to *have* standing with one another (187). Perlocution foregrounds this facet of speech, asserting, in Cavell's phrase, the 'rights of desire'. This phrase should give us pause not only because there are clearly abusive applications of the idea, but also because it suggestively blurs interdependence and individualism, eroticism, assertion and vulnerability. It's an almost posthuman phrase. If desire (rather than the person) claims rights, it marks us as vulnerable where we are most demanding.

I alluded earlier to Cavell's distinction between the performative and the passionate register of speech when I cited his contrast between the 'order of law' and the 'disorders of desire'. The passage from which I draw this juxtaposition is in fact more complex. He writes: 'A performative utterance is an offer of participation in the order of law.

And perhaps we can say: A passionate utterance is an invitation to improvisation in the disorders of desire' (*PDAT*, 185). Passionate utterances recall Cavell's accounts of conversation in the remarriage films, in which the couples' endless talk manifests their endlessly reissued invitations to improvisation. The 'screwball' quality of the films reflects the happy disorder of the form of life they create, and the absence of children signifies the fact that desire claims its own rights, and that the justification for marriage is – must be, according to Cavell – the self-justification of passionate conversation, rather than procreation. Yet, the contrast in the parallel language of the cited passage is not that of opposition: offers and invitations are both performative utterances. 'Participation' is not obedience (I consider myself a participant in the order of traffic laws when I jaywalk or cycle through red lights on empty streets, exercising my own judgement in relation to the law). In Cavell's careful phrasing, performative utterances begin to look more open to vulnerability, desire and disorder, while passionate utterances appear to be mediated by convention.

*The Egoist* shares this understanding, helping us to see that, as Cavell writes, language is 'everywhere revealing desire', no matter how protected it might seem to be by formulas and convention (*PDAT*, 187). The flip side is true, as well: conversations meant to express passion and desire draw on convention, in this novel obsessively. Willoughby turns every passionate moment into a binding ceremonial, and his illocutionary acts cannot help but be 'passionate', exposing 'his naked eidolon, the tender infant Self' he tries so hard to protect (*Egoist*, 346). Indeed, his future with Clara is put at risk not by his demands on her words, but by his demands on her feelings. She resists his claiming of the 'rights of desire', a claim that the novel shows cannot be satisfied by her words anyway.

## Intentionality, Conventions and Acknowledgement

There is a telling irony in Willoughby's compulsive and contradictory relation to speech conventions: he demands that Clara repeat words whose force depends on convention, and he panics when she alludes 'generously' to conventionality. As illocutionary acts, her words are binding, but as perlocutionary acts, they are chilling, because she reminds Willoughby of the very human, mortal rather than divine, conditions of illocution. From an ordinary perspective, her remark that her promises are binding 'as far as [she is] concerned' ought to be reassuring. Willoughby cannot be certain she's telling the truth, but at least she affirms an intention to keep her promise. The fact that her assertion of this intention alarms, rather than reassures, Willoughby points to his uneasiness with what Vernon calls the 'conventional idea of obligation' (*Egoist*, 368). I want to suggest that Meredith indicates Willoughby's anxieties are, at root, anxieties about the idea of convention as such. Willoughby's deepest fear might not be that Clara cannot be relied on to keep her promise, but rather that *language* cannot be relied on. Willoughby, that is, exemplifies the sceptical position I've said ordinary language philosophy helps us both assess and address.

Conventions, in this novel, feel insufficiently binding to Willoughby. He suggests as much when he forces Clara to say that their engagement is 'written above', and again, more vividly, in an exchange in which he tells her about a fantasy of his, in which they've found 'a way of cutting off the world' and becoming 'one another's [. . .] so entirely one, that there never can be question of external influences [. . .] I read your heart [. . . and you are] the one who reads mine! You have me, you have me like an open book, you, and only you!' (98–99). There's a revealing contradiction in the fantasy that they are 'entirely one', apart from the world, and that they are simultaneously privileged readers of one another's hearts. We are separate from the texts we read. This contradiction matches the irony of his endless quest for 'binding ceremonials', which he seeks precisely because he fears that such ceremonials do not bind them enough, at the level of their hearts. These ceremonials, moreover, are only meaningful because they are reinforced by the world and its conventional ideas of obligation.

Such passages resonate with discussions of the fantasy of private language in Wittgenstein's *Philosophical Investigations* and Cavell's gloss of the same, in *The Claim of Reason*. It is as if what Willoughby wants is not (or not only) a mystical union with Clara, but rather a language that only they share, a language in which she alone can read his secret self. As Cavell notes, when Wittgenstein introduces the idea of private language, he does not declare that there is no such thing, but rather poses the question of whether we *can imagine* a private language. This question draws out what we mean by 'language', which is something essentially worldly and shared.[17] When a person like Willoughby fantasises about private language, Cavell proposes, the fantasy indicates resistance to the essential 'publicness of language', uneasiness about the fact that we must rely on '*merely* "conventional"' or 'arbitrary' agreements about how we use language (*CR*, 351, 227). 'Within the mood of the fantasy' of private language is the sceptical question, 'Why do we attach significance to *any* words and deeds, of others or of ourselves?' (*CR*, 351). This is the kind of sceptical question that threatens the possibility of acknowledgement. It fuels doubts about our capacity to know others, doubts that can mushroom into a denial that others exist, or into the more modest, but still destructive, denial that we can understand one another sufficiently. As we've seen previously, Wittgenstein and Cavell answer the sceptical question by saying that 'nothing more and nothing less than shared forms of life' allow us to attach significance to words (CR, 168). Within the mood of scepticism, however, such 'mutual attunement or agreement in our criteria' will seem to be a perilously shaky foundation for our relationships (CR, 168).

In the character of Willoughby, Meredith shows how destructive such scepticism can become. Like many of his literary precursors – Othello and Leontes are two of Cavell's touchpoints – Willoughby's scepticism focuses on a woman's unknowable desires and behaviours.[18] Scepticism, as Cavell summarises:

> breaks into [ordinary or everyday] life, with a surmise that I cannot live with, that the world and I and others are radically unknown to me. I must find a way to put this doubt aside – perhaps through what Pascal calls the taste for distraction, or what Hume depicts as the desire for sociability, or what Kant calls recognizing the necessary limits of human understanding, or what Wittgenstein calls the limits of my language. (*Cities*, 426)

Because its protagonist focuses his anxieties on a woman's word and elaborates fantasies that they might transcend worldly language to perfectly read one another's hearts, *The Egoist* offers an especially clear example of linguistic scepticism. This, according to Cavell, is the variety of scepticism Wittgenstein's work can help us manage. If we can bring our 'words back from their metaphysical to their everyday use', accepting the implications of the fact that language is our form of life, then we can release ourselves not only from a captivating 'picture' of language – for instance, the notion that language is insufficient because it is 'merely conventional', tainted by external influences – but also from ethical liabilities that go along with the 'surmise' of radical barriers to knowledge (*PI*, §116).

In Cavell's terms, 'acknowledgment' is the way we release ourselves from the ethical risks of runaway scepticism. As I discussed in the introduction and previous chapter, acknowledgement is not a 'defeat' of scepticism – which cannot be defeated – but a response that reorients the sceptical surmise. Acknowledgement turns the so-called 'problem of other minds' into the precondition rather than the limit of intimacy. It recasts language as nothing more, but also nothing less, than the medium through which we improvise our desires and understandings. The vulnerabilities and conventionalities of talk contribute to the reason that the conversational form of life, which exemplifies good marriage – and by extension, good human relations – is a life of repetition. The last word can never be reached because the speakers are forever changing, language itself only means in use, and language never can (and should never be an effort to) express everything in the private 'heart' of a person. Cavell writes:

> [W]hat is wanting – if marriage is to be reconceived, or let's say human attraction – is for the other to see our separate existence, to acknowledge its separateness, a reasonable condition for a ceremony of union. Then the opening knowledge of the human is conceived as the experience of being unknown. To reach that absence is not the work of a moment. (*CT*, 22)

The 'absence' he describes is a two-way absence: acknowledgement entails coming to terms with the limits of my knowledge of the other and understanding that I myself am in some profound sense 'unknown'. Only by acknowledging this separateness do we 'make [the other] present [. . .] make them *other*, and face them' (*MWM*, 338). Acknowledgement sees this 'absence' as a prompt to offer the 'articulate responsiveness, expressiveness' signified by the ideal of conversation (*Pursuits*, 87). We acknowledge another when we accept 'separateness' as 'the logic of human intimacy' and 'the field of serious and playful conversation or exchange' (*CT*, 221).

The fraught conversations between Clara and Willoughby are, for Clara, struggles for acknowledgement. She seeks responsiveness, a 'living and frank exchange', but is instead drafted into theatrical performances in which her own words are irrelevant. Here is an exemplary instance of this dynamic, a conversation that begins as a discussion of the impending death of Willoughby's mother, then quickly pivots, as Willoughby demands that Clara performs new vows of faithfulness 'beyond death':

> 'Could you – it agonizes me to imagine . . . be inviolate? mine above? – mine before all men, though I am gone: – true to my dust? Tell me [. . .] I am your husband – say it – eternally. I must have peace; I cannot endure the pain. Depressed, yes; I have cause to be. But it has haunted me ever since we joined hands. To have you – to lose you!'
> 'Is it not possible that I may be the first to die?' said Miss Middleton.
> 'And lose you, with the thought that you, lovely as you are, and the dogs of the world barking round you, might . . . Is it any wonder that I have my feeling for the world? This hand! – the thought is horrible.

You would be surrounded; men are brutes; the scent of unfaithfulness excites them, overjoys them. And I helpless! The thought is maddening. I see a ring of monkeys grinning. There is your beauty, and man's delight in desecrating. You would be worried night and day to quit my name, to . . . I feel the blow now. You would have no rest for them, nothing to cling to without your oath.'

'An oath!' said Miss Middleton.

'It is no delusion, my love, when I tell you that with this thought upon me I see a ring of monkey faces grinning at me; they haunt me. But you do swear it! Once, and I will never trouble you on the subject again. My weakness! if you like. You will learn that it is love, a man's love, stronger than death.'

'An oath?' she said, and moved her lips to recall what she might have said and forgotten. 'To what? what oath?'

'That you will be true to me dead as well as living! Whisper it.'

'Willoughby, I shall be true to my vows at the altar.'

'To me! me!'

'It will be to you.'

'To my soul. No heaven can be for me – I see none, only torture, unless I have your word, Clara. I trust it. I will trust it implicitly. My confidence in you is absolute.'

'Then you need not be troubled.' (85–86)

Here, and throughout the novel, Clara's words have little effect on the course of conversation because Willoughby is caught up in a private melodrama. Instead of responding to her words or her tone, he reaches for performativity, insisting she articulate new vows.

The theatrical quality of such exchanges is significant for several reasons. Cavell explains that we deny acknowledgement to another if we 'convert [them] into a character and make the world a stage for [them]' (*MWM*, 333). 'There is no acknowledgment', he writes, 'unless we put ourselves in [the other's] presence, reveal ourselves to them [. . .] allowing ourselves to be seen' (*MWM*, 332–333). Willoughby's theatricality converts both him and Clara into characters, a conversion that robs her of agency and voice and simultaneously shields Willoughby from being seen by her. He tries to compel her to recite from two scripts, the script of performative ritual and the script of what I've called his private melodrama. The novel implies that the latter is inspired by popular sentimental fiction; at one moment, when Willoughby is envisioning a future conversation with Clara, we read that his imagined 'colloquy' is inspired by 'the language of the imaginative composition of his time [. . .] his popular romances' (279–280).

Such theatricality also recalls the split between speech and intention integral to performative utterances. The more resistance Clara shows to his romantic fantasies, the more fervently does Willoughby demand she repeat words whose significance do not depend on her desires. This implies that his behaviour paradoxically represents a warped form of acknowledgement, even as it refuses Clara acknowledgement. His demands for new, increasingly extreme vows signal his awareness that language has not (yet) closed the gap between them. Acknowledgement is not necessarily 'good', as Cavell indicates in a side remark that murdering someone can be a 'conclusive [. . .] acknowledgment that they are present' (*MWM*, 332). Speech is inadequate in the face of Willoughby's desire for certainty, but speech is all he has, which he acknowledges by insatiably demanding more.

Willoughby, then, swings from one extreme to the other, seeking to deny the publicness of language, then seeking to deny his own position as a source of language: one moment, he resists the fact that we rely on public conventions, and the next, he outsources all responsiveness to the public conventions of promising. Willoughby turns the promise into a tautology – a promise is a promise – exaggerated into absurdly 'bad logic', in Daniel Wright's phrase. Willoughby tells Clara, for instance, that '*affianced* is, in honour, *wedded*', which, as Wright notes, collapses 'the temporal extension of the promise, which may or may not eventually be kept [. . .] so that the promise and the fulfillment of that promise become a single, irreversible act'.[19] This tautology emerges from stressing the 'conventional idea of obligation' past the point of sense. There are obviously justifications for breaking or amending promises, and a betrothal is not as binding as a marriage: if it were, Willoughby might relax. In *Cities of Words*, Cavell criticises inflexible philosophical treatments of the 'institution' of promising, such as Kant's categorical imperative, or utilitarian arguments that similarly apply the principle of utility rather than that of responsiveness to unpredictable, specific situations. He compares promising to talking: 'If promising is a practice, then so is warning, or urging, or asking questions, or let's just say, talking' (88). The point is not to deny that these uses of language are practices governed by convention, but rather to remind us that they are *human* practices, and we must be responsive even when participating in them. As elsewhere, Cavell argues that 'conversation is essential' when we're navigating the obligations of our words, because no abstract rubric can or should guide us in moral life (or political life, as the related vision of the conversation of justice I discussed in the previous chapter shows) (*Cities*, 178).[20] Conversation of the quality Cavell means is precisely what Willoughby avoids at every turn. This is another reason his use of performativity resists acknowledgement, even while subtly offering it: he refuses to face Clara in conversation by instead citing the rules of promising.

The irony of Willoughby's position illuminates the unnecessary self-entrapment of scepticism carried this far, the reason that the response to scepticism offered by Wittgenstein and Cavell is not a refutation but rather a 'turning [. . .] about the fixed point of our real need' (*PI*, §108). Our real need is to communicate across difference, not to obliterate it – to establish trust and confidence in the face of uncertainty, not in triumph over it. Willoughby relies on convention to underwrite the power of speech acts, but it is the conventional – as opposed to divine or otherwise transcendental – basis of language that signals its limits. As in the exchanges cited above, he repeatedly frames his demands on Clara's speech as efforts to protect their love from 'the world', as if he and Clara might build a private world through their vows. Yet promises draw force from their publicness; 'honour' is a value interpreted and upheld in a specific form of life. Like the philosopher led into danger by scepticism, Willoughby resists the very features of language that, from another perspective – when turned on the fixed point of our real need – are the very reason language is a resource for him. The character's unique pathology is that he simultaneously occupies this other perspective: he perceives and exploits the conventionality of language, avoiding the knowledge his manipulative behaviour simultaneously expresses and represses.

## Conventionality and – Versus? – Voice

Clara's level responses to Willoughby's histrionics prefigure the ordinary language philosopher's effort to turn down the temperature of scepticism, accepting separateness and conventionality as constitutive of, rather than obstacles to, our satisfaction of real needs. 'You need not be troubled', she says. Simply accept that my words are according to convention: I mean them as far as I am concerned, which is as far as anyone can mean anything. Willoughby's acceptance of these conditions would allow them to enter the 'field of serious and playful conversation or exchange', in Cavell's words, or 'a living and frank exchange of the best in both', in Clara's. So far, then, *The Egoist* shares several core insights of ordinary language philosophy: language is public, and the perception of this might drive some of us into scepticism about our capacities to express ourselves and understand others, which might further drive us to deny acknowledgement to others. Such problems arise if we struggle to deny what we can't help but already know. It is not only in language use that scepticism poses problems, of course, but it is the manifestation of scepticism in language use which concerns *The Egoist*, as well as the ordinary language philosopher. Yet *The Egoist* complicates its lessons regarding 'our real need' by inviting us to ask the following question: shouldn't *Clara* become a bit sceptical, as she comes to understand the public conventions that underwrite her uses of language? Throughout the flood of talk in this novel, Clara's aim remains to persuade Willoughby to release her, when we know – from Constantia's example as well as common sense – that a simpler and more reliable route of 'jilting' is available. As I'll argue now, it is not 'honour' in the abstract that holds Clara back. She is in a double bind: marrying Willoughby, she would be bound forever to a man with whom she cannot converse; but 'jilting' Willoughby, she'd defy speech conventions that may be necessary for any conversation at all.

As the narrative progresses, Clara grows increasingly indignant not only at herself for committing to an egoist without the appropriate, informed intentions, but also at society, which compels women 'to sign themselves over by oath and ceremony, because of an ignorant promise, to the man they have been mistaken in' (*Egoist*, 142). And it is not only when promising that women in *The Egoist* find a dangerous gap between their intentions and speech. As Clara, Willoughby's long-time friend Laetitia Dale, and the narrator each observe, women are 'differently educated' in the use of language than men (205). Their 'training' makes it difficult for women 'to be straightforwardly sincere in their speech', encouraging them to dissemble rather than 'front an evil with plain speech' (205, 302). This emphasis on education resonates with Cavell's description of learning a language as an 'initiation' into a form of life. The main source of trouble in *The Egoist* is the form of life its characters share: not the structure or publicness of language per se, but its embeddedness in *this* form of life in which, for instance, a woman's ignorance when promising to marry is as conventional as her speech acts. (This is another reason to distinguish the novel's view of performativity from that offered in deconstruction, which is not to say that the novel indicates that uncertainty about intentions can be resolved in an absolute sense.)[21] Clara gave her word with the same degree of freedom and knowledge enjoyed by any other woman in her historical class cohort.

Reinforcing a feminist reading of its central drama, *The Egoist* gives to Willoughby lines that recapitulate a familiar analogy between interpersonal promises and the social contract writ large, which spotlights the jarring position of women in liberalising Britain. He appeals to Clara's father for support against her desire to be released, parroting one of the older man's signature phrases, 'I abhor a breach of faith', then elaborates: 'There are principles which civilized men must contend for. Our social fabric is based on them. As my word stands for me, I hold others to theirs. If that is not done, the world is more or less a carnival of counterfeits' (489). There is heavy irony in the fact that it is Willoughby saying these words: in the immediately preceding chapter, he made an unsuccessful proposal to Laetitia without having released Clara, as part of a late effort to salvage his reputation by marrying *someone*, and I'll return to this convoluted scheme shortly. However hypocritical Willoughby is, though, he is not exactly mis-stating the case: our social fabric is, in fact, based on promises, and, as I've just noted, Clara's ignorant promise is itself representative of a broader phenomenon. Cavell's account of the 'conversation of justice', discussed in the previous chapter, serves in part to temper social contract theory – suggesting that just as interpersonal promises might be navigated in 'conversation' rather than by citing convention, disagreements in a society might be better approached on the model of conversation than contract. *The Egoist* does not explicitly pursue the same reasoning, in part because it does not explicitly depict happy conversation – a matter I'll return to, somewhat indirectly, in my discussion of the ending. Yet the novel does invite us to see Willoughby's inflexible, anti-conversational relationship to Clara's promise as a synecdoche of the unjust social fabric. The 'liberal' social fabric is based on a highly selective view of women's capacities for responsible speech. It is useful to recall that when *The Egoist* was published, one of the disputed principles that 'civilized' men were contending for was coverture, the practice of dissolving a woman's legal identity into her husband's. This 'absurd fiction that two are one' – to use a phrase from Annie Besant's pamphlet on 'Marriage: As it Was, As it Is, and As it Should Be', published the same year as *The Egoist* – meant that a woman's wedding vow was the last meaningful contract she could enter on her own behalf.[22] Under the practice of coverture, a woman ceased to have a separate legal voice after her marriage.[23]

From this perspective, holding herself to her word would erase Clara's legal voice, just as it would bind her to a man who refuses to respond to her human voice. But breaking her word would appear to justify the logic behind coverture and other patriarchal denials of a woman's 'plain speech', the vision of women as unreliable and thus requiring representation by men. Her double bind is exemplary of the bind of women in the era's social fabric, reflecting the ironies and injustice feminist theorists of the social contract have noted. The novel implies that a desire to vindicate her sex is indeed among her motives for seeking to escape her promise without breaking it: 'She had heard women abused for shallowness and flightiness: she had heard her father renounce them as veering weather-vanes [. . .]: for her sex's sake, and also to appear an exception to her sex, this reasoning creature desired to be thought consistent' (225). She paradoxically wishes 'to be exemplary, yet also exceptional; to be perfectly singular, yet also a perfect general proof', as Daniel Wright glosses.[24] This apparent contradiction perhaps expresses a desire to be the exception that *changes*, rather than proves, the general rule: to exemplify women as they might be.

We can also read Clara's struggles with her promise as testing whether she has a 'voice' in her form of life, in Cavell's words, and 'how far [her] responsibility for the language may run' (*CR*, 28). This reading would link her effort to remain true to her word to the novel's insights about the tension between conventionality and acknowledgement. The novel most directly connects the issue of Clara's voice – that is, her capacity for self-expression, and hence the 'articulate responsiveness' or 'frank exchange' of good conversation – and her 'responsibility for the language' in its depiction of her dynamic with her father. Dr Middleton, 'a scholar of high repute', stands in the novel for the conservative consensus (66). He is a flawed yet affectionate patriarch, as well as a pedant who quibbles with other people's uses of language. At one point, he voices the alarming view that 'not to believe in a lady's No is the approved method of carrying that fortress built to yield', which is unfortunately appropriate within the form of life in which women receive the language 'training' *The Egoist* describes (527). As I've mentioned, Dr Middleton frequently remarks that he 'abhor[s] a breach of faith', and this sense of honour, as well as his enjoyment of Willoughby's wine and his appreciation of Vernon's company, make him a strong proponent of the projected marriage. Most pertinent to the novel's study of language use is his response to Clara when she tries to explain her wish to be released from the engagement:

> 'You are engaged to him, a plighted woman.'
> 'I do not wish to marry.'
> 'The apology is inadequate.'
> 'I am unworthy . . .'
> 'Chatter! Chatter!'
> 'I beg him to release me.'
> 'Lunacy!'
> 'I have no love to give him.'
> 'Have you gone back to your cradle, Clara Middleton?' (490)

The conversation is another exemplary instance of a man refusing to acknowledge Clara, yet here the reason is directly linked to her struggle against the 'conventional idea of obligation'. Her father first dismisses her attempts at self-expression as inadequate, then chatter, then evidence of madness, and finally evidence of regression and childish irresponsibility. Clara feels this cascading denial of acknowledgement as a loss of language: 'Language to express her peculiar repulsion eluded her. She formed the words, and perceived that they would not stand to bear a breath from her father [. . .] What could she say? he is an Egoist? The epithet has no meaning in such a scene' (493). If 'egoist' would have no meaning in the scene, it is because her father would refuse to grant meaning to any words that strain against her plighted faith. In such moments, *The Egoist* suggests that Clara's command of language itself is at stake in her efforts to disentangle from her promise.

The conversation that constitutes Clara's 'first direct leap for liberty' reinforces this subtle link between promising and a more basic capacity for expressiveness in language (169). The scene occurs shortly after she and her father relocate to Patterne Hall. Clara has begun to worry about Willoughby's behaviour, and she's also noticed that he has a more natural rapport with Laetitia, who at this point in the novel is still under the sway of a long-time, unrequited attraction to him. Clara tries suggesting to Willoughby that he would be happier with Laetitia, insisting that she – and the world – would even admire him if he were to break off a poorly matched engagement in favour of a true connection. Willoughby at this point considers Laetitia too plain to be a 'prize', and he treats Clara's words as a coy expression of jealousy. He promises to cut Laetitia out of his life if Clara requires it. She responds, 'you must hear me – hear me out', and then: 'women have their honour to swear by, equally with men', even 'girls have: they have to swear an oath at the altar; may I to you now?' (171, 173). Drawing on her capacity to swear in opposition to his dismissal of her words as insincere, she suggests that such a capacity is the foundation of meaning what she says at all, a kind of root certification of intentional speech.

Even as she discovers the difficulty of sincere self-expression, especially when it comes to performative speech, she recognises such speech as her best resource. Rather like Willoughby, but with a different attitude, she embraces the most prototypically conventional form of speech, while also understanding that it aligns imperfectly with her free self-expression. It is crucial to the novel's outlook on the fraught knot of conventionality, scepticism and ethical responsiveness in conversation that *The Egoist* does not outright reject the principles that underwrite illocution, and that it shows Clara's development as far more complicated than a simple process of education about her own desires and the injustice of her situation. In this claim, I depart from readings that treat *The Egoist* as absolutely rejecting the norms of language use enforced by figures like Dr Middleton. Randall Craig, as I've noted, argues that the novel denounces 'the system of rhetorical norms and discursive justice shared by this society and adjudicated by its scholars' because it 'restricts women's voices to ornamental accompaniment, or to silence'.[25] Indeed, the novel critiques the silencing of women's voices, but it also suggests that women might struggle to regain voice, or that women's struggles for self-expression test and potentially reshape the language. Clara learns that to have a voice in her language requires accepting at least some, if not all, of the conventions associated with her form of life.

I earlier quoted Cavell reflecting on moments when we test 'how far [our] responsibility for the language may run' (CR, 28). This line appears in a passage in *The Claim of Reason* that links the publicness of language to the question of mutual responsibility. Sharing a language means, to some extent, speaking implicitly (and sometimes explicitly) on behalf of others and community, sustaining and possibly transforming the form of life we share. Cavell writes:

> If I am to have a native tongue, I have to accept what 'my elders' say and do as consequential; and they have to accept, even have to applaud, what I say and do as what they say and do. We do not know in advance what the content of our mutual acceptance is, how far we may be in agreement. I do not know in advance how deep my agreement with myself is, how far responsibility for the language may run. But if I am to have my own voice in it, I must be speaking for others and allow others to speak for me. The alternative to speaking for myself representatively (for someone else's consent) is not: speaking for myself privately. The alternative is having nothing to say, being voiceless, not even mute. (28)

To share a language is necessarily to participate in its conventions. Participation, again, is not obedience. We do not know in advance of speaking how much freedom and self-expression we're capable of, because of possible divisions or disagreements within ourselves (inhibitions or conflicting desires, for instance), and because of possible divisions between ourselves and the public material of language we must use if we are to communicate. Prior to conversing with others, we do not know how much we share, how they might respond to us, and how our conversation might alter the forms of life we share.

*The Egoist* presents Clara's struggle as a discovery of the stark 'alternative' Cavell articulates.[26] If she finds herself to be voiceless, then she may as well tear the social fabric. But if she tears the social fabric, she might make herself voiceless. As we will see, the novel's concluding gesture – a speechless glimpse of hope in the Alps – can be read as a provocation to radically rethink or even rupture the form of life the characters share with one another, and presumably also with the novel's readers. From this perspective, we can read *The Egoist* as an exploration of 'the content of our mutual acceptance', and an invitation to reject or re-articulate much of it. Ordinary language philosophers insist that forms of life transform as we speak, and *The Egoist* wonders if the possibility of such transformation is adequate to the needs of people in positions like Clara.

### Performative Suspension of Reality

The irony and destructiveness of Willoughby's sceptical position come most powerfully – and absurdly – into focus in the dizzying conversation that constitutes the novel's climax. This conversation shows how an obsessed fear of the publicness of language nearly destroys Willoughby, but also, consistent with his earlier behaviours with Clara, points him towards his primary tool. (The scene also offers a parable that may seem familiar to twenty-first-century readers in the US, the UK and elsewhere: scepticism drives a man with a tenuous hold on power into a deranged effort to deny everyone a stake in the common world.) I read the sequence as a thought experiment: if speech acts can determine relationships, it asks, is the reverse possible? Can speech be not without effect, but with the effect of establishing indeterminacy, and if so, how and to what extent? As I'll explain in a moment, Willoughby tries to suspend the social world in a state of indeterminant potential by undermining the 'world's' confidence in its interpretation of what it observes. In a sense, his behaviour is a perverse instrumentalisation of the anti-instrumental ethos at the heart of Cavell's picture of conversation. Willoughby instrumentalises purposiveness without purpose, and the form of life he generates is one in which participants share a common suspension of reality.

To set the scene up, I should quickly recap part of the novel's convoluted plot. By this point, Willoughby's panic about being jilted a second time has reached a fever pitch. He is especially worried about the happy banter he and the 'world' have witnessed between Clara and a flirtatious visitor to Patterne Hall, Colonel de Craye. The possibility that Clara might jilt him for de Craye is particularly distressing to Willoughby because of the Colonel's popularity with the county Ladies. To save his reputation, Willoughby decides to orchestrate a fiancée swap: he'll propose to Laetitia, who has openly pined for him for years (his careless manipulation of her feelings has long been one of his cruelties). He plans to secure her promise, then 'give' Clara to Vernon, to prevent Clara from marrying de Craye. This arrangement will allow Willoughby to perform the role Clara suggested earlier of a romantic hero overcome by love for his childhood friend, while 'giving' Clara 'up to an extinguisher [...] an old-fashioned semi-recluse' (464–465). As far as he knows, thinking much worse of Vernon than Clara does, no one will be happier than himself: 'Vernon taken by Clara would be Vernon simply tolerated. And Clara taken by Vernon would be Clara previously touched, smirched. Altogether he could enjoy his fall' (570). But Laetitia declines his proposal, having become friends with Clara and consequently losing her romantic illusions about Willoughby. She leaves the house and takes cover in her father's cottage elsewhere on the estate, not explaining to her father what has happened.

The next morning, Willoughby renews his pressure on Clara, but gossip about his proposal to Laetitia begins to circulate. His young ward, Crossjay, overheard the unsuccessful proposal, and he accidently implies as much to Colonel de Craye. De Craye tells Clara, who confronts Willoughby in the presence of her father. Willoughby lies, telling Clara and Dr Middleton that he was speaking on Vernon's behalf, trying to make a match between Laetitia and his cousin. This satisfies Dr Middleton and stirs doubts in Clara: maybe Crossjay misunderstood. Meanwhile, the gossip Mrs Mountstuart arrives, and de Craye intercepts her with news that Willoughby and Laetitia are now engaged. When she sees Willoughby, she whispers congratulations, alerting him to the circulation of the false story. A tense lunch is served, after which Willoughby, Vernon, Mrs Mountstuart and Clara all depart the house, leaving Dr Middleton alone with Willoughby's aunts. Another visitor arrives: Laetitia's father, Mr Dale, who is distressed at his daughter's behaviour and the gossip that has reached him about her engagement with an already-engaged man. Confusion mounts as Dr Middleton, believing that Mr Dale has come after learning that his daughter declined *Vernon*, reassures Mr Dale that Laetitia can yet be persuaded to marry 'the gentleman' whom Dr Middleton so highly esteems (593). He cautions that 'the circumstances' should not yet be treated as 'public', and therefore 'it is incumbent on us [...] not to be nominally precise' (539).

The 'public' then arrives, in the form of the dull-witted county gossips Ladies Busshe and Culmer. They, too, have heard that Laetitia and Willoughby are engaged. The scene becomes increasingly convoluted, with bits of dialogue representing the gradual piecing together of strands of gossip, until Lady Busshe screeches, 'What whirl are we in?' She enjoins the gathering to 'proceed upon system', the first step of which is to state everything known with explicit precision (545). Mrs Mountstuart re-enters the scene, and although she has worked out Willoughby's plan to marry Laetitia himself and couple Clara with Vernon, she luxuriates in the suspension of clarity. As the scene continues, one of the Ladies suggests that their conversation is itself creating the state of affairs: whether or not Vernon has been rejected by Laetitia, the unnamed speaker says, 'is in debate, and at this moment being decided' (549). When Lady Busshe finally articulates aloud Willoughby's plan, and receives Mrs Mountstuart's confirmatory nod, she locates the affair even more firmly in the realm of discourse: the 'ebb and flow' of time and the twists of plot leading to this 'amicable rupture, and [. . .] smooth new arrangement', she remarks, have 'improve[d] the story' (549). Moreover, she appears to credit 'the county' with authorship: 'I defy any other county in the kingdom to produce [a story] fresh and living to equal it.' As we will see, she is not entirely wrong to claim partial, shared authorship.

Willoughby and Dr Middleton return just after Lady Busshe's synopsis, and the former immediately perceives danger. We've now arrived at the most virtuosic conversation in the novel. Without knowing what each person present knows, Willoughby nonetheless recognises that he is caught in a web of contradictory gossip about his engagement status. He also perceives that this entanglement means that, while he is not definitively engaged to either Clara or Laetitia, neither is he definitively disengaged from either woman, at least not in the view of 'the world' whose understanding he perceives as reality. He moves the conversation into a new phase that seeks to preserve this state of indeterminacy, evidently believing that both futures remain open to him as long as he can undermine the observing world's confidence in its interpretation of reality. Just as a performative utterance is neither true nor false, but rather felicitous or infelicitous, neither of the stories about Willoughby's engagement status is entirely true or entirely false.

Feeling like a 'fearfully dexterous juggler', he labours to keep this state of possibility alive, using ambiguous language, significant glances and interruptions to keep the two contradictory stories in motion (563). He reassures Mr Dale that Patterne Hall is '[his] home', for instance, which Mr Dale presumably interprets in relation to his daughter's proposed marriage to Willoughby, while Dr Middleton interprets the words as an allusion to Laetitia's marriage to Vernon, who also lives at Patterne (556). To the county Ladies, this vagueness is a mode of hedging that denies them confirmation of the story they've settled on. At one point, Willoughby glances significantly at Lady Busshe, but 'Lady Busshe would not be satisfied with the compliment of the intimate looks and nods', and she asks directly, 'Which is the father of the fortunate creature?' (556). Willoughby's reply is blatantly evasive: 'the house will be empty to-morrow'. He then bounces away to interrupt a threatening side conversation between Dr Middleton and Mr Dale, intervening with gestures and words of concern about Mr Dale's health just when

Dr Middleton is about to specify by name the man whose 'passionate advocate [he] proclaimed [himself]' (558).

The scene taps into a Victorian renewal of interest in the philosophical implications of vagueness. This line of enquiry is traceable at least as far back historically as Aristotle's contemporary, Eubulides, but it had fallen out of favour until a revival in the nineteenth century.[27] Eubulides is credited with first describing the 'sorites paradox', based on the Greek word for 'heap', *soros*.[28] According to one strand of this tradition, the vagueness of certain uses of language is an epistemic matter, vague language indexing incomplete knowledge of the world. If I am unable to say when, precisely, a 'heap' of objects ceases being a heap and becomes something else – a stack, let's say – the 'epistemicist' position would maintain that my inability is testament to my human limitations. There is some real distinction between a heap and a stack of the objects, the epistemicist would say, and I simply cannot discern it. Other philosophers have seen linguistic vagueness as a problem arising from the intrinsic vagueness of the thing being represented. This second view, sometimes called the 'supervaluationist approach', means that 'for some sentences there is no fact of the matter whether they are true' (like performative utterances, albeit for a different reason).[29] There are intermediary states that are neither definitively heaps nor stacks, and it is neither true nor false to call such an accumulation of objects a 'heap'. This understanding of vagueness can lead to the further view, as Mark Sainsbury and Timothy Williamson summarise, that 'the semantic indeterminacy reflects some real indeterminacy in the non-linguistic world itself'.[30]

The most provocative aspect of Willoughby's vagueness in this scene is its performativity: not merely *reflecting* indeterminacy in the world, or indeterminate knowledge of the world, his ambiguous language *achieves* worldly indeterminacy. If he were to speak truthfully and definitively, there would once more be a 'realist' correspondence between language and world, but since he holds out for a world more advantageous to him than the one that increasingly looks most likely (another broken engagement), he delays. His vagueness, like commissive utterances, opens a horizon for additional plot. One of the two women might change her mind, in which case the appropriate meanings can settle retroactively on indeterminate utterances.

Borrowing an anachronistic analogy from quantum physics, we might say that Willoughby's conversational behaviour turns the drawing room into a social version of Erwin Schrödinger's box, giving his engagement status something like quantum superpositionality. Like the unfortunate cat in Schrödinger's famous parable, Willoughby's engagement status is 'superpositional', spread across possible states, neither alive nor dead but suspended in a state describable only in terms of probability.³¹ In Schrödinger's story, the scientific observer determines the eventual state of the cat: once the observer looks into the box, a quantum, superpositional particle proves to have a distinct position, and that position will either have killed the cat or not. In the scene we're considering in *The Egoist*, the 'world' has the equivalent power to arrest discursive play through interpretation. Willoughby is in some senses engaged to both Laetitia and Clara, as long as the observers – the two fathers and the gossips – remain confused or under false impressions. A word of precision could reveal his duplicity and effectively make him engaged to neither of the women, but until then, a marriage to either remains possible.

Linguistic efficacy can be suspended only while interlocutors will play in the box, as it were, and such rhetorical play is precisely what Ladies Busshe and Culmer will not – indeed *cannot* – do for long. Following one 'exceedingly lively conversation at his table', shortly before the scene at hand, Lady Culmer remarks to Willoughby, 'what it all meant, and what was the drift of it, I couldn't tell to save my life', and Lady Busshe, during the same 'lively conversation', shows 'symptoms of a desire to leave a profitless table' (446, 445). The Ladies seek 'profit' from conversation, clear knowledge of fixed social positions, which will serve them as currency in the social economy of their neighbourhood. Willoughby understands this quality to be especially threatening, because such women cannot be 'hoodwinked' as easily as witty women, like Mrs Mountstuart, who enjoy verbal play: 'These representatives of the pig-sconces of the population judged by circumstances: airy shows and seems had no effect on them. Dexterity of fence was thrown away' (448). The verbal fencing he enjoys with Mrs Mountstuart takes the place of facts and deeds, whereas the dull Ladies resist the distraction of verbal play they do not follow, and 'steadily [keep] on their own scent of the fact', striving to observe a fixed universe, rather than play in the indeterminate space of ambiguous language (447).

*The Egoist* thus traces the source (and limit) of language's performative power to the language community, and specifically to the representatives of the community who insist on fixing language's relation to fact. This underscores the lack of agency enjoyed by the two potentially engaged women. If either woman or Crossjay were present and of a mind to speak, we would see if *The Egoist* imagines a woman or a boy might have a voice capable of successfully challenging Willoughby in his world-suspending language-game. Even if they proved to have such a voice, however, the larger implication of the scene remains the same: in certain circumstances, uses of language that scramble convention and 'hoodwink' observers might suspend the coordinates of social reality.

Talk itself becomes the quantum box, the space in which simultaneous oppositional states are 'true'.

The Ladies adopt several seemingly contradictory positions in the scene: they are judges issuing 'verdictives' that 'decide' the states of the possible engagements at Patterne Hall, authors collectively producing a story, and profit-seeking readers enjoying a romance. When they leave Patterne Hall believing Willoughby to be engaged to Laetitia, Lady Busshe thanks him for the 'lovely romance' and is described to be 'thoroughly imbued [. . .] with his fiction, or with the belief that she had a good story to circulate' (564). The novel suggests that the absurdity of its world is such that the Ladies' apparently contradictory self-understandings are all true. The gossips *do* have the power to dictate the course of events. Their judgements of the increasingly convoluted conversation – or rather, their interpretations, allegorised to reading – attain something like illocutionary force, setting in place the narrative that Willoughby believes he must labour to make felicitous. Interpretation takes place before the final arrangement, not quite making it so; here the Schrödinger analogy is not a perfect match. But it establishes the narrative that Willoughby then strives to render felicitous. His vagueness achieves a temporary indeterminacy, but narrative interpretation exerts stronger illocutionary force. Put in terms of the novel's frequently proposed allegory of reading, the scenario anticipates the poststructuralist 'birth of the reader' with a vengeance. The unnerving implications of this 'birth' linger, as we'll see, in the novel's ambiguous ending.

Willoughby's sense of self is one of the casualties of his performance: 'his partial capacity for reading persons had fled. The mysteries of his own bosom were bare to him; but he could comprehend them only in their immediate relation to the world outside. This hateful world had caught him and transformed him to a machine' (566). Whereas he earlier sought a private language to share with Clara, in opposition to the corruption of the world, he now feels that his own self is expressed in a public language he cannot read. He can only try to comprehend 'his own bosom' by seeing how the 'world' reads him. His fantasy of privacy – linked in the novel to his ironic use and denial of publicness – has morphed into a nightmare of publicity. It is of limited consolation that the 'world' wrests power back from Willoughby through its insistence on normative interpretation, its quest for a lovely romance. Willoughby's theatrical demands on Clara borrowed language from literary romances, after all, which suggests that the same norms that contribute to Clara's near captivity come to her rescue. We might additionally ask – especially from the standpoint of fears of 'post-truth' politics – what happens when the constituents of the 'world' read according to diverging generic conventions, not agreeing in their languages, and thus 'produce' incommensurate stories? We'll revisit these questions in later chapters.

## Noblest Ends? Speech Without Intimacy, Intimacy Without Speech

In the novel's closing pages, the two women at its centre take diverging routes of commitment. Willoughby has discovered that Clara, unrelenting in her aversion to marrying him, might be willing to marry Vernon. She does not promise to do so – I'll return to this detail in a moment – instead dodging illocution with the utterance, 'I could engage to marry no one else' (569). This negative almost-promise gives Willoughby confidence that he is near to achieving the second-best (to his mind) scenario, having apparently prevented his rival Colonel de Craye from marrying Clara. He resolves to secure Laetitia's engagement, thereby realigning reality with its representation in circulating gossip. The conclusion pairs off two new couples in scenes with sharply, and significantly, different representations of speech.

Laetitia takes the path of conventional responsibility, agreeing to marry Willoughby in a conversation that underscores the ceremonial and formal aspect of speech. She stipulates the presence of witnesses, Willoughby's aunts, and she addresses them rather than Willoughby, making the semi-public record reflect that she marries for money, not love, and will be 'irresponsive and cold':

> He asks me for a hand that cannot carry a heart, because mine is dead. I repeat it. I used to think the heart a woman's marriage portion for her husband. I see now that she may consent, and he accept her, without one. But it is right that you should know what I am when I consent. (595)

Laetitia's 'consent' recalls Clara's, replacing the former instance of a woman reciting words without appropriate intention with a new instance of a woman reciting the performative formula along with a full disclosure that the 'appropriate' intention is absent. Words are our bonds, she reaffirms, and she wishes all to know that she binds herself in words that derive their power from convention rather than sensibility: 'Ladies. You are witnesses that there is no concealment, there has been no reserve, on my part [. . .] I would not have you change your opinion of him; only that you should see how I read him. For the rest, I vow to do my duty by him' (597). In a sense, Laetitia's marriage will begin on the other side of scepticism: there is no need for Willoughby to doubt and fear her loving faithfulness, because she has already said it exists in legal but not sentimental form. Her faithfulness will be on the order of the law, not desire.

While Laetitia's engagement vows insist on the separateness of speech and sensibility, the understanding that passes between Clara and Vernon is a speechless demonstration brimming with sensibility finally acknowledged. The pairing of these two would seem to represent the best-possible authentication of marriage in the world depicted by *The Egoist*. He finds her witty and charming as a conversational partner, and she finds him enlarging and erudite, as well as kind. But in the final sentences of the novel, which suggest a union of sorts between the two, the narration conspicuously declines to make explicit claims: 'Two lovers met between the Swiss and Tyrol Alps over the Lake of Constance. Sitting beside them the Comic Muse is grave and sisterly. But taking a glance at the others of her late company of actors, she compresses her lips' (602).

The scene through which Vernon and Clara affirm their mutual attraction is likewise full of ellipsis and implication, rather than assertion, which in this novel represents a critical deferral of the performativity that both threatens and signals the possibility of conversation. Their conversation mediates their future through Clara's father – the novel's principal arbiter of linguistic convention – by purportedly concerning whether Clara will join Vernon and her father on a journey the two men plan to make through the Alps:

> 'To the Italian Alps! And was it assumed that I should be of this expedition?'
> 'Your father speaks dubiously.'
> 'You have spoken of me, then?'
> 'I ventured to speak of you. I am not over-bold, as you know.'
> Her lovely eyes troubled the lids to hide their softness.
> 'Papa should not think of my presence with him dubiously.'
> 'He leaves it to you to decide.'
> 'Yes, then: many times: all that can be uttered.'
> 'Do you consider what you are saying?'
> 'Mr. Whitford, I shut my eyes and say Yes.'
> 'Beware. I give you one warning. If you shut your eyes –'. (586)

In this passage, Clara says yes to Vernon without him having proposed. Her yes contains 'all that can be uttered', an ironic assertion that reinforces her distrust of speech. This 'all' is precisely what cannot be uttered: it may be indicated, but not contained, in elliptical language. Laetitia enters the scene a few lines later and witnesses 'their union of hands', an embodied expression of tenderness that suggests they have carved a space for intimacy surrounded by, but not enacted through, language. In this case, linguistic vagueness preserves intimacy by refusing to perform, by shaping a space for indeterminate union. The final page's image of the Comic Muse 'compress[ing] her lips' likewise represents the strength of Vernon and Clara's connection by refusing to name it, which would draw it into the conventions of marriage and/or of narrative. In contrast to the unethical ambiguity of the scene I've analogised to Schrödinger's box, here ambiguity allows for intimacy whose language is not possible, somehow, in the novel's form of life. Having shown how dangerous scepticism can be, the novel nonetheless seems to close on a sceptical note.

For me, this ambivalent closing calls to mind a famous 'scene of instruction' from *Philosophical Investigations*, in which the philosopher-speaker runs out of justifications for following a rule, drawn short by a question from a newcomer to the language:[32]

> 'How am I able to obey a rule?' – if this is not a question about causes, then it is about the justification for my following the rule in the way I do.
> If I have exhausted the justifications I have reached bedrock, and my spade is turned. Then I am inclined to say: 'This is simply what I do.' (*PI*, §217)

According to a common interpretation of this passage, Cavell explains, 'the teacher's (or speaker's) gesture [. . .] [is] a show of power, a political gesture [. . .] speaking for the community and its settlements, demanding agreement, [and] threatening exclusion' (*PDAT*, 113). This reading conforms with the perception of ordinary language philosophy as conservative in its appeal to 'what we say'. Cavell reads the passage otherwise, noting that Wittgenstein's speaker expresses an inclination, rather than a duty or a resolution, and suggesting that the 'response to hitting bedrock is meant as weak, temporary, open to continuation' (*Cities*, 186). By this reading, the speaker does not fall back on his own authority, but rather 'places confidence in the other', the student in the scene of instruction, whose questions might prompt the teacher to 'shift [their] ground, or take a new approach, or blast [their] way through, or exclude the site and this block from [their] plans altogether' (*CHU*, 76, 82). In other words, we might take the metaphor of the spade turning as an invitation to imagine many possible sequels, the most attractive of which are those in which the teacher learns something and perhaps passes the spade on to the next generation. This reading distils what Cavell 'think[s] of as the moral of the moment of recurrent silence' that he detects at the end of each section of the *Investigations*: 'at some point in teaching the pupil must go on – and want to go on – alone. Another way is to say that the teacher has to know both when, even how, to fall silent and when and how to break her silence' (*PDAT*, 114).

We might read *The Egoist* along these lines, taking its 'everlasting flood of talk' – its characters' repetitive struggles over, and through, performative speech – as the exhaustion of justifications for holding Clara to her promise. Suggesting we do so, I am also suggesting that the novel continues the aversive, self-questioning conversation of justice launched by Austen, adding a complication by warning us that we risk voicelessness when we contest the social fabric. This might be conservative, or at best a tepid, liberal case for moderation and slowness. But let's not forget that this novel 'jilts' any reader expecting a 'lovely romance'. Let's also not forget that the issues raised in the drawing room's quantum box linger after the scene ends. The novel's conspicuous closing silence would thus seem to be a gesture prompting the reader to carry on, alone, with a more challenging task than embracing a flexible approach to promises, or undertaking liberal social reforms that would enable women to mean what they say more consistently. The gossiping 'readers' force the indeterminant world back into shape, but it was not guaranteed that they would glean a coherent 'lovely romance' that happens to support Clara's chances for happiness. Moreover, the happiness of the ending is only partial: Laetitia's married life seems unlikely to be fulfilling. If words mean in use – if the meanings of our words and our conversations depend not only on how we use them, but also, as the novel reminds us, how members in our community interpret our uses of words – how can we use words in new ways, ways that do not reinforce the governing norms? How can we understand those 'initiated' into other forms of life in an increasingly inclusive, liberalising society? How can conversation be worldmaking without reproducing repressive interpretive norms, yet also without repressing the truth of scepticism, our reliance on shared forms of life to mean anything at all? The subsequent chapters of this book continue tracking the central questions with which *The Egoist* leaves us. That is, we can read Woolf, Rushdie and Smith as 'going on' in directions *The Egoist* prompts.

Chapter 3

# Conversation and Common Sense: Woolf, Russell and Kant

'English people have been trained not to see but to talk', observes the speaker in Virginia Woolf's 'Walter Sickert: A Conversation', a piece that blends fiction with commentary on Sickert's paintings, presented as a dinner party conversation.¹ Woolf here suggests that visual art arrests English chattiness by drawing its perceivers into the 'zone of silence in the middle of every art'. The 'artists themselves live in it', she writes, and they give expression to the view from within this silent space. Silence presumably lies at the heart even of verbal arts like Woolf's novels. As she writes in *A Room of One's Own*, the writer (like the visual artist) must strive to be receptive to a 'reality' that is 'more real than the world of speech', and then 'communicate it to the rest of us'.²

In Woolf's fiction, silence is also 'in the middle' of the most verbal, ordinary and allegedly 'English' art of conversation. As the Sickert story in fact reflects in its ironic adoption of the form of a fictional conversation about ineffable aesthetic experience, Woolf consistently represents conversation as a practice far more complex than any swift juxtaposition of aesthetic sight and talk implies. She develops a vision of conversation as an art in its own right, and she also proposes that, as an artistic practice, conversation can transform perception, including vision, thereby also transforming our orientation to 'reality'. Most extensively in *To the Lighthouse* and *The Waves*, Woolf integrates the activities of looking and talking in scenes of conversation, developing a vision of community founded on artistic efforts that link the social features of talk to the silent attentiveness of looking. This results in a conversational model of community, I claim, the backdrop of which is scepticism.

Indeed, Woolf's representations of conversation extend the reservations about cultivating intimacy through language that we saw in *The Egoist*, shifting from Meredith's concerns about the historical contingencies of language use to a characteristically modernist, deeper-running scepticism about language, communication and mutual understanding.

From her first novel, *The Voyage Out*, to her posthumously published *Between the Acts*, Woolf's fiction demonstrates keen awareness of the limits of language as a means of connecting with others. Richard Dalloway's exclamation to Rachel Vinrace in *The Voyage Out* encapsulates this sense that language inevitably falls short: '"Here I sit; there you sit; both, I doubt not, chock-full of the most interesting experiences, ideas, emotions; yet how communicate?"'[3] At times in Woolf's fiction, the limitation of speech offers relief, as in Clarissa's appreciation in *Mrs Dalloway* for the 'solitude' she can enjoy in her marriage with Richard, who famously cannot 'bring himself to say he loved her; not in so many words'.[4] Richard's silence on the subject of love suits Clarissa's sense that 'there is a dignity in people; a solitude; even between husband and wife a gulf; and that one must respect' (120). Along similar lines, the first section of *To the Lighthouse* ends with a curious, wordless struggle between the Ramsays, as Mr Ramsay craves his wife telling him 'just for once that you love me', and Mrs Ramsay resists.[5] Against the 'arid scimitar', the 'beak of brass' that is her husband's enervating need for sympathy and reassurance, Mrs Ramsay's occasional moments of resistant silence suggest that she withholds her voice as a means of self-preservation, which adds ethical and political dimensions to the novel's linguistic scepticism (38). The latter is expressed, for instance, when Lily thinks that 'words fluttered sideways and struck the object inches too low', and correctly surmises that Mrs Ramsay might feel we are somehow 'more expressive' when silent (178, 172). An abiding concern in *The Waves* is 'how little known' one's friends are and a view, to which I'll return, that 'speech is false', and we are 'only superficially represented' by our words.[6]

The moments of greatest connection between Woolf's characters are frequently moments when such imperfect verbal communication occurs alongside a different sort of conversation, the figurative conversation of the word's etymology. Woolf's depictions of conversation evoke the Latin roots, which, as I noted in the introduction, suggest a sense of togetherness generated by shared perception rather than communicated content, by 'turning with' others towards and through shared experiences. A line in *To the Lighthouse* encapsulates this kind of togetherness, describing Mrs Ramsay's feeling of connection to Augustus Carmichael while they both look at a bowl of fruit: 'That was his way of looking, different from hers. But looking together united them' (97). Woolf frequently pairs this wordless conversational attunement with the variously flawed efforts of characters to communicate through speech.[7] The opening of *To The Lighthouse* offers a sharp example, spacing a six-line conversation about going to the lighthouse over the course of many pages, as the narration plunges into the minds of the characters listening to and participating in the conversation, and everyone turns, in their different ways, towards the lighthouse. Woolf does not exactly contrast these modes of conversation, as though the figurative 'turning together' boasts an authenticity lost in ordinary speech. Rather, it is when the two senses of conversation come together that her characters experience a reprieve from scepticism. This idea, I suggest, animates the form of Woolf's most unusual novel, *The Waves*, a cycle of utterances in six voices that are abstract, lyrical and bearing only obscure relation to each other. Woolf described *The Waves* in her diary as a 'play-poem'.[8] The soliloquies that make up the body of *The Waves* are not, it seems, spoken aloud, and they frequently express reservations about the limitations of speech. A lifelong 'conversation' of sorts nonetheless holds the work's characters together, as the novel's texture of utterances insists.

In what follows, I read pivotal scenes in *To the Lighthouse* and *The Waves* as explorations of the convergence of literal conversation with its figurative counterpart. In each scene, companions gather around a dinner table, making conversation and also, in the process, making community. I begin with the dinner scene in *To the Lighthouse*, which establishes complex parallels between conversation and other forms of art. I then turn to *The Waves*, which I argue reconfigures two philosophical debates that were themselves the subject of vibrant conversation in Woolf's Bloomsbury circle: sceptical epistemology, especially as elaborated in Bertrand Russell's work, and aesthetics as developed by Immanuel Kant.[9] The novel suggests that conversation elevated to the level of an art can affirm a common sense of reality in the face of sceptical doubt by generating a feeling similar to Kant's *sensus communis*. Drawing from *The Waves* something like an implicit conversation between Russell and Kant, I elaborate a vision in which conversationalists create – rather than 'impute' or consult – a unique variant of *sensus communis*, which gives Woolf's characters a fleeting sense of sharing a common world.

As in every chapter of this book, my argument is not so much that Woolf sets out to develop a theory or philosophy of conversation, but rather that a revealing expression of the conversational outlook becomes legible when we reconstruct the implicit conversation her work stages with Kant and Russell. Reading *The Waves*, and to a lesser extent *To the Lighthouse*, with attention to the figure and practice of conversation, we can perceive a vision at the heart of Woolf's work that draws together aesthetics, epistemology and ethics. Conversation, for Woolf, is a means of facing others by not quite facing them: by facing the world *with* them, and by establishing a common ground on which to stand in mutual opacity. This vision of conversation encompasses a Cavellian acknowledgement of separateness, and in tune with Cavell, and Wittgenstein as read by Cavell, it proposes that talk undertaken in a state of aesthetic disinterestedness can relieve (but not defeat) scepticism about the common world. It recognises language as both a means and limit of intimacy and commonality, locating its potency in aesthetic features that simultaneously prefigure Hannah Arendt's account of public life as constituted in conversation. As such, Woolf's work offers a distilled encapsulation of the conversational outlook and a bridge between the ethical concerns about ordinary language use I elaborated in Chapters 1 and 2, and the political concerns about democratic speech and shared reality that I foreground in Chapters 4 and 5. Scholars typically locate Woolf's political salience in her feminism or subtle critiques of the British Empire, but tracing her representation of conversation reveals a new, foundational link between politics and her aesthetic vision. Conversation, Woolf suggests, generates a specific form of *sensus communis* that affirms the commonality scepticism warns our other senses cannot ensure. This vision, I show, anticipates Arendt's account of the public realm, and thus also this book's own political turn.

## Conversation and Aesthetics in *To the Lighthouse*

The famous dinner scene in *To the Lighthouse* characterises Mrs Ramsay as an artist, working with the media of dinner party conversation: talk, but also candlelight, the table settings, Boeuf en Daub and carefully timed social interventions, such as when her husband's vanity or temper threatens to derail her 'effort of merging and flowing and creating' (83). Described by Woolf as holding herself 'outside' the 'eddy' of talk and emotion in order to see 'things truly', her portrayal clearly resonates with classic accounts of aesthetic impersonality, in Woolf's work as well as the aesthetic tradition she inherits from Kant, which also clearly inform the novel's descriptions of Lily painting. Lily, too, must detach herself from 'gossip' and 'community with people' in order to see, without the distractions of self-consciousness and self-interest, the 'truth [. . .] at the back of appearances' she wishes to capture in her work (159). The dinner scene thus establishes ambiguous parallels between the novel's literal artist and the character who embodies the 'Angel in the House', the feminine ideal that Woolf famously argues a woman artist must murder, figuratively, if she is to see clearly and express her vision truthfully.[10] In *A Room of One's Own*, Woolf establishes the striking image of the 'androgynous' and 'incandescent' mind of successful artists, who transcend specifically gendered self-consciousness in favour of impersonal perception. The normative force of gender is key to Mrs Ramsay's domineering charm, in tension with the novel's admiration not only for her beauty, but also for her artistic potential. Such ambivalence is central to the dinner scene.

The party gets off to a rocky start, as characters 'all [sit] separate', alienated from one another and the premise of dining together. 'There was no beauty anywhere', Mrs Ramsay thinks while surveying her raw materials, as it were (82). Reinforcing the domineering aspect of her creative efforts, Woolf likens her to the 'chairman' of 'some meeting', who insists 'that every one shall speak in French', knowing the artifice will 'impose some order, some uniformity' (90). Woolf is subtly Wittgensteinian, here: Mrs Ramsay imposes a distinct form of life, analogous to an artificially adopted language, and its class and gender norms chafe those least initiated to it – Lily, William Bankes and Charles Tansley. Tansley feels excluded and behaves with petulant egotism. Bankes is bored with 'family life', the 'waste of time' of social chat, the interruptions of children and servants. Lily wants to rebel against the gendered 'codes of behaviour' that dictate she be nice to Tansley, relieving his vanity even though he taunts her with the sexist refrain, 'women can't paint, women can't write' (91). She complies, though. They all fall in line under the power of Mrs Ramsay's 'social manner'.

The group begins to 'merge' when Mrs Ramsay calls for the lighting of candles. The shift in lighting reorients their perception, drawing the party into a coherence the chairwoman's 'language' alone does not achieve:

> Now all the candles were lit up, and the faces on both sides of the table were brought nearer by the candle light, and composed, as they had not been in the twilight, into a party round a table, for the night was now shut off by panes of glass, which, far from giving any accurate view of the outside world, rippled it so strangely that here, inside the room, seemed to be order and dry land; there, outside, a reflection in which things waved and vanished, waterily.
> 
> Some change at once went through them all, as if this had really happened, and they were all conscious of making a party together in a hollow, on an island; had their common cause against that fluidity out there. (97)

In this passage, the characters gain new consciousness of their formal relations, as though discovering they are inside a work of art, looking outwards through the glass at the 'fluidity' of a world without intentional form, which seems vaguely threatening in its formlessness.

They are at once the materials of Mrs Ramsay's art and the judges, whose perception of themselves as 'making a party' transforms them into a party. In other words, the moment shows their aesthetic judgement to be circularly integral to their transformation into a living artwork. Visual formalism accomplishes what verbal form alone did not, but rather than separating the achievement of coherence from conversation, the passage shows a convergence of aesthetic and linguistic attunement. Mrs Ramsay's 'social manner' is supplemented by the candles' alteration of perception, which transforms the characters from disconnected individuals into 'a party round a table'. Towards the end of the scene, Mrs Ramsay assesses what she has helped to make, declaring it a 'community of feeling with other people' (113).

A description of Mrs Ramsay at the height of the party establishes a somewhat puzzling link between this social achievement and an earlier scene, which in many respects appears to be its opposite. In the earlier passage, Mrs Ramsay steals a moment of solitude and freedom before dinner, savouring an opportunity to 'be herself, by herself' (62). This, we read, is 'what now she often felt the need of – to think; well not even to think. To be silent; to be alone. All the being and the doing, expansive, glittering, vocal, evaporated; and one shrunk, with a sense of solemnity, to being oneself, a wedge-shaped core of darkness, something invisible to others' (62). In ordinary life, responding to the demands of her familial and community roles, she is expansive, glittering and vocal; alone, she is distilled into a dark, silent wedge. She imagines that her 'sense of unlimited resources' must be shared by others, that others must similarly feel that their vocal and glittering, social selves are nothing but 'apparitions, the things you know us by', 'childish' and superficial glimpses of a self that moves in 'dark', 'spreading' and 'unfathomably deep' regions, occasionally surfacing in ordinary conversation. The passage oscillates between defiant 'triumph' and freedom, and a darker, almost death-courting embrace of the 'peace' available when 'life sank down for a moment':[11]

> There was freedom, there was peace, there was, most welcome of all, a summoning together, a resting on a platform of stability. Not as oneself did one find rest ever, in her experience (she accomplished here something dexterous with her needles), but as a wedge of darkness. Losing personality, one lost the fret, the hurry, the stir; and there rose to her lips always some exclamation of triumph over life when things came together in this peace, this rest, this eternity. (62–63)

This feeling paradoxically returns to her during the dinner sequence, when she is at her most expansive, glittering and vocal. Here is the paired moment from the dinner scene:

> She hovered like a hawk suspended; like a flag floated in an element of joy which filled every nerve of her body fully and sweetly, not noisily, solemnly rather, for it arose, she thought, looking at them all eating there, from husband and children and friends; all of which rising in this profound stillness [. . .] seemed now for no special reason to stay there like a smoke, like a fume rising upwards, holding them safe together. Nothing need be said; nothing could be said. There it was, all round them. It partook, she felt, [. . .] of eternity; as she had already felt about something different once before that afternoon; there is a coherence in things, a stability; something, she meant, is immune from change, and shines out [. . .] in the face of the flowing, the fleeting, the spectral, like a ruby; so that again tonight she had the feeling she had had once today, already, of peace, of rest. Of such moments, she thought, the thing is made that endures. (105)

The surprising link between these scenes suggests that Mrs Ramsay transmutes the glittering and vocal labours of social life into an aesthetic medium. While performing in her most 'expansive, glittering, vocal' way – chatting and intervening in the conversation, drawing stragglers into the flow of talk, lighting the candles to deflect her husband's grumpiness, charming Lily into flattering Tansley, and so on – she simultaneously mediates a timeless truth beyond such apparitional being and doing, the sense of peace and stability she earlier accessed as a wedge of darkness.

In the earlier scene, she likewise double-tasks, performing the gendered labour of knitting stockings for the lighthouse keeper's son while 'shrinking' into a dark, core self beneath personality. Her moments of freedom thus coincide with – perhaps are contingent on – her conformity to her social role, as if her glittering, vocal self screens her invisible, silent self, allowing both to mingle in the moment. The irony of the dinner party's aesthetic achievement is less a contradiction than a complication, a linkage between the aesthetic power of conversation under Mrs Ramsay's guidance and the strict 'codes of behaviour' that dictate her life, and which she strives to dictate for future generations. It recalls 'compromises' we experience, according to Cavell, in consenting to any form of life, as well as the 'creative force' Woolf elsewhere describes women as having developed by 'the most drastic discipline' while sitting 'indoors all these millions of years'.[12] Conventions are inescapable, necessary for the 'community of feeling with other people', yet frequently standing in need of change.

As I alluded at the beginning of this section, the passages above are echoed in Lily's successful completion of her painting in the third section of the novel, and again in *A Room of One's Own*, in which Woolf describes the writer, or artist, as living 'in the presence of' an elusive quality she calls 'reality', a 'very erratic, very undependable' quality that 'fixes and makes permanent' 'whatever it touches', and 'makes the silent world more real than the world of speech' (110). Woolf writes that it is 'the business' of the writer (or artist, we can generalise) to 'live in the presence of' the silent, timeless 'reality', to 'find it and collect it and communicate it to the rest of us' (110). Lily does precisely this, although her creative process is more harrowing than Woolf indicates in *A Room of One's Own*. She feels 'drawn out of gossip, out of living, out of community with people into the presence of this formidable ancient enemy of hers – this other thing, this truth, this reality, which suddenly laid hands on her, emerged stark at the back of appearances and commanded her attention' (*To The Lighthouse*, 159). Whereas Mrs Ramsay's freedom from the 'glittering, vocal' rhythms of ordinary life leads to a sense of peace and stability, and *A Room of One's Own* describes the writer as having 'the chance to live more than other people in the presence of this reality', Lily's experience is 'half unwilling', an 'exacting form of intercourse' with 'reality' (159). The description of this rather ominous, exacting form of intercourse simultaneously evokes communication and sex, as the word conversation historically has. In any case, for Lily painting is indeed an attempt at communication, or rather, two attempts at communication: a three-way encounter between the artist, reality and 'the rest of us', as she tries to express on the canvas something of the 'truth' so exacting in its intercourse.

In its depictions of both Mrs Ramsay and Lily, *To the Lighthouse* establishes a complex set of links between impersonality and communication. On the one hand, glittering and vocal performances – talk and gossip, community with other people – obstruct the person's communication with 'this truth', something timeless or eternal. On the other hand, conversation is a metaphor for Lily, and perhaps a synecdoche for Mrs Ramsay: a model and a medium in which she 'communicates' her privately glimpsed truth beneath surface apparitions, the 'coherence in things' whose rendering into the public medium of the dinner conversation allows a 'community of feeling with other people'. Ten years after this party, when Lily returns to the house and finishes her painting, she recalls Mrs Ramsay as having 'ma[de] of the moment something permanent (as in another sphere Lily herself tried to make of the moment something permanent)' (161). Indeed, as Lily's paintbrush attempts to convey something she glimpses in impersonal conversation with 'reality', Mrs Ramsay's words and the perceptual 'turns' of conversation attempt to convey a formless stability similarly visible to her when she is 'suspended' outside the flow of talk.

Mrs Ramsay does not claim that she has made 'the thing [. . .] that endures': she has made something like a rough draft, or gathered the perceptual materials into a moment from which further communication of 'this reality' might be made. In her view, the scene she has made begins to dissipate immediately: 'as she moved and [. . .] left the room, it changed, it shaped itself differently; it had become, she knew, giving one last look at it over her shoulder, already the past' (111). Lily in fact recognises the difference between material artworks and the 'sphere' of memory, in which Mrs Ramsay's achievement endures. She imagines that Augustus Carmichael – the grumpy poet with whom Mrs Ramsay feels briefly united by 'looking together' at a bowl of fruit, at the height of the dinner party – might explain to her 'how "you" and "I" and "she" pass and vanish; nothing stays; all changes; but not words, not paint' (97, 179). Yet, as Mr Ramsay remarks, simultaneously tormenting and soothing his fragile ego, 'the very stone one kicks with one's boot will outlast Shakespeare' (35). The differences between conversation and canonical works of art may be traceable in terms of degree, rather than kind. Nothing endures without end; conversations, like paintings or poetry, can stamp the everyday with enduring but not everlasting significance. Under aesthetic stewardship, fleeting conversation may reveal – or perhaps generate – an elemental social coherence.

### *The Waves'* Twofold Conversation

*The Waves* makes this vision of conversation as an art into a formal principle, stylistically evoking and subverting ordinary ideas about conversation, and developing Woolf's paradoxical conjoining of social life, talk and impersonality. As I have noted, the language of the six voices in Woolf's 'play-poem' is lyrical and repetitive, unlikely to be uttered aloud, although each soliloquy begins with the conventional markers of speech: 'Bernard said', 'Susan said', and so forth.[13] In her study of conversational poetics in modernist fiction, Elizabeth Alsop proposes that the style of *The Waves* serves to denaturalise the individuating function of dialogue in conventional novels, thus also denaturalising the vision of autonomous personhood reinforced via conventional novelistic characterisation. In Alsop's view, Woolf develops a mode of representing 'speech as something other than a discrete performative act by a single speaker', making it instead 'a kind of communal practice or property'.[14] The reading that follows largely complements Alsop's, but I propose that the full significance of this depiction of speech as a 'communal practice or property' comes into focus when read in the context of the novel's invocations of scepticism.

As in Woolf's other fiction, characters in *The Waves* frequently express both linguistic and epistemological scepticism, directing attention to the limitations of language use in everyday conversation and to the uncertainty of sense perception as a means of knowing reality. Consistent with previous studies of the philosophical dimension of Woolf's work, especially Ann Banfield's pathbreaking analysis of Woolf's engagement with British epistemology, I locate in the conversational form and vision of *The Waves* an extended reworking of Bertrand Russell's response to scepticism. As is well known, Woolf and Russell were friends, and Russell's thought was influential on the former 'Cambridge Apostles' in the Bloomsbury Group. Among other ambitions, Russell sought to update epistemology to accommodate the revelations of modern physics, which dealt new challenges to confidence in human perception. He drew on mathematics, logic and ordinary sense experience to develop a new 'theory of knowledge', which, Banfield argues, Woolf adopts in her fiction.[15] I propose that Woolf in fact reframes Russell's ideas, especially in *The Waves*, where both textual form and a repeated dinner scene invoke and rework Russell's theory. *The Waves* suggests that conversation undertaken in a disinterested, aesthetically sensitised frame of mind can relieve scepticism by creating a specific kind of common reality. In other words, not only might conversation at times become communal 'property', but it might, moreover, *make* something akin to communal property, a common world. Via aesthetic affordances, conversation can transform the uncertain world perceived by our fallible senses into a 'dwelling-place', as Rhoda calls it (*The Waves*, 228).

Woolf's reworking of Russell's epistemological scepticism begins in the novel's opening pages, with the move from an italicised, third-person description that begins, '*The sun had not yet risen*', to the first soliloquies:

> 'I see a ring', said Bernard, 'hanging above me. It quivers and hangs in a loop of light'.
> 'I see a slab of pale yellow', said Susan, 'spreading away until it meets a purple stripe'. (9)

From this opening forwards, sections of soliloquy alternate with brief, italicised descriptions of the progress of a single day near the sea, from sunrise to sunset. The form juxtaposes the life stages of individual people against a daily cycle that repeats: the characters are children when the sun rises, they are in their prime at noon, and most have died by the evening. It also instantiates what Russell calls, in *An Outline of Philosophy* (1927), 'a question of very great importance': 'What difference is there between the propositions "there is a triangle" and "I see a triangle"?'[16]

What is the link, that is, between first-person experience – which the sceptical tradition teaches us to suspect – and objective, common reality?

The alternating sections of *The Waves* reproduce the gist of Russell's question, yet the voice of the third-person interludes in *The Waves* does not offer a neutral, objective perspective. This voice is itself idiosyncratic and prone to historically charged metaphors, such as an analogy linking the sound of the waves crashing to 'turbaned warriors' drumming. The echo of Empire here and elsewhere is significant considering the novel's subversive treatment of an imperial, masculine ideal in its accounts of Percival, a silent object of admiration for the six characters, who dies in India after falling off a horse. Percival's fate deflates the fantasies he embodies, encapsulated by Bernard in the idea that Percival is 'a God', who would 'appl[y] the standards of the West, using the violent language that is natural to him', and thereby 'solve' the 'Oriental problem' (136). The imperial 'God' dies, just as the imperious Angel dies in *To the Lighthouse*, suddenly and off-page.[17] It is outside my scope to pursue the full implications of these deaths, beyond observing that they produce similarly central absences in each novel and link idealism to repressive political and social practices. Here it is also worth noting that the slippage of imperial imagery into the third-person interludes in *The Waves* suggests that even the 'objective', third-person narratorial voice associated with conventional, realist novels is entangled in specific ideological and material relations. The absence or inaccessibility of a narratable position beyond history and power is another facet of the epistemological uncertainty Woolf's novel explores.

In Russell's treatment, scepticism poses problems for community, as we tend to 'want the same object for different people', in part to ensure that different people inhabit the same reality.[18] In *The Problems of Philosophy* (1912), he situates this desire in a scene of 'ten people [. . .] sitting round a dinner-table', which Woolf echoes in the repeated dinner scene in *The Waves* (*Problems*, 21). Here is Russell's version:

> When ten people are sitting round a dinner-table, it seems preposterous to maintain that they are not seeing the same tablecloth, the same knives and forks and spoons and glasses. But the sense-data are private to each separate person; what is immediately present to the sight of one is not immediately present to the sight of another: they all see things from slightly different points of view, and therefore see them slightly differently. (*Problems*, 21)

In his 1914 *Our Knowledge of the External World*, Russell states a bolder version of the 'preposterous' implications of the fact that our 'sense data are private': 'There is absolutely nothing which is seen by two minds simultaneously', he writes; 'the three-dimensional world seen by one mind therefore contains no place in common with that seen by another'.[19]

According to Russell, the ordinary conviction that people sitting around a table do in fact see the same tablecloth, cutlery, and so on is not exactly wrong, but its truth requires several intervening steps of explanation. For us to see the same objects, there must exist 'something over and above the private and particular sense-data which appear to various people' (*Problems*, 21). There must be a common world, populated with what he calls 'public neutral objects' (ibid.). He develops an account of the relation between human observers and such 'public neutral objects' that characterises individual observation as a 'purely structural position', in Banfield's words, 'one already there before an observer arrives'.[20] There are infinitely different perspectives through which different people might look upon public neutral objects, and each of these perspectives discloses its own 'world', in Russell's terminology. 'If two men are sitting in a room', he writes, 'two somewhat similar worlds are perceived by them; if a third man enters and sits between them, a third world, intermediate between the two previous worlds, begins to be perceived' (*Our Knowledge*, 70). And although a 'world' is contoured according to the position from which it may be observed, an actual observer is not necessary to that world's 'existence': each world 'exists entire exactly as it is perceived, and might be exactly as it is even if it were not perceived' (ibid.). Russell thus describes worlds not in terms of what is 'seen' by a particular subject, but what is 'seeable' by perspectives both occupied and unoccupied, potential views on objects by potential, non-specific subjects. We are constantly moving through different 'worlds' that await our arrival, and we do not share the same world with one another. We perceive the public, objective world in glimpses, from specific angles, which we can imaginatively integrate 'by inference' and mathematical logic. Our knowledge of the world is a 'logical construction', he writes, an extrapolation of a 'relation between the perspectives' (*Our Knowledge*, 72, 71).

Now consider the first of the two dinner table scenes in *The Waves*. The characters have gathered for a farewell meal before Percival leaves for India:

> 'But here and now we are together', said Bernard. 'We have come together, at a particular time, to this particular spot. We are drawn into this communion by some deep, some common emotion. Shall we call it, conveniently, "love"? Shall we say "love of Percival" because Percival is going to India?

'No, that is too small, too particular a name. We cannot attach the width and spread of our feelings to so small a mark. We have come together (from the North, from the South, from Susan's farm, from Louis's house of business) to make one thing, not enduring – for what endures? – but seen by many eyes simultaneously. There is a red carnation in that vase. A single flower as we sat here waiting, but now a seven-sided flower, many-petalled, red, puce, purple-shaded, stiff with silver-tinted leaves – a whole flower to which every eye brings its own contribution.' (127)

The parallels to Russell are clear. Woolf gathers seven people 'round a dinner-table' (the six 'speakers' of the novel and Percival) and draws attention to their slightly different points of view. Bernard's curious specification that the flower in the centre of the table is 'seen by many eyes simultaneously' offers a complicated rejoinder to Russell's 'preposterous' suggestion that people sitting around a table are not, in fact, seeing things simultaneously. The claim partly reads as a shorthand version of Russell's theory: the many-sided flower they perceive while dining together is a public object whose existence the friends can infer from the similarities of their distinct 'worlds'. Each eye sees a unique, non-shared world, or 'side' of the flower, but the composite of their worlds is evidence of the inferable 'public' flower.

Matters are complicated by Bernard's suggestion that an urge to make such a Russellian public object has drawn them to the dinner in the first place. He insists they have come together not simply to bid Percival farewell, and that 'love' is also 'too small, too particular a name' for whatever compels them. The emotion drawing them together is the urge 'to make one thing [. . .] seen by many eyes simultaneously'. The line is doubly strange for its pre-emptive defence against scepticism – *this thing* is seen by many eyes simultaneously! – as well as for its conflation of looking and making, a conflation that makes some sense in light of Russell's theory of public objects, insofar as a public object is constitutively many-sided. Yet Woolf modifies Russell in several crucial ways. First, for Russell, looking is decidedly not an act of creation: the public object's many sides pre-exist observers. Second, Woolf integrates Russell's theory with aesthetics, not only by insisting on the creativity of coordinated perception but also in the characters' varied accounts of the scene, beginning with Bernard's fixation on a flower, a paradigmatic symbol of beauty. By linking Russell's sceptical formulations to a flower – Immanuel Kant's exemplary 'free natural beauty' in the *Critique of Judgement*, the work that set the terms for much subsequent thinking about aesthetic experience, including in the Bloomsbury Group – *The Waves* offers not only an aesthetic expression or extension of Russell's ideas, as Banfield argues, but also an aesthetic *reorientation* of scepticism, a response to sceptical doubt that draws on aesthetic theory where Russell draws on mathematics and logic.[21]

References to flowers are abundant in the *Critique of Judgement*, but the more pivotal link between *The Waves* and Kant's aesthetic theory is in the set of connections both establish between aesthetic experience and the sense of commonality affirmed when we share experiences of beauty – a sense we might call communion, following Bernard. When we pronounce an object beautiful, Kant writes, 'we believe that we speak with a universal voice, and we claim the assent of every one' (*CJ*, §8, 50). Herein lies the difference between saying 'this flower is beautiful' and 'I like this flower', the latter phrase making no claims on others' tastes. We '*imput*[e] this agreement [about the flower's beauty] to everyone', Kant explains, expressing a peculiar universalising tendency even though we cannot conceptually or logically account for our judgement (§8, 51). According to Kant, we do not judge a flower to be beautiful via logical deduction or induction, and our judgement proceeds 'without the mediation of a concept' (§40, 138). 'There can be no rule according to which anyone is to be forced to recognise anything as beautiful', he writes, and 'we cannot press upon others by the aid of any reasons or fundamental propositions our judgement that a coat, a house, or a flower is beautiful' (§8, 50). This is curious: we believe that anyone who perceives the flower (or coat, house, or other object) will immediately, 'preconceptually', judge that it is beautiful, despite our inability to explain why or attempt to logically force them to do so, should they not. Here is the foundational Kantian link between aesthetics and communion: to judge an object beautiful is to imagine you perceive it as others would, with the 'universal voice' of what Kant calls the *sensus communis*, the 'subjective principle which determines what pleases or displeases only by feeling and not by concepts, but yet with universal validity' (§21, 75). In fact, when we judge something beautiful, the main thing we 'postulate' is this communion itself: 'in the judgment of taste nothing is postulated but such a *universal voice*', although the postulation of this universality only occurs in '*singular*', specific and sensual responses to beauty (§8, 50 and 49, original emphases). Lacking abstract concepts from which to derive our judgements – abstractions that theoretically might be accessible in isolated, rational contemplation – we need the singular, specific object. But when we judge that object, we are affirming nothing quite so powerfully as the possibility of communion, the existence of a universally valid, yet subjectively and concretely accessed, 'voice'.

There are numerous links between Kantian aesthetic theory and ordinary language philosophy, especially the conversational ideal in Cavell's writing. As I mentioned in the introduction, Sianne Ngai has pointed out that Kant's theory begins with a 'turn toward ordinary conversation', and includes a 'veritable catalog of speech acts', proceeding like an ordinary language philosopher from observation about how we use language when attempting to account for beauty to propositions about the form of life – the *sensus communis* – through which we speak thus.[22] And just as, for Cavell and other ordinary language philosophers, there are no rules or fixed formulae to guarantee mutual understanding, Kant warns that our initial responses to objects like flowers are not guaranteed to be shared. Lest we mistake our personal, idiosyncratic tastes for those of the universal voice – or lest we believe that the 'preconceptual' nature of aesthetic judgement is a licence for subjective relativism in aesthetic matters – we should 'compare' our tastes 'with the collective reason of humanity, and thus [. . .] escape the illusion arising from the private conditions that could be so easily taken for objective' (*CJ*, §40, 136). Here we reach a second important link between aesthetic experience and community, the method Kant proposes follows the communal foundation of aesthetic judgement. To loosen the grip of 'the limitations which contingently attach to our own judgment', Kant recommends we test our judgements by comparing them with the 'possible rather than the actual judgments of others' via a procedure he calls 'representation', in which we imaginatively 'represent' the outlooks of others (§40, 136). We should imagine that we encounter the same object from different perspectives, 'putting ourselves in the place of any other man' and seeking to discover the judgement to which we would assent from each of these different outlooks (ibid.). This judgement, accessed via imaginative travel between positions in the world, is the curiously subjective – individually experienced – yet universally valid judgement of pleasure or displeasure that we suppose the *communis* would share. Judgement developed through representative thinking is what Kant calls 'reflective' judgement. Pronouncing a flower to be beautiful, we risk rebuke, just as the ordinary language philosopher risks rebuke when describing what 'we' say.

Moreover, Kant's 'representative thinking' can be analogised to the figurative, etymological sense of the word conversation. We 'turn' towards the same object from different imagined standpoints, looking at its various sides and seeking a common verdict: staging an imaginary conversation about the object with versions of ourselves, stripped of contingent attachments. I develop this interpretation of reflective judgement as premised on figurative conversation in the next chapter, but Woolf lays the foundation in her dinner party scenes, which evoke both ordinary and etymological senses of conversation, as characters talk to each other while turning together towards centrepieces of fruit or flowers. For Kant, a 'many-sided substance' of beauty is affirmed in both ordinary conversation – the compulsive sharing of aesthetic judgement so strikingly prevalent in his 'turn toward ordinary conversation' in the third *Critique* – and in acts of imagination that serve as a kind of figurative conversation with possible rather than actual others. Here Woolf illuminates a commonality between Russell's logical response to epistemological uncertainty and Kant's aesthetic theory (which, it is worth noting, some have argued is Kant's response to his own sceptical conviction that our knowledge of the world is mediated by the structures of our minds).[23] As described by Kant, aesthetic judgement treats beautiful objects as quintessentially 'public' objects, in Russell's sense: objects whose reality – or whose aesthetic value – is affirmed only in a 'correlation' of points of view. A Kantian might say that one of the essential features of aesthetic judgement is that it asserts that a beautiful object can be seen from many 'sides' and yet be judged with a singular verdict. Our judgement of a flower is strengthened by representative thinking, which gives us an imaginative sense of its many sides. Imagination serves a similar function for Kantian aesthetics as mathematics for Russell's epistemology. An implication of the subtle encounter Woolf invites us to imagine between Kant and Russell is that aesthetic judgement offers a kind of reassurance Russell locates in mathematical extrapolation.

Yet Bernard is the only character to mention a flower, and for him it does not provide a causal account for their feeling, as it would in a more traditionally Kantian scenario. According to Bernard, they are drawn into 'communion' to *make* the flower, the judgement of which, Kant would say, reaffirms their communion. Bernard's account of the dinner implies a circular generation of aesthetic common sense, the sense of sharing a flower whose 'many sides' attest to its perceptibility from 'the place of any other man'. This iterative interchange between creativity and judgement recalls the dinner scene in *To the Lighthouse*. Bernard's conflation of looking and making occurs alongside speaking – there is no reason to believe the characters in *The Waves* are talking about a flower, but they are talking, and we will return momentarily to the issue of their talk – which implies an analogy between talking *about* beautiful objects and conversation itself. The form of *The Waves*, its invocation and subversion of expectations surrounding speech, reinforces this analogy between aesthetics and conversation. Just as each 'eye' contributes a side to the 'many-sided' flower at dinner, each 'I' of *The Waves* contributes a side, an aspect, to the many-voiced substance of the play-poem. Just as the flower is a quintessential emblem of beauty, the scenes of the 'many-sided substance' produce a synecdoche or emblem for the novel itself.

Like the 'community of feeling' created in *To the Lighthouse*, the communion in the dinner scenes of *The Waves* arises through a coalescing of attention in which ordinary speech is neither irrelevant nor sufficient to account for the powerful sense of togetherness. As the first dinner scene in *The Waves* proceeds, other characters' differing accounts of the experience reinforce and develop the analogy between conversation and aesthetic experience. Bernard asserts that they have gathered to 'make one thing' early in the scene, but initially the others seem to resist communion by resisting the impersonality that Woolf and Kant both ascribe to aesthetic experience. They cling to what Kant would call the 'contingent' attachments of personal identity. 'We differ', Louis declares early in the sequence of soliloquies; 'I am not single and entire as you are' (127). 'When I sat down you put your hands to your ties, you hid them', Jinny says, joining Louis in laying stress on personal difference: 'But I hide nothing' (128). Neville 'speaks' next, as if chastising Jinny for the qualities she emphasises: 'You inflict stillness, demanding admiration', and a few lines down he begins defining his own unique 'rapidity that [you] lack' (129). Whatever they are literally saying to each other, Louis suggests, it amounts to self-assertion driven by 'vanity', 'fear' and 'a desire to be separate', which makes them attempt 'to accentuate differences' (137). This process continues until, in Rhoda's words, 'comfort steals over us. Gold runs in our blood. One, two; one, two; the heart beats in serenity, in confidence, in some trance of well-being' (136–137). Louis, picking up the thread, proposes that they have realised 'that these attempts to say, "I am this, I am that", which we make, coming together, like separated parts of one body and soul, are false' (137). They begin to let go of their 'passions [. . .] pain and jealousy, envy and desire' (142). In Bernard's words, they enter a 'wide margin of indifference', a 'margin of unknown territory', which opens in them 'a thousand eyes of curiosity' (143).

In short, the scene that begins with Bernard declaring they have come to make a many-sided object of beauty proceeds through a sequence in which the characters enter the 'trance' of Kantian (and Woolfian) disinterestedness, the 'indifference' about ego that allows aesthetic perception and creation. The 'thousand eyes' Bernard describes are analogous to the 'eyes' or 'I's of representative thinking, the perspectives from which we can imaginatively perceive objects when unencumbered by the contingent passions and desires of the personal self. This phrase recalls a reflection by Lily Briscoe in *To the Lighthouse*, that 'one wanted fifty pairs of eyes' in order to adequately 'get round' Mrs Ramsay, including eyes 'stone blind to her beauty' (198). In response to Lily, Kant would suggest two points, echoed partially by Bernard: first, to judge we must imaginatively look through fifty – a thousand – or as many pairs of eyes as we can manage, and seek the consensus view that would be shared by all those pairs; and, second, this imaginative effort of representative thinking gives us immunity not to beauty, but to our personal claims on that beauty. Fifty pairs of eyes would help Lily not because one pair would be 'stone blind' to Mrs Ramsay's beauty, but because the effort of sampling so many standpoints would release Lily from her personal interests in Mrs Ramsay, the mix of adoration and resentment that reads as erotic and demanding. And in *The Waves*, the 'thousand eyes' of disinterested curiosity prepare the characters to perceive the many-sided substance they make together.

It is not within the 'unknown territory' that they perceive what they have made, but instead on the threshold of individual identity, as they begin to be conscious once more of themselves as distinct persons. Louis says: 'Something is made. Yes, [. . .] a little nervously, we pray, holding in our hands this common feeling, [. . .] the thing that we have made, that globes itself here, among these lights' (145). Jinny affirms: 'Let us hold it for one moment [. . .] this globe whose walls are made of Percival, of youth and beauty' (145). Rhoda adds, 'forests and far countries [. . .] are in it'. Neville adds 'happiness' and 'the quiet of ordinary things'. Susan adds time: 'week-days are in it', she says, 'Monday, Tuesday' (145). Bernard adds anticipation: 'What is to come is in it', he says, then underscores the aesthetic achievement of the moment by asserting, 'We are creators. We too have made something that will join the innumerable congregations of past time' (146). Each of these contributions reflects the abiding interests associated with each character: whatever 'it' is – the common feeling, the globe or flower – its sides reflect the characters, from Susan's domesticity to Jinny's emphasis on youth and sexual appeal, Neville's desire for companionship and Bernard's preoccupation with narrative progress and creative achievement. Here, as Bernard says of the seven-sided flower, every 'eye' makes a contribution, and they make rather than perceive an indeterminate 'something' as their disinterested attentions converge at the dinner table. To speak with *To the Lighthouse*, each of them has a 'way of looking', and each way of looking contributes something to the substance they make together. The 'something' they make demands disinterestedness, yet it reflects their individual interests and depends on their separate ways of looking, a paradox akin to Kant's insistence that aesthetic judgement is universal and subjective at once.

It remains to be explained how it is that *looking* becomes *making* in Woolf's vision of communion, and how the personal and impersonal mix. In Russell's account, looking together allows us to infer, but not *make*, the public object. And for Kant, the act of judgement does not make the beautiful object being judged. This conflation is part of Woolf's implicit invocation of the etymological as well as ordinary meanings of conversation: the characters make conversation by turning together, perceiving together while talking. What they make emerges through this combination of first-person expression – each 'I' articulating what it sees – and coalescing attention – each 'eye' turning towards the same objects. The second scene of dinner table conversation not only elaborates on this curiously creative power of turning and talking together; it also indicates an additional way this twofold conversation reorients epistemological doubt.

### A Dwelling-place, a Place in Common: Conversational *Sensus Communis*

The second scene of dinner table communion begins, like the first, with a transitional period, as the characters feel themselves becoming 'impartial', 'dissolved utterly', 'featureless and scarcely to be distinguished from [one] another' (224). Describing the transition as an instance of 'moments when the walls of the mind grow thin, when nothing is unabsorbed', Rhoda declares that the friends 'enjoy this momentary alleviation' from the burdens of personal identity, as 'the walls of the mind become transparent' and 'the still mood, the disembodied mood is on us' (224, 228). Jinny feels 'as if the miracle had happened [. . .] and life were stayed here and now' (225). Others describe the experience less favourably, however. Louis suggests a link to death: 'our separate drops are dissolved; we are extinct, lost in the abysses of time, in the darkness', and Bernard asks, along similar lines, 'What do we oppose, with this random flicker of light in us that we call brain and feeling, how can we do battle against this flood; what has permanence? Our lives too stream away' (227). Here, as in *To the Lighthouse*, a scene of conversational creation is linked to a deathly, impersonal 'incandescence', a sensation of stepping out of 'the being and the doing' of ordinary, hence mortal, life. Creation, of course, is one mode of 'opposition', of insisting on making something permanent that withstands the dissolution of individual lives, but here and elsewhere Woolf suggests that the impersonality required for creation – the famous androgynous or 'incandescent mind' of *A Room of One's Own* – is a foretaste of dissolution.

As in the previous scene, the characters begin to perceive that they have 'made' something in another liminal moment, when 'time comes back' as they walk together after dinner, remaining poised on the threshold between dissolution and ordinary, individuated life (227).

Lingering in a semi-disembodied mood, they turn not towards each other but towards what they feel they have made, which again is indeterminant, signified somewhat differently for each. Bernard describes 'a six-sided flower; made of six lives', recovering his earlier image but subtracting one side due to Percival's absence (229). Louis refers to a 'mysterious illumination', and Jinny describes something 'built up with much pain, many strokes'. Rhoda calls it a 'dwelling-place' (228). Bernard elaborates: it is 'a many-sided substance cut out of this dark; a many-faceted flower', a 'blaz[ing]' substance that contains their different experiences of 'marriage, death, travel, friendship [. . .] children and all that' (229). The illumination flickers out as soon as the characters' attentions dissipate and personalise. They turn attention once more towards themselves and each other, with judgement that is no longer disinterested. Jinny and Neville speak of love and look theatrically at water lilies (or so it seems in Louis's critical appraisal). Susan murmurs self-pityingly to Bernard. Louis and Rhoda observe the others from a distance, resisting the claims of their own identities but ultimately suffering a 'shrinkage' and a 'shriveling' as they become themselves once more under the gazes of their friends: 'Illusion returns as they approach down the avenue', Louis says. 'Rippling and questioning begin. What do I think of you – what do you think of me? Who are you? Who am I? – that quivers again its uneasy air over us, and the pulse quickens and the eye brightens and all the insanity of personal existence without which life would fall flat and die, begins again' (232). As in the first scene of communion, the activities of creation and judgement are separated by a thin margin. They create while dining and talking, losing consciousness of identity and becoming 'disembodied', attuned – vulnerably exposed – to something like a 'reality' that transcends individual lives and thus hints of death. They confirm this creation as they leave the moment behind, affirming something like a *sensus communis* accessed on the threshold of self-awareness.

Rhoda's account of this second moment of communion suggests how such conversation might reorient epistemological scepticism, especially as articulated by Russell. I have proposed that Bernard's 'many-sided substance' responds to Russell's declaration that 'There is absolutely nothing which is seen by two minds simultaneously', establishing a link between Russell's proposed response to scepticism and Kant's aesthetic theory (*Our Knowledge*, 70). While walking past the palace at Hampton Court following dinner and continuing to reflect on the friends' moment of communion, Rhoda suggests a response to a second claim of Russell's cited earlier, that 'The three-dimensional world seen by one mind contains no place in common with that seen by another' (ibid.). While the other characters reflect on what they have made at dinner, Rhoda gazes at the palace and links it, and thus their sense of communion, to a music recital she attended on the afternoon she learned of Percival's death: 'Wren's palace, like the quartet played to the dry and stranded people in the stalls, makes an oblong. A square is stood upon the oblong and we say, "This is our dwelling-place. The structure is now visible. Very little is left outside"' (228). To Russell's declaration that we perceive 'no place in common', we can juxtapose Rhoda's discovery of a 'dwelling-place'.

In the scene that Rhoda recalls after dinner, she produces the strange image of the square and oblong 'dwelling-place' after first struggling to describe her response to the recital in more conventional, representational terms. She attempts and rejects a series of similes for the singer's voice, analogising it to an arrow piercing a musical note/apple, then to an axe 'split[ting] a tree to the core', and finally to a woman's call to a lover, 'leaning from her window in Venice' (162). The violins, she ventures, make a 'ripple and laughter like the dance of olive trees and their myriad-tongued grey leaves when a seafarer, biting a twig between his lips where the many-backed steep hills come down, leaps on shore' (162). She becomes frustrated with these attempts to translate her experience of music into similes: '"Like" and "like" and "like," but what is the thing that lies beneath the semblance of the thing?' (163). Rhoda's language seems to blend Kant's accounts of epistemological scepticism – in which 'we can have cognition of no object as a thing in itself, but only [. . .] as an appearance' – and aesthetic experience.[24] The latter, which Kant argues transpires 'without the mediation of a concept', would presumably resist mediation by similes (*CJ*, §40, 138). Rhoda abandons her effort to provide an account of the music and instead describes intuiting a 'perfect dwelling-place':

> Now that lightning has gashed the tree and the flowering branch has fallen and Percival, by his death, has made me this gift, let me see the thing. There is a square; there is an oblong. The players take the square and place it upon the oblong. They place it very accurately; they make a perfect dwelling-place. Very little is left outside. The structure is now visible; what is inchoate is here stated; we are not so various or so mean; we have made oblongs and stood them upon squares. This is our triumph; this is our consolation. (163)

Rhoda reaches an expressive solution that is doubly Kantian. The 'gift' Percival's death has yielded by driving her to the music hall, seeking consolation, is her perception of a 'perfect dwelling-place' with others who are 'not so various or so mean'. We can recast this gift as the intuition of something like a *sensus communis*, a sense of being already in community with others. And by offering a metaphor that expresses this sense of commonality, rather than describing the music or its beauty directly, she relieves a frustration consonant with Kant's insistence that aesthetic judgement cannot be accounted for via concepts. 'The thing' she sees in this moment of revelation is not the noumenal truth of the music (the thing in itself), which she would not be able to conceptualise or express anyway, but rather the strange figure of the square and oblong. Rather than use inescapably conceptual language to describe a non-conceptual aesthetic experience, Rhoda uses language to attest to the experience's affirmation that she 'dwells' with others. If language seems inadequate to account for the experience of beauty, perhaps it can account for the *sensus communis* that thereby seems confirmed.

Reviving the image of the 'dwelling-place' when other characters try to describe the 'thing' they have made in conversation at the dinner table, Rhoda describes the implications of their experience, rather than the shared object they ostensibly make. In doing so, she comes closer than the others to describing what is 'made' in conversation: not a flower or globe or illumination, but a communion like that which is affirmed by experiences of music and other instances of beauty. The significance of this conversational *sensus communis* is underscored by the fact that it is Rhoda who gives it this articulation, as she is the character who 'wish[es] above all things to have lodgment' but typically feels tortured by the presence of others (131). She daydreams of wild seas, marble columns and cold landscapes she shares only with a swallow, private fantasies that help her recover from the sense of being 'broken into separate pieces' when forced into company (106). This gives poignance to the possibility that conversation, like other aesthetic experiences, might reassure such a person of the common 'dwelling-place', a 'lodgment' in shared reality rather than private fantasy.[25] One of the tragedies of *The Waves* – and an indication that the commonality constructed in conversation is temporary, like conversation itself – is that Rhoda does not 'dwell' in this place long enough, committing suicide before the end of the novel. Her sense of alienation ultimately defeats its alleviation by music and the similarly aesthetic 'conversation' with her friends.

A crucial distinction between the conversational aesthetic sensibility developed in *The Waves* and the *sensus communis* Kant describes is that Woolf's *sensus communis* is produced collectively, rather than evoked by the beautiful object.[26] It is created in conversation by those who talk and turn together, rather than consulted and imputed by spectators. In aesthetically purposive conversation, Woolf suggests, we oscillate between two roles, that of the artist and that of the judge, which are subtly different in degrees of self-awareness, but which equally require intense attention on a shared object, in a disembodied or disinterested frame of mind. What we make in this collective, conversational aesthetic practice is not a material work of art. Rather, to invoke again Mrs Ramsay's words, aesthetic judgement affirms or even circularly makes a 'community of feeling with other people', which is difficult to distinguish from the object mediating our attunement. If Bernard's account of their motives for Percival's farewell dinner is accurate, something like aesthetic intention, pitched against scepticism, brings them into conversation. *The Waves* links and reconfigures Kant and Russell to suggest that conversation might relieve an urge to share a common world by creating the sense that we already share such a world, not through empirical or mathematical verification but aesthetic sensibility. In this sense, Woolf's aesthetic conversations resonate with Cavell and the pivot of late Wittgenstein, turning our attention away from uncertainty about the *a priori* existence of 'one thing seen by many eyes simultaneously' and towards the fact that we are already in a 'dwelling-place', as long as we continue turning together.

Individual voice and perspective hold dubious but significant value in this project. Woolf's characters at once crave and doubt the 'insanity of personal existence', repeatedly describing speech as 'false', especially when it is used to distinguish an individual self. Yet, while claims to personal identity are dubious, the backdrop to the characters' assertions of self is ominous: a 'chain whirling round' beneath them (per Louis), a 'coal-black stream that makes us dizzy if we look down into it' (Susan), a foretaste of death (Bernard), 'roaring waters' in opposition to which 'we reason and jerk out these false sayings, "I am this; I am that!"' (Neville) (138). Moreover, *The Waves* is of course a cycle of individual articulations, a complex enactment and adjustment to Bernard's Kantian claim to 'a thousand eyes of curiosity', and a formal elaboration of the truth behind Lily Briscoe's notion that 'one wanted fifty pairs of eyes' in order to adequately see Mrs Ramsay. There are more sides to a person or flower, or reality, than any single pair of eyes can see, and the flower or 'dwelling-place' only has as many dimensions as we acknowledge by acknowledging the contribution of other eyes or 'I's.

In its conversational form, *The Waves* thus alludes to Kant's vision of imaginatively multiplying the eyes through which we 'get round' the objects of our world, testing and developing our judgements' consistency with the *sensus communis*. Simultaneously, it indicates a limit to this imaginative travel, a necessity to recall the situatedness of our perspectives and enter into conversation with actual others, situated elsewhere. The specific 'dwelling-place' and 'many-sided substance' generated in *The Waves* depends on the 'insanity of personal existence', one's own and that of others. Kant, too, indicates that imaginative conversation about aesthetic objects only makes sense in the context of communication with actual others. He writes that 'the beautiful interests us only in society', that 'a man abandoned by himself on a desert island would adorn neither his hut nor his person; nor would he seek for flowers' (*CJ*, §41, 139). Aesthetic experience, like language, is only conceivable in a shared world; we would struggle to imagine a private aesthetic judgement, as understood by Kant, just as (as noted in the previous chapter) we would struggle to imagine a private language.

Aesthetic judgement keeps us in the common world by invoking, yet also chastening, individual perspective, reminding us that the world is seen by many eyes simultaneously, not only because we possess the thousand eyes of disembodied imagination but also because we share the world and its objects with actual, embodied others. Woolf's lyrical, figurative 'conversation' represents togetherness premised on this complex balance between impersonality and multiplicity. The chains of connection and threats of dissolution the characters perceive with such ambivalence transform through conversational attunement into a *sensus communis*, which counters the isolation of epistemological doubt and the egoistic impulse to distinguish oneself from others, without fully extinguishing the self. Like the conversational form of life traced in earlier chapters' studies of ethical acknowledgement, such *communis* must be endlessly renewed, day after day. At the same time, this fragile *communis* enjoys permanence in the form of *The Waves* itself: a many-sided play-poem, 'built up with much pain, many strokes', cut out of the dark, and inviting readers to turn with its voices in a dreamlike, repeating cycle.

## The World, Displayed

During the early stages of their first dinner table conversation, Neville suggests that the community the characters make entails a kind of worldly awareness, which in turn enables the companions to converse in the ordinary, verbal sense: '"After the capricious fires, the abysmal dullness of youth," said Neville, "the light falls upon real objects now. Here are knives and forks. The world is displayed, and we too, so that we can talk"' (127). 'The world', here, is a distinctly communal world: not the given space of knives and forks ('and spoons and glasses', as Russell writes in the passage Woolf invokes), but that same space transformed into 'the world' by shared attention. Like the party in *To the Lighthouse*, growing conscious of the aesthetic nature of their community, the characters in *The Waves* see themselves 'displayed' in a similarly revealed world of 'real objects', and this consciousness prepares them to talk. The experience is again circular, as it is only because they are already turning together – already sharing a form of life – that they are able to refresh and continue it.

The echo of Russell in the scenes of communion seems intentional, but these passages also suggestively anticipate the description of worldly reality Hannah Arendt offers in *The Human Condition*. As I noted in the introduction, Arendt's work pivots around a concern that the 'common world' is threatened in modernity by epistemological scepticism. The famous Cartesian response to doubt is emblematic for her of the general modern response: a turn inward, towards the ideas one can be certain one has, in contrast to our uncertain, external reality. In the predominating view of sceptical modernity, she writes, 'What men now have in common is not the world but the structure of their minds, and this they cannot have in common, strictly speaking; their faculty of reasoning can only happen to be the same in everybody' (*HC*, 283). Her vision of the 'public realm', or 'common world', is strikingly like Woolf's conversational dwelling-place, a space created through a process of talking and turning with others:

> The reality of the public realm relies on the simultaneous presence of innumerable perspectives and aspects in which the common world presents itself [. . .] This is the meaning of public life [. . .] the reality rising out of the sum total of aspects presented by one object to a multitude of spectators. Only where things can be seen by many in a variety of aspects without changing their identity, so that those who are gathered around them know they see sameness in utter diversity, can worldly reality truly and reliably appear. (*HC*, 57)

Like Russell, Arendt proposes the existence of 'public objects' that are constitutively 'many-sided'. But like Woolf, she also indicates that the 'reality of the public realm' is itself many-sided, discovered and made through conversation. This reality does not pre-exist our meeting one another 'in the manner of speech and action', as Arendt puts it, but rather 'rises out' when and where we talk and turn together. The model for political life she finds in the ancient Greek *polis* is a kind of conversational spectatorship, a process of 'incessant talk' by which individuals come to understand that they look, from many sides, at the same world, and that 'the world we have in common is usually regarded from an infinite number of different standpoints, to which correspond the most diverse points of view' ('Concept', 51). Through conversation in both ordinary and etymological senses, Arendt's exemplary Greeks learned 'to see the same in very different and frequently opposing aspects' ('Concept', 51).

Woolf's representation of a process of 'making' the common 'thing seen by many eyes simultaneously', and in the process also making a dwelling-place, suggests a similar model of worldmaking, conversational spectatorship, given aesthetic form by *The Waves* itself. Linking talk, perception and aesthetic experience, Woolf's 'many-sided substance' intuits the link between such worldmaking conversation and aesthetic experience that Arendt herself would begin to develop in her eventual turn to Kantian aesthetics for a model of political judgement, which I take up in the next chapter. Reciprocally, Arendt's earlier work articulates political implications that Woolf leaves unnamed; as we will see, for Arendt, worldmaking conversation akin to that depicted and enacted in *The Waves* is the foundation for democratic life.

An ambivalence at the centre of Woolf's vision anticipates other political concerns as well. As I have noted, the occasions on which characters generate a 'community of feeling' in *To the Lighthouse* and *The Waves* are shaped in part by ideals that are at once oppressive and compelling. Mrs Ramsay evokes the Victorian Angel whose death might be necessary for Lily's artistic vision to clear, but whose power and attractiveness lingers. And Percival functions as a silent icon of imperial masculinity, whose death in India registers the sun setting on the Empire, but whose romance continues to compel the characters years later and constitutes one of the reasons they meet for dinner. Both novels are often read as ambivalent elegies, and the conversational *sensus communis* sketched by Woolf is neither immune from, nor identical with, political ideology. The next chapter pursues the links between this book's outlook on conversation, aesthetics and politics further, asking, with Arendt and Salman Rushdie's *The Satanic Verses*, what happens to the possibility of common sense once there are no more shared illusions – or ideals – unifying the postcolonial British public sphere?

# Chapter 4

# Public Conversation and Judgement: Rushdie and Arendt

Near the culmination of the first scene of dinner table communion in *The Waves*, Neville observes: 'We sit here, surrounded, lit up, many coloured [. . .] We are walled in here. But India lies outside' (135). This is one of many instances in which Woolf acknowledges that there are borders to the reality generated by her characters' converging perceptions, that India – along with Britain's other colonies – lies outside the scope of her play-poem's illumination. The ambivalent idealisation of Percival further underscores the text's awareness that a vast, troubling Empire sustains the 'dwelling-place' its characters make.

Moving from Woolf's *sensus communis* to Salman Rushdie's representation of the fractious Thatcher years, this chapter travels distinctly into the public sphere, taking up the political affordances of conversation, and of the metaphor of conversation, by focusing on public unrest related to the breakdown of clear boundaries between (post)colonial and British common sense. In *The Satanic Verses* (1988), people relegated to the 'outside' of British political life – arrivals from former colonies and their descendants – demand inclusion. These Londoners live in what the novel terms the 'undercity', where they are harassed by police and white supremacist skinheads, and misrepresented by the mainstream media, yet they actively build a resistant community. Their efforts to gain public recognition culminate in a violent riot though which the novel evokes real-world conflicts between Black and South Asian communities and the British state throughout the postwar, postcolonial half of the twentieth century. To speak in the register of ordinary language philosophy, the novel represents a situation in which the dominant language or form of life governing the public realm is called radically into question, and any possibility of conversation would require some form of resolution between conflicting languages.

In what follows, I argue that through its depictions of the undercity and riot, *The Satanic Verses* subtly interweaves the ideas of several strands of political philosophy, suggesting a new vision of the worldmaking or world-denying power of public discourse – a vision expressed, I argue, in the figure of conversation, reworked as the novel invites. I demonstrate that Rushdie's representation of Black resistance sketches what critical theorists call a 'counterpublic', and that the undercity's function in the novel is similar to the work performed by the concept of counterpublics in political philosophy: it highlights problems in the theory and practice of the supposedly liberal public sphere. Moreover, from the riot sequence I draw an alternative vision of public life, in which it is not rational discussion that structures (or even ideally *ought* to structure) public discourse, but rather conversation in the twofold sense implicit in Arendt's work. The novel's depiction of the riot helps me link her early writing on public speech to her late turn to Kant's aesthetic theory, through which she began to develop an account of how we should judge political issues. By clarifying the continuity between Arendt's early work on the power of conversation to generate the public realm, and her late turn to aesthetic theory for a model for political judgement, this reading of Arendt and Rushdie articulates a complex relationship between democratic worldmaking and judgement, the latter of which is often deemed to exist in tension with democratic openness. Moreover, by interweaving Arendtian concepts and Rushdie's postcolonial London, it pushes her ideas past the limitations set by her strict demarcation of boundaries between 'public', 'private' and 'social' realms, which led her to take especially troubling positions on racial justice politics.[1]

Proposing new readings of *The Satanic Verses* and Arendt's political thought, this chapter also argues for the conceptual power of the conversational outlook as a means of understanding public life. After situating *The Satanic Verses*' representation of the undercity and dominant British public sphere in relation to the theoretical literature on public discourse, I draw on Arendt to demonstrate that a framework positing public life as forged in conversation rather than rational discussion clarifies the work required for perceiving and judging collectively in situations in which there is no prior consensus regarding the criteria by which to judge: situations, that is, when the norms of liberalism – rationality, civility, appropriate topics of public speech, and so on – have not been agreed upon, or are suddenly disputed. Arendt helps us see that there are alternatives to liberalism besides relativism and the disavowal of judgement, on the one hand, and authoritarianism on the other. Moreover, framing public life as a conversation prepares us to do something of great importance to both Arendt and Rushdie: to recognise when 'newness' enters the world and to respond appropriately. On this point, the form of Rushdie's novel makes an essential contribution, as the magical elements of Rushdie's narrative parallel the role of 'the miraculous' in Arendt's work. Magical realism, I claim, solicits the interpretive practice that conversational public life requires. This conclusion simultaneously urges a new assessment of the politics of this literary form and underscores the ambivalent stakes of turning the conversational outlook towards public life.[2]

### 'That otherworld, that undercity': Rushdie's Counterpublic

The novel's central story follows the divergent fates of two Indian-born actors who land in England after falling from an exploded, hijacked airplane, miraculously unharmed but having gained characteristics of an angel and a devil during the fall. Saladin Chamcha (born Salahuddin Chamchawalla), a British citizen who has lived in England since the age of thirteen, despises India and has worked hard 'to be transformed into the foreignness he admires' (441). He has devoted himself to a 'picture postcard' version of England that does not exist; in the words of his estranged wife Pamela, 'you couldn't get him to look at what was really real' (181). Falling through the sky in the novel's opening pages, he is transformed again, this time into the horned and hooved incarnation of xenophobic fears of migrants. Gibreel Farishta is his opposite, 'preferring, contemptuously, to transform' England, and embraced by England nonetheless (441). While Chamcha is rejected by his wife, Farishta is welcomed by the Englishwoman he travelled to England to see; Chamcha loses his career, and Farishta's gets a temporary boost. Yet the latter suffers from episodes of acute, paranoid schizophrenia, which, in the novel's hybrid magical-realist form, are simultaneously depicted as genuine visions in which he is the Archangel Gibreel.[3]

Chamcha's transformation initiates him to what the novel suggestively calls 'that otherworld, that undercity', the 'really real' England experienced by 'browns-and-blacks' (426, 295). When he lands in his newly devilish body, he is illegally detained and abused by immigration police, and he later takes refuge in the multi-ethnic London neighbourhood of Brickhall. This neighbourhood is an allusive mix of three areas of London associated with large and active Black and Asian communities: Brixton, where many people of Afro-Caribbean descent live, Southall, home to many South Asians, and Brick Lane, the heart of the British Bangladeshi community. In the novel, the undercity's Black residents – the identity 'Black' being adopted in the period by people of African, Caribbean and South Asian descent – are excluded in numerous ways from British public life.[4] Their social and political community forms in separate, 'shadow' institutions; they are considered too 'tinted' to appear in visual entertainment media; they are targets of racist violence; and their political demands are rendered incomprehensible by the news media and police suppression. Towards the end of the novel, a riot erupts in Brickhall, resembling events throughout the second half of the twentieth century in Britain, when residents of real 'undercities' repeatedly clashed with racists, fascists and the police.[5]

In its depiction of the undercity, *The Satanic Verses* evokes, and largely anticipates, critical accounts of the modern public sphere as a space of conflicting discourses, rather than a unified space of critical discussion from which some are temporarily excluded.[6] The seminal account of the ideal of a unified public sphere is, of course, Jürgen Habermas's *The Structural Transformation of the Public Sphere*, which describes the rise and fall of the ideal and partial historical reality of a discursive arena characterised by virtual equality, in which citizens could (in theory) meet on equal footing and deliberate over common interests. Social inequality is bracketed for the sake of public discussion, in this ideal, and reason rather than economic or other power carries the day. According to Habermas, this idealised sphere never really existed, and its partial existence was sustained by a conflation of the interests of bourgeois men with those of the general public. Habermas nonetheless admires the underlying commitment to public rationality and laments the decline of the ideal: across the twentieth century, he argues, public deliberation increasingly gives way to public consumption (of entertainment and consumer goods), and – as the sphere of politics becomes more inclusive – allegedly private interests blend with public authority in the form of (for instance) the welfare state, eroding the autonomy that in principle gives the public sphere its capacity to host virtual equality.

We'll return to criticisms of the historical and ideological commitments of the public sphere momentarily, but first I'll note that the official British public realm in *The Satanic Verses* tracks with Habermas's description of a postwar public sphere degraded by consumerism and mass media manipulation. In its account of Chamcha's acting career prior to his transformation, *The Satanic Verses* depicts the British culture industry as vapid and racist. Chamcha's boss, the advertising and television executive Hal Valance – an acolyte of Margaret Thatcher – describes to him the 'facts' of the media industry: it is guided rightly by the market, and in this case consumer preference restricts opportunities for people 'of the tinted persuasion' (275–276). Chamcha accepts the market's terms and works primarily as a voice actor on the radio and for animated television commercials, using skills of vocal mimicry honed in his efforts to assimilate as a child. There is an ironic upshot to the media market's racism: 'With his female equivalent, Mimi Mamoulian, he ruled the airwaves of Britain [. . .] but [they were] crippled legends, dark stars [. . .] shedding bodies to put on voices' (61). In the figure of the postcolonial migrant who 'rule[s] the airwaves of Britain' because of a racist stipulation that he shed his body in order to obtain a voice, the novel inverts the jingoistic message of 'Rule, Britannia!', mimicking the inversion of the Empire itself via postcolonial migration. There is no triumph in this inversion, at least in Chamcha's experience. His starring role on Valance's controversial programme, 'The Aliens Show', earns him the nickname 'Brown Uncle Tom'. And as we'll see, the novel's critique of British public culture becomes sharper and more overtly political during the riot sequence, in which the news media 'chooses sides' and reinforces the exclusion of 'tinted' inhabitants of Britain from the public realm.

As the neologism 'undercity' indicates, *The Satanic Verses* depicts its 'tinted' Londoners as participants in a shadow society, with its own institutions and narratives of collective identity. To borrow language from Nancy Fraser, the novel explores the discursive mechanisms and institutions through which Brickhall's inhabitants 'elaborat[e] alternative styles of political behaviour and alternative norms of public speech'.[7] Fraser's 1990 essay 'Rethinking the Public Sphere' remains one of the most influential accounts of the function of counterpublics in 'actually existing democracy', although the term 'counterpublic' was coined two decades earlier by Oskar Negt and Alexander Kluge in *Public Sphere and Experience*, first published in German in 1972 and translated into English in 1993.[8] Negt and Kluge critique and expand on Habermas's study of the bourgeois public sphere by directing attention to the 'proletarian public sphere'. They argue that acknowledging the existence of proletarian public and counterpublic institutions highlights what we might call the political economics of publicity and publicness: the alleged realm of discursive equality in the public sphere is not class neutral, because (among other reasons) the norms of discourse are not class neutral. Fraser sketches a broader account of 'subaltern counterpublics', drawing especially on feminist and queer histories, and she advocates the benefits of the existence of 'parallel discursive arenas' rather than one, unified public realm.[9] Democracy is strengthened, she argues, when groups can finesse their narratives of identity and need in their own arenas before entering a meta-discourse with other groups' narratives and demands.

In critical theory, the study of counterpublics has challenged the standard liberal account of the public sphere on at least three fronts. First, attention to counterpublics foregrounds the conflation of class-specific, culturally masculine, secular and individualist styles of speech with rational and civil discourse as such. Negt and Kluge, for example, argue that the liberal standard for publicness, rationality or reasonableness, is in practice an ideological construction, a 'mechanism for controlling the perception of what is relevant for society', rather than a neutral cognitive ideal.[10] Fraser observes that the demarcation of what is suitable for public discourse is itself a political question, which should be taken up *in* public discourse rather than serving as a precondition that lays down rules for public speech in advance. Second, counterpublics challenge the ideological privilege given to the institutions of the bourgeois public sphere. Public squares and the coffee houses of the emerging European middle class are not the only spaces in which people have converged to elaborate the values and aspirations of their communities, and bourgeois norms of speech are neither universal nor fundamentally democratic. Numerous scholars have used these two sets of claims to criticise the 'constitutive exclusions' of the bourgeois public sphere and the (related) ideological pretence of neutrality in bourgeois norms of discourse, which, they maintain, are inadequately theorised in the liberal tradition.[11] Power has already shaped the terms by which issues are considered to be of 'public' interest; power has already shaped the rhetorical habits and skills of those who seek to intervene in public discourse; power has already affected the material conditions underwriting a person's capacity to participate in 'disinterested' exchanges of ideas. Invocations of the ideal of disinterested, rational and polite discourse thus often function to negate the legitimate concerns of people who have been excluded from the space and/or denied the means to participate in the accepted discursive terms.

A third challenge implicit in the counterpublic model concerns the unit of political participation: whereas liberalism tends to represent the struggle for consensus as an activity between individuals, a counterpublic model reframes disagreement as unfolding between *groups* rather than individuals, suggesting that some degree of agreement has formed within a constituency (forged along class, racial, gender or other lines that are not necessarily 'rational'), prior to the voicing of interpretations in public. This is equally true of the group whose interests are passed off as neutral or universal. In societies like Britain, whiteness, economic security, heterosexuality, Christianity, and so on, are the unmarked qualities of the group whose interests are developed in official 'public' deliberation.

*The Satanic Verses*' depiction of the undercity includes numerous scenes in which Brickhall's residents 'formulate oppositional interpretations of their identities, interests, and needs', in Fraser's words, according to terms that spotlight race and ethnicity (67). These scenes lay a foundation for the riotous confrontation between their interpretations and those of the dominant British public, whose interpretations are similarly group based. The central counterpublic institution in the novel is the Shaandaar Café and Boarding House, the heart of Brickhall's South Asian community. One of its proprietors, Muhammad Sufyan, was a schoolteacher before the family left Bangladesh and now 'serves as mentor to the variegated, transient and particoloured' people who gather in the café and stay in the boarding house (251). A second institution, less central to the narrative but seemingly serving similar functions as the Shaandaar, is a nightclub called Hot Wax, where clubbers celebrate the otherwise invisible achievements of Black Britons honoured as wax effigies – including Mary Seacole, Abdul Karim and Ignatius Sancho – while ritualistically avenging themselves on effigies of 'villains' like Sir Oswald Mosley, Enoch Powell and Margaret Thatcher. The dance club supplements the café; there, collective, festive and emotionally charged performances (alternative norms of political expression) reinterpret Britain's past and present politics.

The Shaandaar is not exactly idealised. Muhammad's wife Hind has contrived (without her husband's knowledge, and with help from their two teenage daughters) to collect large sums of money from the government in exchange for providing 'temporary accommodations' to displaced people who cannot be accommodated by public housing (272). The 'temporary human beings' are crowded into small rooms at the boarding house, while the Sufyan family is paid by the government on a per-person basis. In addition to casting a doubtful eye on the women in the Sufyan family, this arrangement alludes to varying degrees of class precariousness within the migrant diaspora. It also alludes to Thatcherite housing policies, particularly in the Tower Hamlets borough of London, where many Bangladeshi immigrants lived. As Peter Kalliney has described, the rates of homelessness more than tripled in the area during the 1980s in correlation with a Thatcher-government push to privatise and gentrify large swathes of its housing.[12] It is to this somewhat compromised ethnic enclave, divided by class differences that go unmentioned by most characters, that 'Jumpy' Joshi, Pamela's new lover, brings Chamcha, after the latter shows up at his own home looking like a devil, and Pamela refuses to allow him to stay.

Joshi's arrival with Chamcha at the Shaandaar provokes 'an impromptu crisis summit' that bears playful resemblance to what Fraser would call 'strong publics', deliberative political bodies like Parliament. The family discusses what to do with the devilish goat-man, while a 'gallery of nightgowned residents' from the boarding house looks on: the shadow public regarding the shadow Parliament (259–260). The conversation is going nowhere definitive until Joshi intervenes:

> 'The central requirement', he announced, 'is to take an ideological view of the situation.'
> That silenced everyone.
> 'Objectively', he said, with a small self-deprecating smile, 'what has happened here? A: Wrongful arrest, intimidation, violence. Two: Illegal detention, unknown medical experimentation in hospital', murmurs of assent here, as memories of intra-vaginal inspections, Depo-Provera scandals, unauthorized post-partum sterilizations, and, further back, the knowledge of Third World drug-dumping arose in every person present to give substance to the speaker's insinuations, – because what you believe depends on what you've seen, – not only what is visible, but what you are prepared to look in the face, – and anyhow, something had to explain horns and hoofs; in those policed medical wards, anything could happen – 'And thirdly', Jumpy continued, 'psychological breakdown, loss of sense of self, inability to cope. We've seen it all before.' (260–261)

With what we might call 'alternative norms' of political speech, Joshi elicits solidarity based on shared, embodied and personal experiences, defying the classic insistence in theories of public discourse that the tone and subject matter of public speech be disinterested and universal, or at least subject to common interest. Matters of the body have often been discounted as too particularising, private and personal to be aired in the public sphere; this logic has supported the wholesale exclusion of women and racial minorities from political life, or the insistence that we 'bracket' our embodied, personal experiences in order to participate in public life with impartial reasonableness.[13] The phrase 'shedding bodies to put on voices', used to describe Chamcha's voice-acting work, also summarises this requirement for participation in the public sphere. The passage above, however, insists that bodily experiences are part of political understanding: the nightgowned Parliament and counterpublic judge based on first-hand exposures to biopolitical abuses and degradations. These experiences, the narrator suggests, make them 'prepared to look in the face' at the political implications of Chamcha's devilish appearance. Some truths must be acknowledged in addition to seen, an operation that in politics, as in Cavellian conversational ethics, 'goes beyond knowledge'. I will return periodically to this suggestion that discerning the meaning of what we see is an operation distinct from mere perception on the one hand, and rational persuasion on the other.

If the Shaandaar summit scene flouts a simplified liberal narrative in which we shed bodies to put on voices, it also sharply satirises its counterpublic (as does the sequence in which dance clubbers celebrate or melt waxwork figures). An 'ideological' view cannot also be 'objective', and Joshi takes liberties in advancing his ideological interpretation. Objectively, Joshi's audience has *not* 'seen it all before'. Joshi mentions neither horns nor hooves in his speech, and he makes no reference to one of the more remarkable details about Chamcha's condition: he survived a fall of 29,002 feet.[14] Moreover, Chamcha's transformation began during the fall, not in the hands of his abusive detention officers. In the effort to derive an ideological account, Joshi disregards much of the evidence at hand. He interprets a symbolic and coincidental resonance as a causal explanation, and he ignores whatever does not support this ideological view. As a consequence, he either fails to perceive or ideologically obscures a genuine instance of what the novel calls 'newness enter[ing] the world'. We will revisit the importance of 'newness', in the novel and in what Arendt calls 'political thought', but for now it is enough to notice that in a text that opens with a 'big bang' and a series of questions about newness – 'How does newness come into the world? How is it born?' (8) – Joshi's reading of Chamcha's body is among other things a refusal to acknowledge the genuinely new.

The novel itself persistently courts this conflation of figurative and literal explanation, suggesting that one target of the parody advanced in Joshi's speech is a reductively ideological reader of *The Satanic Verses*. A fellow inmate at the immigrant detention centre tells Chamcha, 'They have the power of description, and we succumb to the pictures they construct', implying racist metaphors have performative power, which magical realism literalises (174). Numerous critics have cited this line as though it is a straightforward comment about the dehumanising power of racist language, which to some extent it is, but in Chamcha's case the transformation begins sooner and interweaves magical and sociopolitical elements that exceed this interpretation.[15] The scene of the Shaandaar summit signals that the reader should be wary of accepting such invitations to see the novel's characters and their fates as straightforward allegories, and that we should hold onto multiple threads and logics – both magical and realistic – without seeking to subordinate one to the other. In this scene, at least, the supernatural elements signify complexity that surpasses Joshi's heavy-handed reading.

Joshi's speech is nonetheless successful, and it foreshadows a period in which Chamcha's devilish likeness becomes an icon of Black resistance in the undercity. Inexplicably, magically, he begins appearing to Brickhall residents in their dreams, a hulking devil destroying the 'perfectly restored residences' of gentrifying white people who have moved in, presumably with encouragement by Thatcher's privatisation schemes (295). To the 'non-tint neo-Georgians', this dream is a nightmare, but 'nocturnal browns-and-blacks found themselves cheering, in their sleep, this what-else-after-all-but-black-man, maybe a little twisted up by fate class race history, all that, but getting off his behind, bad and mad, to kick a little ass' (295). The 'browns-and-blacks' begin wearing buttons and T-shirts emblazoned with the devil, as well as rubber devil horns: 'a defiance and a warning' to the 'white society' that has rejected them. As Hind and Muhammad's teenage daughter Mishal Sufyan explains to Chamcha: 'you're a hero. I mean, people can really identify with you. It's an image white society has rejected for so long that we can really take it, you know, occupy it, inhabit it, reclaim it and make it our own' (296).

There are several sources of ambivalence here. There is the fact that Chamcha himself does not wish to be a representative of Black radicalism; he is a conservative man filled with disdain for his cultural and racial background, a man who championed the Falkland War and sneered at the activist epithet levelled against him, Brown Uncle Tom. This is perhaps a warning about the 'death of the author' in political rhetoric: the untethering of meaning from man, and more generally of narrative from material reality, is one source of the novel's scepticism towards the eager activists in the undercity. Another source of ambivalence is the magic itself, the inexplicable forces that are repeatedly absorbed into and flattened by socio-political interpretation. Horns are unquestioningly treated as a metaphor for Blackness rejected by 'white society'. Chamcha's new heroic stature repeats the pattern Joshi set, generated by an interpretation that requires selectively repressing details.

The undercity gains a concrete political purpose when one of its most prominent figures, the activist Dr Uhuru Simba, is arrested and charged, without any evidence, for a series of murders of elderly women. Simba is a cartoonish figure. Like Chamcha, he is a self-remade man. Originally 'plain Sylvester Roberts from down New Cross Way', he has renamed himself with the Swahili words for freedom and lion, and characters speculate that his 'Dr' is also a product of self-naming (294). According to Simba and his supporters, his arrest is an effort to silence an activist, an agitator who has 'not been willing to seem reasonable' in various campaigns against racism, including protests he led against Chamcha's television show (428). He claims to 'occupy the old and honourable role of the uppity nigger', implying he's been imprisoned for refusing to stick to the terms of liberal public speech (428).

A community meeting takes place to devise a collective response to his arrest. Filtered through the perspective of Chamcha, who has regained human form and attends to ogle young Mishal Sufyan, the scene is heavy on inflated political rhetoric and light or lacking in concrete strategy. Simba is quoted promising to 'remake this society, to shape it from the bottom to the top' (429). Attendees sing freedom songs from the US South and 'Nkosi Sikelel' iAfrika', a Xhosa hymn associated with the anti-apartheid movement. To Chamcha, these songs signify not a legitimate effort to articulate international anti-racist solidarity and mutual inspiration, but rather 'an attempt to borrow the glamour of other, more dangerous struggles' (429). He also notes the differences between Simba as a symbol and Simba as a man: crucially, Simba has a pattern of violence against women. This, Joshi replies, is 'a problem in the family', something to repress when more public stakes are involved: recognisable logic that has been strenuously critiqued by feminists.[16] Although Chamcha's scorn at the meeting is itself a subject of satire, his critiques of the political rhetoric and flattening of details specific to Simba as an individual man are consistent with the novel's general reservations about the counter-discourses shaping the undercity. The scene, in other words, seems to both mock and raise sincere concerns about the rhetorical strategies by which this radical movement coalesces.

The narrative of the undercity's development into a collective organised against what Joshi calls 'the Man' is thus simultaneously a rebuke to idealised notions of a unified public sphere and a more general warning about narratives of collective identity. The novel's target is not only the undercity, and it is not suggesting in an underhanded way that the old arguments used to justify 'constitutive exclusions' of women and racial or cultural minorities from public discourse are valid. The mainstream narratives of British identity are similarly ideological and flawed, 'picture postcard' fantasies that are sustained by denying the realities and consequences of the nation's imperial past, demanding that its non-white citizens shed bodies to put on voices. The satirical portraits of both British media and the undercity flaunt the flaws of heavy-handed ideological interpretations of identity and political situations, simultaneously tempting readers to undertake, and catch themselves undertaking, similarly flawed interpretations of the novel's apparent allegorising of migrant experience. The satire thus elicits uncertainty about collective identity as such, and by extension, about collective movements.

## The Riot as Conversational, (Counter)Public Discourse

The tensions between the undercity and mainstream public culminate in the riot that consumes Brickhall. As Janice Ho observes, readings of the riot sequence tend to 'replicate' the novel's own 'ambivalence toward the dangers of rioting and violence' (167). Her compelling analysis focuses on the 'trope of tropicalization' in Gibreel Farishta's contributions to the conflict. While the undercity gathers political bearings in the manner I've described above, preparing to resist the police's treatment of Simba and the community as a whole, Farishta is under the sway of either hallucinations or visions, imagining himself using his angelic powers to 'tropicalize' London. He seeks to transmute its meteorological indeterminacy, and by extension its political and moral vagueness, into heated, passionate extremes. 'The trouble with the English', Farishta muses, is '*their weather*':

> 'When day is not warmer than night', he reasoned, 'when the light is not brighter than the dark, when the land is not drier than the sea, then clearly a people will lose the power to make distinctions, and commence to see everything – from political par-ties to sexual partners to religious beliefs – as much-the-same, nothing-to-choose, give-or-take. What folly! For truth is extreme, it is *so* and not *thus*, it is *him* and not *her*; a partisan matter, not a spectator sport. It is, in brief, *heated*'. (365, original emphasis)

As Ho demonstrates, through Farishta the novel articulates a critique of temperate liberalism that resembles Carl Schmitt's (ultimately fascistic) argument that politics is rightly antagonistic, a 'partisan matter', in which views are bolstered by passion that neither can nor should be tamed by liberal protocols. It also evokes (although Ho does not pursue this route) attempts to draft a leftist alternative to both Schmittian antagonism and, in Chantal Mouffe's words, 'a moralizing liberalism which pretends that antagonisms have been eradicated and that society can now be ruled through rational moral procedures and remaining conflicts resolved through impartial tribunals'.[17] Farishta's effort to tropicalise London, and its embedded critique of liberalism, mirrors the rising temperature of the undercity's anger. In Ho's view, Farishta's critique provides the novel's inner interpretive framework for the riot, which becomes a repudiation of liberal temperateness: the refusal to 'seem reasonable', as Simba says.

Farishta's ambition to tropicalise the city is also central to Ian Baucom's earlier, influential reading of the riot, although Baucom reads the trope as a model for hybridity rather than radicalism. The '"tropicalizing" riot' brings British colonial history back into the nation's space, mixing the weather patterns of the North Atlantic island and the tropical places its rulers once colonised. By 'recalling it to that which it has attempted to displace', Baucom argues, tropicalisation is a way to 'redeem'

Britain, 'revealing the nation as a space of "fusions, translations, conjoining"'.[18] Whereas revolutionary moments of crisis 'can be invoked but not depended upon', tropicalisation, Baucom suggests, is a climatological palimpsest that stands for a cultural palimpsest, which can endure (216). By this reading, the novel endorses multicultural hybridity against the 'picture postcard' fantasies of white, monocultural Britishness.

When we shift focus to the collective acts of the undercity, rather than the acts of an individual who may or may not be angelically empowered, different but not necessarily incompatible implications of the riot come into view. The riot is the culmination of escalating injustices against the undercity. Simba dies in police custody, and the British public, primed by the media to believe him guilty, accepts the police's implausible explanations of his death with indifference. Conflict begins when 'differing estimations' of Simba and his death meet in the streets, in a violent version of the meta-discourse Fraser envisions for democracies. Focusing on the collective dimension of the riot enables us to discern the novel's hints about how a counterpublic might challenge norms governing political discourse and transform public life. Crucially, however, the transformation remains only potential.

The straightforward reading of the riot is that it fictionalises real events that sent British public life into a frenzy of concern about immigration and racial diversity. Here is Stuart Hall's summary of decades of racial conflict in postwar England, the 'ancient story, banal in its repetitive persistence' that forms part of the backdrop of *The Satanic Verses*:

> From the early race riots of Nottingham and Notting Hill in 1958, through the 1970s campaigns against 'sus' laws (permitting arbitrary stop-and-search), the death of [antifascist activist] Blair Peach from a police baton at a 1979 demonstration in Southall, the uproar following the death of Colin Roach in Stoke Newington police station in 1983 and the lack of explanation for many other black deaths in police custody, the Deptford Fire and the arson of Asian shops and homes, the 1980s 'disorders' in Brixton and at Broadwater Farm, Tottenham, to Stephen Lawrence's murder in 1993 [. . .] black people have been the subject of racialized attack, had their grievances largely ignored by the police, and been subjected to racially-inflected practices of policing. Each of those events was followed by a campaign, unofficial inquiries (I sat on two), recriminations from the authorities, promises of reform. Very little seems to have changed.[19]

According to Hall, two distinguishing features of the surge of violence in the 1980s were the intensification of policing in Black neighbourhoods immediately *prior* to 'disorder', and the introduction 'for the first time [of] para-military policing tactics (including full riot-gear, plastic bullets and CS gas)', which, Hall posits, were introduced 'not to contain the violence' but more theatrically to '"win" the public-order "war"'.[20]

Press coverage during the period promoted a mainstream sense of moral and political crisis. As tracked by the Birmingham Centre for Contemporary Cultural Studies (CCCS), the press frequently linked social unrest to a 'threatening black presence' within England, 'always codified as "immigration"'.[21] This intensified following the advent of Margaret Thatcher's Conservative government in 1979, the CCCS claims. An exemplary headline in *The Financial Times* likened the spread of unrest to that of an 'alien disease', observing that 'the body politic has no immunity' to this external contagion.[22] Another article in the same paper asserted that the 'street fighting' showed 'consensus' to be 'in dangerously short supply'.[23] Alfred Sherman, an advisor to Margaret Thatcher, declared that the period's unrest threatened 'all that is English and wholesome'.[24] Such rhetoric draws together anxieties about race, cultural identity and – in remarks about the body politic and scarce consensus – ideals of a deliberative public sphere threatened by racial and cultural diversity.[25]

*The Satanic Verses* intermixes many aspects of this history, including an aggressive police presence in a multi-ethnic neighbourhood, frequent stops-and-searches, unpunished vigilante attacks on Black people, the death of a Black person in police custody, the absence of official acknowledgement of community anger about any of these events, and the use of para-military equipment in response to 'unrest'. As in many of the real-world episodes, the novel's riot is prefaced by more 'civil', or liberal, efforts by the undercity to gain justice. They gather outside the police station to demand answers about Simba's suspicious death and are ignored. The police's community liaison officer, Inspector Kinch, tactlessly describes Simba's death as 'a million-to-one shot', a careless metaphor that suggests he speaks neither to the undercity, nor with any consideration for its inhabitants' perspectives (nor does the metaphor express, as Simba's mother puts it, 'respect for us as human beings') (464–465). When the murders of elderly women continue following Simba's death, the police brazenly claim that there must be a 'copycat killer' who mysteriously possesses knowledge of Simba's 'trademark' arrangement of victims' organs, which was never publicly disclosed (466). The police 'quadruple' their presence in Brickhall, and 'stories of police brutality' circulate in the undercity. Meanwhile, racist violence against the undercity's residents 'beg[ins]' to occur more frequently: attacks on black families on council estates, harassment of black schoolchildren on their way home, brawls in pubs' (466). Young South

Asian and Afro-Caribbean men form self-defence patrols to protect the undercity from both police and racists. One of these patrols captures the real 'Granny Ripper', and rumours fly through the undercity about a planned 'cover-up' by the police (478).

The riot itself is the consequence of the police's escalation. After the real 'Granny Ripper' is caught, fights break out between white pub-goers and crowds angered by the police's behaviour. There is 'some damage to property', and then 'the divisional superintendent of police, in consultation with higher authority, declared that riot conditions now existed in central Brickhall, and unleashed the full might of the Metropolitan Police against the "rioters"' (468–469). The superintendent's declaration functions as a performative utterance, unleashing the 'full might' of the police and thereby guaranteeing a riotous conflict. The novel directs special attention to the media's biased construction of the ensuing events, stressing that the media's material interests align with those of the police: 'A camera is a thing easily broken or purloined; its fragility makes it fastidious. A camera requires law, order, the thin blue line. Seeking to preserve itself, it remains behind the shielding wall, observing the shadow-lands from afar, and of course from above: that is, it chooses sides' (470).[26] Having chosen sides, and restricting the positions from which it aims its supposedly objective lens, the media's camera 'cannot understand, or demonstrate, what any of this achieves. These people are burning their own streets' (470–471). To the television viewer, the 'rioters' are fundamentally alien.

The narrative form of this section of the novel emphasises what Baucom calls the 'hermeneutic indeterminacy' of the riot, its availability to numerous interpretations (213). The perspective shifts with abrupt, camera-like 'cuts' between the experience of the so-called rioters in the streets and the point of view cultivated by news media. By 'staging' the riot 'as an event on television', Baucom notes, the sequence stresses the significance of perspective in construing its meaning (213). The gratuitously destructive police raid of the Hot Wax nightclub, for instance, is depicted from the camera's perspective as the dramatic bust of a criminal enterprise, while readers know that the people arrested are activists and community leaders, as well as Hind and Muhammad Sufyan's younger teenage daughter. The undercity's outcry in response, a declaration of 'Now it's *war*', 'happens, however – as does a great deal else – in places which the camera cannot see' (472). As a result, the meaning of the riot is unstable, a conflict of motivated interpretations, like individual and collective identity in this novel.

To trace the novel's proto-political philosophy, however, we need to back up and closely consider the immediate prelude to the riot, which suggests that something like 'hermeneutic indeterminacy' is in fact the *cause* of conflict. Here is a longer extract from the passage that presents the mounting tensions in Brickhall as a matter of conflicting 'estimations':

> As Simba had in effect already been tried and convicted in what he had once called the 'rainbow press – red as rags, yellow as streaks, blue as movies, green as slime', his end struck many white people as rough justice, a murderous monster's retributive fall. But in another court, silent and black, he had received an entirely more favourable judgment, and these differing estimations of the deceased moved, in the aftermath of his death, on to the city streets, and fermented in the unending tropical heat. The 'rainbow press' was full of Simba's support for Qazhafi, Khomeini, Louis Farrakhan; while in the streets of Brickhall, young men and women maintained, and fanned, the slow flame of their anger, a shadow-flame, but one capable of blotting out the light. (465)

The narrative thus establishes that one of the principal causes of conflict is the difference between 'estimations' manufactured by the mainstream press, which equates radical anti-Western politics with criminality, and judgement developed in the undercity's 'silent and black' court of counterpublic opinion. As we know, the undercity is hardly 'silent' prior to this moment. The paradoxical image of a shadow-flame captures the cognitive disconnect experienced by a 'public' when a 'silent and black' counterpublic takes its estimations into the public realm, insisting on their public expression.

As we began to see at the end of the previous chapter, the public expression of 'differing estimations' could double as a gloss on Hannah Arendt's characterisation of the formation of the 'reality of the public realm'. According to Arendt, the public realm is constituted by speech and action: activity that freely initiates new states of affairs, and speech – explaining, justifying, promising, and so on – that draws activity into communicable meaning and therefore, for Arendt, into the shared reality in which political life takes place. This shared reality, the 'space of appearance' or the 'common world' in her phrasing, comes into being 'only where things can be seen by many in a variety of aspects without changing their identity' (*HC*, 57). The common world's foundation is conversation, in both ordinary and etymological senses: people gather in public and talk to each other, expressing how the world looks from their perspectives, and through conversation with others, we come into awareness that we 'turn with' each other towards a shared world that is always available to multiple, and often conflicting, perspectives. Our 'incessant talk', she writes, teaches us 'that the world we have in common is usually regarded from an infinite number of different standpoints, to which correspond the most diverse points of view' ('Concept', 51). Like the ancient Greeks who figuratively model many of Arendt's ideas, we learn 'to see the same in very different and frequently opposing aspects' ('Concept', 51). Talk attunes us to 'reality rising out of the sum total of aspects presented by one object to a multitude of spectators' (*HC*, 57). In short, for Arendt talk is the medium in which we affirm that we turn together towards a world and objects we have in common, and through this twofold conversation, we actually *generate* this common world.

Like Habermas, Rawls and other theorists of public life affiliated with political liberalism, Arendt views speech as central to politics, especially in a democracy, but she differs by rebuffing the notion that our 'incessant talk' should be restricted in accordance to norms such as those associated with rational discussion. She does not claim that public conversation should aspire towards 'communicative rationality', in Habermas's phrase, nor that it be regulated by a competitive 'marketplace of ideas'. When Habermas distinguishes the proto-public sphere of literary salons from the liberal, political public sphere, he writes that 'reason [. . .] turns conversation into criticism and *bons mots* into arguments', whereas for Arendt, political speech need not be rational, critical nor argumentative.[27] As we'll see, her less normative conceptualisation of public speech complements her commitment to a political realm in which 'newness' can appear, where we can be 'prepared to look in the face', as Rushdie's narrator puts it, at modes of expression and sources of common interest that lack precedent. A too-strict commitment to 'reasonableness' – or secularity, or a given definition of the 'common', and so forth – can pre-emptively short-circuit 'newness' and, with it, the fullness of political life. Here we can discern an affinity between Arendt's understanding of public speech and the ideal of conversation we have traced in Cavell's work, both in his descriptions of the 'form of life' of 'articulate responsiveness, expressiveness', which is signified, generated and perpetuated in interpersonal conversation, and in his proposed adaptation of Rawls's theory of justice. For Cavell, as we saw in the first chapter, the phrase 'conversation of justice' describes his vision of a perfectionist, democratic society, in which no shared project should be presumed, and in which we should not insist on shared definitions of what is reasonable or unreasonable. 'The virtues most in request here are those of listening, the responsiveness to difference, the willingness for change', he writes, and without 'difference' – including different ways of describing a shared reality – a society cannot know itself, its 'reality' cannot be roundly assessed, and thus its own relation to 'justice' cannot be drawn onward in the endless labours of perfectionism.

The central purpose of conversation, for Arendt as for Cavell, is disclosive and creative, rather than logically persuasive. Arendt's public realm is a political parallel to the 'form of life' generated and sustained by Cavell's conversing couples: not a pre-existing, permanent arena, but instead a space that 'arises out of [people] acting and speaking together', appearing 'between people living together for this purpose, no matter where they happen to be', and lasting only as long as people continue to converse (*HC*, 198). Conversation – in the double sense Arendt implies – is poetic, performative, generating the shared common world wherever people turn together towards common interests. It is crucial, here, to keep track of her distinctive use of terms. She distinguishes 'reality', the 'space of appearance' and 'the common world' from that which is purely given, factual or truthful. When she writes that reality 'ris[es] out of the sum total of aspects', she refers to this creative outcome of speech and assembly, the constitutively shared 'space of appearance' rather than 'reality' in its more conventional sense. This vision of conversation's performative power is especially pertinent in the context of Arendt's concerns about the threat to the common world posed by scepticism, the modern turn inward since Galileo's 'telescopic discoveries' and Descartes's *cogito*. She warns that by stressing the commonality of 'the structure of [our] minds' rather than the objective world, modern philosophy has proposed a route of recovering from sceptical doubt that imperils the foundational premise of public life. Conversation counters this threat from scepticism, for Arendt, because the 'common world' is itself the product of conversation. We need not question the objectivity of the 'common world', the specific world that matters for politics, because *that reality* comes into being wherever and whenever we speak with one another.

As Linda Zerilli has argued, Arendt's thought recasts the pluralism many see as a principle threat to modern democratic politics – the diverging conceptions of value and truth that people bring to bear in a multicultural and diverse public realm – as the precondition for politics: 'plurality [is] the condition of, rather than the problem for', the work of politics.[28] Here, again, we find a crucial distinction between Arendt's work and conventional liberal theory (as well as an echo of Cavell's description of separateness – plurality and difference – as the 'logic of human intimacy' and hence the 'field of serious and playful conversation or exchange' [*CT*, 221]). Arendt argues that one of the greatest problems for politics is the exclusion or suppression of perspectives on the world. Such exclusion can result from oppression, conformity and censorship, cynical disengagement, or the normative regulation of political speech. Any reality that arises where specific voices and perspectives have been excluded is vulnerably partial and unstable. (This is one reason that her peremptory exclusion from politics of views deemed 'social' – such as demands for integrated education – may be read as a contradiction of her own thinking.)[29] Excluded standpoints continue to exist and, in what *The Satanic Verses* might call a 'shadow' sense, they threaten worldly reality, or they build worlds invisible to those who have excluded them – worlds, like that of the undercity, which might burst into the hegemonic 'reality'. Riots, but also political events like the 2016 EU referendum in Britain and recent illiberal, populist developments in supposedly liberal societies, attest to the vulnerability of any 'worldly reality' constructed in terms that exclude supposedly illiberal standpoints or modes of expression. By this view, disruptive events like the riot in *The Satanic Verses* may be more than mere breakdowns of public order: they may offer momentary glimpses of hitherto suppressed aspects of political 'reality'. Insofar as such events express 'differing estimations' of reality, they at least temporarily, performatively, alter the common world.

Drawing on Arendt to make this case, but also to challenge Arendt's prioritisation of speech in public life, Judith Butler has argued that both orderly and riotous public assemblies alter the 'space of appearance' by altering what she calls 'the relation between the recognizable and unrecognizable'.[30] Whereas the norms of a political system may 'recognize' only political expression that is made according to the norms governing political speech (civility, reasonableness), when people 'enact their plural existence in public space', Butler argues, their presence itself makes demands 'to be recognized, to be valued' and performatively enacts 'a right to appear, to exercise freedom' (26). Public assemblies frequently both *assert* something (a collective grievance or demand) and *perform* something (the group's contribution to the public 'space of appearance'). Such assembly also implicitly critiques the system that has excluded those assembled, raising into visibility the exclusionary norms governing the space of appearance. As Butler puts it, 'plural performativity' can 'produce a rift within the space of appearance, exposing the contradiction by which its claim to universality is posited', and this rift can potentially 'establish new forms of appearance' (50–51). Butler critically extends Arendt's view of public life by stressing that plural performativity 'may or may not take linguistic form; speech and silence, movement and immobility, are all political enactments; the hunger strike is precisely the inverse of the fed body standing freely in the public domain and speaking', but this does not make it less political and performative (172). How, she asks, might we 'understand public assembly as a political enactment that is distinct from speech?' (155).

In *The Satanic Verses*, the space of appearance indeed transforms when the undercity brings its differing estimations of Simba into public, estimations that are not acknowledged as 'speech' by the existing political order. The novel stresses this refusal to hear the undercity's claims as speech in its attention to the uncomprehending news camera, and it is pessimistic about the power of assembly in such circumstances. The 'rift within the space of appearance' produced by the undercity is promptly sutured by state violence, and the scar is erased by a media industry whose material as well as ideological interests align with the police. By the time the 'differing estimations' of Simba clash in the streets, numerous rounds of misconduct by both police and media have ensured that the estimations of the undercity conflict with the sense of reality grasped by the majority of the British public. Unleashing its 'full might' against the undercity, the police force interrupts whatever liberatory power the undercity's performative assembly may have possessed. Moreover, once the 'riot' is in full swing, a statement by Inspector Kinch strives to reinscribe the boundaries of the British public sphere:

> These kids don't know how lucky they are, he suggests. They should consult their kith and kin. Africa, Asia, the Caribbean: now those are places with real problems. Those are places where people might have grievances worth respecting [. . .] People should value what they've got before they lose it. Ours always was a peaceful land, he says. Our industrious island race. (470)

Kinch explicitly positions the undercity outside the racial geography of British consensus, its grievances not meriting 'respect'. The camera again takes sides, framing Kinch as 'a good man in an impossible job. A father, a man who likes his pint' (470). As one character in *The Satanic Verses* observes, the 'modern city [. . .] is the locus classicus of incompatible realities' (325). In the course and aftermath of the riot, Kinch, the police in the streets, and the media are successful in shoring up the walls of British consensus against a possible reckoning between realities, or a conversational, performative convergence of 'aspects' of reality.

Insofar as the riot represents the momentary breakdown and swift reestablishment of a governing language of public conversation, it provides us with an allegory for the limits of the conversational ideal. We encountered a version of these limits in the first chapter's consideration of the 'conversation of justice', pre-empted in *Persuasion* by the incompatibility of Anne's and the nurse's forms of life. However flexible 'conversation' is in comparison to 'rational discussion' or 'communicative reason', as an ideal for public life it still presumes a shared language.

The ideal of public conversation can seem at best utopian, and at worst the source of normativity and thus, perhaps, suppression. In the words of David Rudrum, whose extension of Cavell's work I mentioned in Chapter 1, 'Conversation cannot be a model if one party is not considered capable of speech' (171). This is precisely the situation described in *The Satanic Verses* and, in a subtler way, in *Persuasion*. As we've seen, in Rushdie's novel, the camera that mediates the official British public realm 'cannot understand, or demonstrate, what any of this [unrest] achieves', and the undercity's response to the police's militarised action 'happens [. . .] – as does a great deal else – in places which the camera cannot see' (470–472). In the terms of Jacques Rancière, the theorist on whom Rudrum draws to supplement and temper Cavell's conversational idealism, the 'quarrel' in Rushdie's novel 'has to do with the consideration of speaking beings as such'.[31]

Does Rancière, then, offer a better handle than Arendt, or Cavell, on what happens in *The Satanic Verses*, and by analogy in any moments of political breakdown? Yes and no – or rather, yes, but in a way that I'll resist by carrying the conversation between Arendt and *The Satanic Verses* further. Rancière argues that politics 'is first of all a way of framing, among sensory data, a specific sphere of experience, [. . .] a partition of the sensible, of the visible and the sayable'.[32] 'Politics', he writes, 'is aesthetic in principle'.[33] In *The Satanic Verses*, the 'partition of the sensible' by the 'camera' is indisputably a political and aesthetic act, as is the undercity's insistence that, in Rancière's words, 'there is something "between" them and those who do not acknowledge them as speaking beings who count'.[34] With Rancière, the novel suggests that new political possibilities arise when 'another court, silent and black', ceases to allow the fantasy of its silence to persist, bringing its 'differing estimations' of the common world into a pitch that cannot be denied, even if its status as speech continues to be denied. For Rancière, such *dissensus* is the 'rupture in the logic' of the space of appearance that doubles as 'the very institution of politics itself', earning the name 'democracy'.[35] *The Satanic Verses* invites readings along these lines, summarised by Ian Baucom as representing 'a desire of those black Britons who take to the streets [. . . to] be recognized before the law as legitimate inhabitants of the national community'.[36] 'The riot, in this reading', Baucom continues, denotes the novel's 'insistence that black Britons must be recognized to occupy spaces within the island's towns and cities and a legitimate place within the geography of citizenship'.[37] Butler and Rancière would presumably amend this reading by claiming that the novel's activists are not only 'insisting' on recognition: they are achieving – performing – a kind of publicity that remaps the 'geography of citizenship'. Even if they are not granted full recognition, they have transformed (if fleetingly) the British 'space of appearance'.

This is not Baucom's reading, however, nor is it mine, as the novel's pessimism about riotous assembly counters any impulse to ascribe utopian interpretations to such ruptures in the space of appearance.[38] Several prominent characters die in the riot: Jumpy Joshi, a pregnant Pamela Chamcha, and the Shaandaar proprietors, Hind and Muhammad Sufyan. In its aftermath, the narrative perspective travels with Chamcha and Farishta back to India, leaving London behind with vague, unexplored suggestions that the younger generation of 'browns-and-blacks' have taken on the work of rebuilding Brickhall. Farishta commits suicide, and Chamcha looks primed to return for good to India, reconnecting with his Indian girlfriend and inheriting his father's wealth after making peace with the fertiliser tycoon. This conclusion appears to express not only cynicism about racial justice movements in Britain, but also a retrenchment in conservative rather than hybrid values. Peter Kalliney has argued that Chamcha's 'just-passing-through' experience in Brickhall gives the novel 'access [to] questions around racial and postcolonial anxieties' while allowing it to 'disentangle itself from the painful class dynamic'.[39] By this reading, the novel indulges in a kind of literary tourism of postcoloniality as it is experienced by working-class migrants, and it ends with a return to the 'homelands' of India, heterosexual union between two Indians, and, with Chamcha's inheritance, economic privilege. Whatever its intended politics regarding the experiences of working-class Black and Asian British citizens, the novel declines to represent the 'space of appearance' following the riot, suggesting indifference to whether or not this space rebuilds in terms more auspicious for the undercity.

The murkiness of the novel's politics in fact parallels one of the central tensions of democratic political theory, the conflict between 'dissensus' and political institutions, and, in my view, this tension points to the resources offered by the conversational outlook sketched by this book's exemplary novelists and philosophers. As Aletta Norval puts it, 'Democratic theory is torn between two moments: that of the extraordinary, the moment of founding and of constituent power, and that of the ordinary, the institutional and constituted power'.[40] Rancière manifests the former tendency, not only prioritising 'extraordinary' moments of dissensus, but also casting into suspicion any form of constituted power, which he aligns with 'the police'. This stress on the normative and repressive elements of shared conventions renders it difficult to imagine transitioning from the 'extraordinary' to the 'ordinary', to the daily efforts of building and sustaining institutions, efforts without which we cannot sustain a (more) egalitarian world. The latter requires the conventions of shared language and the normativity of judgement, assertions that some ways of life are better, fairer, more egalitarian than others. If Cavell and Arendt too readily presume a shared (enough) language for conversations of justice and worldmaking political speech, Rancière and similar theorists of rupture focus perhaps too emphatically on moments that expose communicative responsiveness and coordination as impossible or entailing repression.

Throughout this book, I've claimed that philosophers and novelists drawn to the ideal of conversation propose conversation as a risky middle ground between versions of the two 'moments' Norval describes, a relay between the conventionality of shared language and the openness of transformation. Forms of life, for ordinary language philosophers, are flexible and open, and we must accept conventions and the 'publicness of language' – with its limitations – if we are to communicate at all. An overly acute suspicion of the normativity of speech and language, in politics as in ethics, can itself invite world-denying or -destroying scepticism. In the political realm, a commitment to conversation, rather than rational discussion or liberal 'cooperation', for instance, entails a commitment to responding, articulately, even to expressions that arise in a language we don't yet understand. This responsiveness must encompass acting – building institutions, inscribing principles of justice into a political order – while remaining open to further and unexpected critiques. Cavell's ethos of conversation, founded on ordinary language philosophy and linked to perfectionist critique and acknowledgement, outlines a hope applicable to democracy, but as critics observe, it leaves ambiguous the path forwards in situations like the one depicted in *The Satanic Verses*. Norval joins Rudrum in making what Cavell would call a 'continuation' of his thought by integrating it with Rancière's attention to disruption.

Arendt provides an alternative continuation, a supplement to the conversational ideal as expressed in both her work and Cavell's, which I'll now put into dialogue with Rushdie's vision of fractured public life. This is the lens through which I read her turn to Kant's aesthetic theory for a model of political judgement in the absence of fixed rules. Arendt does not herself connect her account of the public realm 'rising out' of speech and action to her reworking of aesthetic theory, but there are important continuities. If the public realm is a performative achievement of twofold conversation rather than a neutral, pre-existing space for deliberation, it establishes what we might call, in Kant's phrase, 'merely formal purposiveness', internal, shifting and contingent criteria. If we are committed, like Arendt, to responding to others within a political realm that is disclosed and reconfigured through our incessant talk, we need a manner of judging responsibly, despite lacking the foundation of fixed concepts. Arendt's turn to Kant's aesthetic theory lays a blueprint for a 'democratic theory of judgment', in Linda Zerilli's phrase, a way to judge without deference to mediating concepts of what is 'reasonable', 'civil', 'common', or anything else, but also without abandoning conviction in the validity of our judgements.[41] Building on Zerilli, I propose that Arendt's turn to Kant not only outlines procedures for improving our judgements, but also meets a need implied by her understanding of a performatively, conversationally generated common world.

## Differing Estimations: Judging the Conversational Common World

Up to this point, I have been considering 'differing estimations' primarily as the indices of differing points of view. *The Satanic Verses* insists on the importance of perspective and position in the construction of estimations, particularly through its emphasis on the location of the media camera that 'chooses sides'. But the word estimation signifies judgement, a stage beyond the perception of an 'aspect', and in this detail, too, the novel's implicit understanding of political conflict resonates provocatively with Arendt's work. Elaborating Arendt's understanding of judgement and its continuities with her implicit commitments to conversation takes us temporarily away from *The Satanic Verses*, but we'll shortly see that Rushdie's novel at once affirms Arendt's view of judgement and, in its attention to racist prejudice, prompts a reformulation of her work for conditions in which inequality and prejudice render conversation across forms of life impossible.

Arendt intended to make *Judging* the final volume of *The Life of the Mind*, following *Thinking* and *Willing*, but she died before writing more than its two epigraphs. In the postscript to *Thinking*, she writes that the planned volume on judgement

> shall show that my own main assumption in singling out judgment as a distinct capacity of our minds has been that judgments are not arrived at by either deduction or induction; in short, they have nothing in common with logical operations – as when we say: All men are mortal, Socrates is a man, hence, Socrates is mortal. We shall be in search of the 'silent sense', which – when it was dealt with at all – has always, even in Kant, been thought of as 'taste' and therefore as belonging to the realm of aesthetics. (*LMT*, 215)

As we saw in Chapter 3, a curious feature of aesthetic judgement, in Kant's account, is that we 'believe we speak with a universal voice' when we pronounce an object beautiful, despite having no metric to reference other than our own taste and the inner 'silent sense', the *sensus communis* that assures us others do, or would, share our taste (§8, 50). We 'imput[e] this agreement to everyone', expecting 'not confirmation by concepts, but assent from others' (§8, 51). Arendt argues that this seemingly unwarranted universalisation without conceptual foundation applies also in the political realm, where, as Kant observes of aesthetic experience, 'there can be no rule', nor 'any reasons or fundamental propositions' by which we can 'press [upon others]' our judgements (*CJ*, §8, 50). If we do not see beauty or the same political implications that another person does, logical argument will not make a difference. For Arendt, then, politics is 'aesthetic in principle' not only because (per Rancière) the political realm emerges via the 'partition of the sensible' in speech and assembly, but also because the ways in which we respond to political issues are similar in principle to the ways in which we respond to objects of aesthetic interest.

In her *Lectures on Kant's Political Philosophy* and several essays, most notably 'The Crisis in Culture' and 'Truth and Politics', Arendt began to sketch how she would extend such ideas from Kant's *Critique of Judgment* into politics. She derives from Kant not only an original account of the commonalities between aesthetic and political experience, but also guidance for how best to judge politically, despite lacking external metrics or logical rules. As we have seen, Kant proposes that we test and refine judgements by 'comparing [them] with the possible rather than the actual judgments of others, and by putting ourselves in the place of any other man, by abstracting from the limitations which contingently attach to our own judgment' (§40, 136). Political judgement, Arendt argues, demands a similar method of imaginative comparison:

> Political thought is representative. I form an opinion by considering a given issue from different viewpoints, by making present to my mind the standpoints of those who are absent; that is, I represent them. This process of representation does not blindly adopt the actual views of those who stand somewhere else, and hence look upon the world from a different perspective; this is a question neither of empathy, as though I tried to be or to feel like somebody else, nor of counting noses and joining a majority, but of being and thinking in my own identity where actually I am not. The more people's standpoints I have present in my mind while I am pondering a given issue, and the better I can imagine how I would feel and think if I were in their place, the stronger will be my capacity for representative thinking and the more valid my final conclusions,

my opinion [. . . ]. The very process of opinion formation is determined by those in whose places somebody thinks and uses his own mind, and the only condition for this exertion of the imagination is disinterestedness, the liberation from one's own private interests.[42]

Representative thinking, as Arendt adapts the concept from Kant, is crucially different from the standard understanding of democratic political representation, in which 'counting noses' to learn the majority opinion guides decision-making. Everyone participating in political life must think for themselves, but ideally in a manner that imaginatively 'represents' alternative standpoints. As she stresses, representative thinking is not a civic extension of empathy: we should not swap our own personal interests and feelings for those of others, but rather should sample so many perspectives in our own identity that our interests loosen their grip on our judgements. Representative thinking in politics, as in aesthetics, is meant to induce what Kant calls the 'enlarged mentality' of disinterestedness, but not the disinterestedness of abstract 'rationality', which presupposes a concept of rationality. Arendt comments, appealingly, that 'to think with the enlarged mentality means that one train one's imagination to go visiting' (*LKPP*, 43).

There are two distinct, but intertwined, operations involved in political judgement as Arendt understands it. We judge immediately, instinctively and without reflection, upon encountering the object at hand: we feel pleasure or repugnance, outrage or ennoblement. For Kant, we know a response is aesthetic judgement rather than strictly personal taste if we impute it to others, despite lacking a solid rationale. We should then test and refine this judgement via representative thinking, which allows us to assess the 'communicability' of the judgement, regardless of where we stand. Communicability, here, means consistency with the *sensus communis*: 'The criterion is communicability', Arendt writes, 'and the standard of deciding about it is common sense' (69). The two operations work together, and because of its intrinsic link to community and imagined communication, Arendt writes that judgement reassures us we are 'at home in the world' (76).

The procedure Kant recommends implies that the object to judge is 'usually regarded from an infinite number of different standpoints', as Arendt describes the 'reality of the public realm' ('Concept', 51). In other words, it is a procedure well suited to the conversational common world as Arendt characterises it, although she does not herself remark on this continuity. Whereas her earlier descriptions of 'reality' emphasise talking with others to learn and share the many 'aspects' of common issues, 'representative thinking' proposes something like an independent and depersonalised 'conversation' with oneself. It is a form of 'anticipated communication with others with whom I know I must finally come to some agreement'.[43] Travelling into alternative standpoints, we turn towards the world with imagined versions of ourselves, in anticipation of turning and talking with actual rather than imagined others.[44] Representative thinking presumably draws on talk – which, by teaching us that the world we have in common is infinitely many-sided, helps to map our imagination's routes of travel – but imagination travels more freely than voices, and we might visit standpoints occupied by people excluded from a political community's conversations. To anticipate a point I'll return to, Kant's insistence that we try to judge, eventually, as a member of the 'world' community suggests one way in which Arendt's adoption of Kantian judgement might mitigate the restrictiveness of her emphasis on speech: to judge as a member of the world community means learning to judge across languages or forms of life, learning to find a *sensus communis* or form of life in which others' unfamiliar expressions count as speech.

Liberal protocols for public deliberation – giving reasons and hoping others will respond to what Habermas calls the 'forceless force of the better argument' – are not prohibited in Arendt's vision of public life.[45] But these protocols will not carry the day. More provocatively, not only does Arendt tell us it is unrealistic to hope to reach consensus through rational discussion – because political judgement, like aesthetic judgement, does not submit to rational persuasion – she also insists this is a *good thing*, that we shouldn't want to resolve political disagreement through appealing to logic or additional information. This latter, normative rather than descriptive claim is where her work most sharply deviates from liberal thought. For Arendt, like Rancière, the essence of politics *is* disagreement, differing estimations, and not the discovery of logically or empirically indisputable truth. 'Truth carries within itself an element of coercion', Arendt writes; it is 'beyond agreement and disagreement', and disagreement is the 'very essence of political life' (TP, 239, 241). Any aspiration to resolve disagreement by appealing to reason, factual or logical 'truth', or what Rawls calls 'comprehensive doctrines' like religious belief, is in essence anti-political.[46] As Jürgen Habermas and other critics of Arendt have charged, her work fails to close the 'yawning abyss between knowledge and opinion'.[47] Although accurate, such complaints miss her central point: closing the 'abyss' between truthful knowledge and political opinion would negate politics as such. Thus, whereas Habermas agrees with Arendt that 'the public sphere ideal is not perfectly reachable', her view is premised not on human fallibility, but rather on a different understanding of the nature of politics.[48]

At the same time, disagreement about facts (or truthful knowledge) threatens the very possibility of politics by jeopardising 'common and factual reality itself' (TP, 237). Public life depends on factual reality: our disagreeing judgements must be *about* something, and we must distinguish between that which is indisputable – the facts – and that which is constitutively disputable – the implications of those facts, our opinions about what to do given our material conditions. Insofar as the shared reality we judge is constituted performatively, in our speech and action (which ideally are guided by judgement), the common reality we turn towards and judge is itself unstable, shifting. Instead of closing the 'yawning abyss' between truth and opinion, Arendt offers, in Cavell's words, 'a thin net over an abyss', insisting that the exchange of opinion constitutes the kind of reality we must judge. The 'net' her work stitches with its vision of public life as constituted in conversation, and judged as an aesthetic achievement, simultaneously retains and mitigates scepticism's threatening presence in public life. To again invoke Cavell, 'nothing insures' political conversations or the common world they generate, the world in which we continue to speak, judge and act. Nothing insures we will speak the same language as those with whom we must converse; this is one way to gloss the plight of Rushdie's undercity, and we will return to this issue momentarily. Likewise, nothing insures our 'estimations': political judgements are constitutively unsettled. Any political agreement we reach is not final, as the world we judge changes, and the community with whom we judge is in flux. These features of vulnerability are precisely why we must keep talking to one another, turning towards a world constituted by our talk, and repeatedly sending our imaginations visiting to new standpoints, or revisiting old standpoints looking out over a changing world. We ultimately have nothing more, and nothing less, than conversation at our disposal, if we seek to constitute and maintain a democratic political realm. (We must, of course, provide material supports for conversation, so I do not mean that literally nothing more than talk is required for democracy. Talk of the sort Arendt envisions requires, to name just a few of its material conditions, education, time not spent working, and a mind not beleaguered by economic anxiety. Such reflections have at times compelled people to defend exclusionary or elitist political practices – as Arendt's ancient Greece exemplifies – but they might instead compel egalitarian distributions of resources.)

So, what should we do when our judgements differ, if we should not rely on presenting each other with evidence or logic? We might try urging others to look at the objects under consideration again. We might try providing them with new information, or we might describe to them a new standpoint from which to consider the object. Our appeal, in other words, would not be that others *reason* differently, but rather that they *perceive* differently, with the conviction that as soon as they see what we see, they will share our judgements. As Cavell writes of aesthetic judgement, 'It is essential [. . .] that at some point we be prepared to say in its support: don't you see, don't you hear, don't you dig?' (*MWM*, 93). Arendt claims something similar of political judgement, drawing again on Kant's language: one can try to 'woo' rather than compel another's agreement, and when doing so, 'one actually appeals to the "community sense"', she writes (*LKPP*, 72). *Don't you dig?* If not, look again, and refer to the same sense that guides me. If you keep looking, you'll see the validity of my estimation that, for instance, Simba's death was a crime.

Arendt focuses on Kant's guidance for how we *ought* to judge, but *The Satanic Verses* directs our attention to the importance of the *descriptive* register of her (and Kant's) account of judgement, which clarifies the difficulties of retaining or regaining a common world in conditions of intense inequality and polarisation. Following the stages of reflective judgement 'indicates a man of *enlarged thought*', Kant writes: an aspirational rather than a universal or typical man (§40, 137, original emphasis). Yet those of us who fall short of the 'enlarged' mentality still make aesthetic and political judgements, perhaps after consulting the *sensus communis* in a less rigorous way, not travelling very widely in our imaginations and judging in common with a narrower set of people, those whose positions we are most readily inclined to imagine. When we reach a political (or aesthetic) judgement even by less rigorous reflective activity, we still 'believe that we speak with a universal voice' and 'impute' the judgement to others, assuming they perceive what we perceive.[49] Simba's death is judged 'rough justice' by 'many white people', whose *sensus communis* and sense of factual 'truths' have been shaped by the discriminatory news media. The amorphous 'many white people' have not visited the standpoint of 'another court, silent and black', which sees and judges differently, and with somewhat similar tendencies to repress facts. In judging Simba's death to be just, these 'many white people' presumably believe they speak with a universal voice: this is simply what it means to judge, whether or not we have exerted much imaginative effort to form the judgement.

According to Arendt's account of political judgement, people whose estimations differ may find each other to be perverse, deficient in sensibility, or 'alien'. They are not merely uninformed or irrational, but beyond the pale, outside our *communis*. This is Pamela's charge against Chamcha, prior to the metamorphosis: 'You couldn't get him to look at what was really real', by which she means the injustices of his 'picture postcard' England (181). It might also be the charge against anyone who passively accepts either the police's implausible account of Simba's death or the undercity's romanticised account of Simba's life. The implications of this account of judgement are alarming: if the other simply cannot *dig*, cannot see what I see and hear what I hear, I might conclude we are so different from each other we ought to cease trying to communicate. We share neither form of life nor *sensus communis*. This suggests that the nature of judgement can undermine its own foundations, its requirement that we take into account alternative standpoints. The differing estimations of Simba and his death become 'incendiary', to borrow the prescient adjective used by undercity activist Hanif Johnson, precisely because their mutual contradiction is matched by the strength with which each is believed to be true.

We are returning to the perilous edge of scepticism that Arendt walks, which in this case points to a paradox inherent to political judgement as she (and this book) understands it: we feel as though we speak with a universal voice, but even while speaking so confidently, we must begin judging anew unless we are satisfied to pass judgements only on the objects and events of the past, and in *communis* with past generations. Neither human affairs nor beautiful objects are immutable; flowers wilt, paintings fade and political conditions endlessly transform. More importantly, the *communis* itself continuously transforms. We judge both aesthetic styles and racial justice by markedly different, yet not rationally deducible, terms today than one or two hundred years ago. Our 'we', too, has changed in multiple ways. Arendt stresses 'natality' in her work, linking mortality and birth to the ever-renewing newness of the world, newness guaranteed as long as new people are born and come of age, move into a community, or become part of its talkative constituency for the first time after discriminatory norms or exclusions break down. People themselves change. The material conditions that form the standpoint of a person or group change. To remain properly 'political' in our thinking, according to Arendt's terms, we must not attribute transhistorical truth to our political judgements (we might attribute transhistorical truth to *moral* judgements, but Arendt would locate these in the private or social, rather than public, sphere).[50] We must never cease to imaginatively visit. The work of representative thinking must be repeated despite the satisfaction that accompanies judgement.

Arendt hints at this constitutive challenge for political judgement when she discusses the nature of prejudice. A prejudice, she writes in 'Introduction *Into* Politics', is a previously made judgement that has been 'dragged through time without [. . .] ever being re-examined or revised'.[51] Prejudices encapsulate the 'estimations' of a particular community at a particular moment in history. They are time capsules of judgements derived from standpoints that no longer exist, regarding a world that no longer exists. Arendt notes that prejudices are not entirely bad: we are limited in our intellectual resources, and we cannot judge everything for ourselves. Representative thinking is quite demanding, and inherited judgements provide shortcuts. When our speech or actions are motivated by prejudice, we 'can count on the ready assent of others, without ever making an effort to convince them' – prejudices rest on a presumed *sensus communis*, and, like judgements, they help 'people recognize themselves and their commonality' (ibid., 100). But prejudices outlive their usefulness, and they are the anti-political fate of judgements that outlive and resist representative thinking and reflective judgement. Eventually, 'it is the task of politics to shed light upon and dispel [them]' (ibid., 99). Any community that lapses in the relentless labour of representative thinking risks falling into prejudice.

According to this understanding of prejudice, bigotry becomes prejudice only when the *sensus communis* encompasses the standpoints of those who disagree with the bigoted view, possibly those who have been dehumanised. To put this another way, within a racist *communis*, there is nothing 'anti-political' about racism. The racist view will be supported by Arendtian 'political thinking' and will not actually be 'prejudice' in the sense of unreflective judgement. Views that outsiders to one's *communis* recognise as prejudicial do not feel like prejudices to those within the *communis*; they feel like preparation to 'look in the face' at the 'reality of the public realm'. Where they hold sway, prejudices shape the ways we perceive the world, determining at once the standpoints we imaginatively visit, the aspects of the world we turn towards, and our capacities to look in the face at what we see. Although she does not say so, Arendt's Greeks exemplify this aspect of political thinking, as well. The judgements sustaining the exclusion of women and slaves from the public realm were entirely consistent with that political community's *sensus communis*. Representative thinking is no guarantee of inclusive pluralism. Arendt alludes to a haunting example of murderously exclusionary political thinking in her study of the Eichmann trial, in which she notes that any individuals in Nazi Germany who exercised independent, non-genocidal judgement would have needed to 'be completely at odds with what they must regard as the unanimous opinion of all those around them'.[52] In such conditions, prejudice itself is worldmaking, or world-reinforcing. For the person whose humanity is denied, the other's prejudicial standpoint is world-denying, and for the person whose *communis* is animated with prejudice, the other's standpoint is not even on the imagination's map.

This is the situation represented by the riot in *The Satanic Verses*. Like anyone might whose powers are aligned with a governing *sensus communis*, Kinch and the cameras respond to moments of conflict by doubling down on their imaginative map, unwilling to try to see the world they have in common with those who contest their understanding of justice. Rushdie portrays the British public realm of the 1980s as a carefully policed reality, or rather, a carefully policed reality atop an incompatible, 'shadow' reality. Imaginations do not travel between these standpoints; the geographic hierarchy expressed by the metaphor of the 'undercity' hints at the difficulty of representative thinking when vastly unequal experience prepares us to look in the face at the reality of the public realm. From the 'facts' that restrict Chamcha's acting career to the news camera that 'chooses sides', the media is worldmaking, and thus world-denying to those whose standpoints are structurally beneath the realm of public representation and imagination. The riot indexes the forced exclusion of undercity activists from worldmaking public conversation, as well as the perpetuation of a prejudiced *sensus communis* that polices the reality of the public realm. The camera 'remains behind the shielding wall [of the riot police], observing the shadow-lands from afar, and of course from above' (470). Confined to the 'shadow-lands', the undercity remains indiscernible in the imaginative map of British life.

Arendt suggests that the solution to the problem thus framed is a civic ethic that urges us to be what Kant called a 'world citizen', striving constantly to expand our imaginative 'reach', the 'realm in which [we are] able to move from standpoint to standpoint' (*LKPP*, 43). Imagination can be trained for wider travels. We can read, engage with diverse media and art, and otherwise fuel and educate our imaginations. This capacity to exercise the imagination is a premise behind engaging in 'incessant talk' with others, especially those whose outlooks are profoundly different from our own. 'One judges always as a member of a community, guided by one's community sense, one's *sensus communis*', Arendt writes. 'But in the last analysis, one is a member of a world community by the sheer fact of being human' (*LKPP*, 75). This is as attractive as it is practically unhelpful. It requires flexible communicative habits, beginning with a capacity to sense when and how such flexibility is needed. *The Satanic Verses* depicts a more violent version of the difficulty we saw in *Persuasion*, that of talking, imagining and judging across forms of life. The cosmopolitanism to which Arendt gestures is effortful and reliant on individuals assuming burdens for the sake of a collective that does not naturally exist; indeed, for the sake of trying, without guarantee, to conjure a collective into existence. Moreover, many people are distinctly prejudiced *against* such cosmopolitanism, as exemplified by Theresa May's declaration several months after Brexit that, 'if you believe you are a citizen of the world, you are a citizen of nowhere'.[53] This does not make cosmopolitan judgement any less essential to the pursuit of justice, especially in an era in which political and personal fates are globally interconnected by climate and capital, as Seyla Benhabib and Lyndsey Stonebridge argue in recent works that invoke Arendt to discuss twenty-first-century emergencies.[54] It would be reasonable to decide that only in conversation with a 'world community' can we move towards justice in an interconnected world, but as Arendt insists, reason and evidence do not compel politics.

For Linda Zerilli, the commitment to enlarging one's mentality is crucial to the democratic aspect of Arendt's view of judgement. If responsible democratic citizenship entails this commitment, then when we find another's vocalisations or physical acts to be senseless – when, like the news media in *The Satanic Verses*, we 'cannot understand, or demonstrate' what another's acts or speech mean – we should take our incomprehension as evidence that we need to renew our imaginative travels. Zerilli analogises Arendt's vision of political judgement to the accounts of language use offered by Wittgenstein and Cavell, proposing that judging the world can expand – reattune – our shared forms of life. When we send our imaginations visiting, it is like 'learning new meanings for words', or 'new ways in which objects can be disclosed, and in this way [we are] enlarging our sense of worldly reality' (*DTJ*, 267). Arendtian judgement, Zerilli writes, is a 'world-building' practice, in which imaginatively consulting the perspectives of possible others can extend the scope of the shared public realm, rerouting our mutual attunements.[55] The more standpoints we visit, the larger and more complex, or 'many-sided', our world becomes. Building on Zerilli, I read Arendt's model of judgement as essential to democracy for two reasons: first, we must ground our acts and institutions somehow, which means that we must judge. Second, Arendt's model indicates how we can do this without ossification into the anti-democratic logic that Jacques Rancière names the police.

Democratic life, viewed from the conversational outlook, takes the form of a chiastic synecdoche, in which talk is a representative part of the whole of democracy, which, in turn, entails actions guided by both imagined and literal conversation. This restless, endlessly repeated activity of conversation and judgement is the always changing, vanishing and re-established, foundation of democratic life, a foundation shaky enough to allow change, but normative enough to allow worldmaking. There are no guarantees that those in power will judge with an enlarged mentality, of course, as *The Satanic Verses* dramatises. The fate of Rushdie's undercity emphasises the breakdown or impasse – the radical dissensus – that can render conversation between certain groups, in certain times and places, impossible. Yet, as I'll argue in drawing this chapter to a close, the magical-realist form of the novel simultaneously suggests a more hopeful vision.

### How Does Newness Come into the World, and How Does it Survive?

We have already answered a question that both Rushdie and Arendt repeatedly pose: How does newness enter the world? Newness enters the world, or the world takes on a new reality, when new aspects are expressed in the twofold conversation of public life. This answer is shared by Butler and Rancière, as well. But an equally important question is: How does newness *remain* in the world, or how does the transformation of the public realm register as more than a disturbance quickly repressed? This is where judgement and interpretation come in, for Arendt: we must learn to perceive and judge newness, and to judge in ways that update our capacities to perceive and judge the world. And although the newness generated by the undercity's expression of its 'differing estimations' fails to take hold, the novel's form itself offers hints about how it might.

As I have mentioned, *The Satanic Verses* broaches the newness question in its opening pages as its narrator recounts the miraculous transformations and survival of Chamcha and Farishta, falling to the earth from the exploded airplane:

> How does newness come into the world? How is it born?
> Of what fusions, translations, conjoinings is it made?
> How does it survive, extreme and dangerous as it is? What compromises, what deals, what betrayals of its secret nature must it make to stave off the wrecking crew, the exterminating angel, the guillotine? (8–9)

Over the course of its hundreds of pages, the novel gives multiple different glosses to these central questions. Does newness arise because of magic, divine or diabolical intervention, inscrutable historical forces, or deliberate human action (collective or individual)? When an event appears to be new, is it genuinely new, or is it in truth a mutation, a change in existing materials rather than the inauguration of an entirely new form? Finally, in the political realm: is extremism, ideological inflexibility, necessary to change the world, or must radicals in fact betray their ideals – compromise – in order to retain power?

*The Satanic Verses* largely has it both – or all – ways: *it was so, it was not*, as goes a familiar phrase in Arabic storytelling, which is frequently repeated in the novel.[56] The extremists in the novel – the prophet, an exiled Imam evocative of the Ayatollah Khomeini, the activist Uhuru Simba, a mystic named Ayesha, and Gibreel Farishta during his 'tropicalizing' efforts – are simultaneously admirable and deeply flawed, driven by ideals as well as personal vanity or madness. Even Margaret Thatcher is included in the novel's list of visionary extremists: she is a 'radical', Hal Valance tells Chamcha, and her government's neoliberal transformation of Britain amounts to 'a bloody revolution. Newness coming into this country that's stuffed full of fucking old *corpses*' (279). In each case, inflexible dedication appears to be one way that newness can enter the world, for better and for worse.

According to Rushdie in one of his many responses to the controversy stimulated by the novel, *The Satanic Verses* celebrates one source of newness above all others: diasporic hybridity. It affirms 'intermingling', he claims, disavowing rigidly 'pure' identities, whether religious or national: 'mélange, hotch-potch, a bit of this and a bit of that is *how newness enters the world*'.[57] In a lecture delivered via proxy during his time in hiding, Rushdie suggests that fiction is an ideal site for such intermingling. Novels, he asserts, mirror the 'way in which different languages, values and narratives quarrel'.[58] Unlike the news media portrayed in *The Satanic Verses*, a novel does not take sides, it 'does not seek to establish a privileged language, but it insists upon the freedom to portray and analyse the struggle between the different contestants for such privileges'.[59] A novel, in this view, is a kind of virtual public sphere, its Bakhtinian heteroglossia a synecdoche of modern plurality. Re-presenting the 'quarrel' of voices in the British public sphere – and via satire and magical realism, resisting a singular, simple reading along the lines of fantasy, straight realism or political protest – *The Satanic Verses* challenges readers to make something out of a reality generated by profuse, divergent, unmanageable voices. Rushdie implies that the novel is the inclusive public sphere that liberalism never has managed, and also the public sphere that an Arendtian would desire: not taking sides, welcoming all standpoints, indeed 'rising out' of the differing estimations it brings together. The act of reading becomes an act of learning to perceive coherence, order and direction out of the multiplicity of novelistic discourse: training the imagination in the worldmaking work of conversation. There is a flipside to this argument in favour of fiction, however, which parallels the novel's scepticism towards counterpublic radicalism. It allows for the suspicion, encouraged by the novel's depiction of the undercity, that hybridity can be worldmaking in the magical-realist postcolonial novel, but not in Britain in the 1980s. A novel can represent the depth and complexity of people and communities, the roundness of characters and counterpublics, whereas, at least according to *The Satanic Verses*, such complexities are ironed out of politics.

Moreover, the offence and pain the book caused in its depictions of the Prophet 'Mahound' remind us that novels are not actually as inclusive and egalitarian as Rushdie at least purports to believe.[60] The novel as a literary form has a historical affiliation with colonial modernity and liberal individualism.[61] Free indirect discourse and magical realism make a novel like *The Satanic Verses* a speech act that can refuse straightforward notions of accountability, as hybridity and heteroglossia become alibis. As Tariq Modood noted at the time of the original controversy, *The Satanic Verses* was particularly painful to South Asian Muslims, whose sensitivity about the representation of 'Mahound' 'ha[d] nothing to do with Quranic fundamentalism but with South Asian reverence of Muhammad [. . .] and cultural insecurity as experienced in Britain and even more profoundly in India'.[62] The liberal value of free expression came into conflict with cultural, economic and bodily vulnerability, Modood claims.[63] In an ironic repetition of the fate of the undercity, the 'estimations' expressed by precarious South Asian Muslims – in assemblies and book burnings – largely failed to register within the existing terms of political discourse. I do not make these observations to condone the fatwa and acts of violence committed in its name (including the appalling attack on Rushdie on stage in Chautauqua, which took place as I was revising this book), but rather to note parallels between the insistence a novel 'does not seek to establish a privileged language' and the erasure of normative values at work behind the scenes in liberal claims of neutral reason. In both cases, only certain 'languages' are admitted to the public sphere, and counter-discourses are pre-emptively refused.

Magical realism itself has a complicated status within postcolonial theory. Decades ago, Homi Bhabha called it 'the literary language of the emergent post-colonial world', while others have critiqued magical realism for reifying supposedly colonial categories of 'the real' versus the magical and commodifying the seemingly exotic.[64] According to Janice Ho, the use of magical realism in the riot sequence also enables Rushdie to dodge the crucial political question of whether violence is necessary for radical political transformation by blurring the lines between supernatural and violent, material causes. Thus, Ho argues, *The Satanic Verses* 'rewrites a liberal Englishness in order to repoliticize it, but also dreams of a radical politics that can retain its radicalism without recourse to violence' (226). Through magical realism, she suggests, the novel evades the implications of its radical critiques of liberalism, and in a roundabout way tepidly endorses liberal protocols for collective life. *It was so, it was not.*

From another perspective, however, the novel's magical realism is its strongest contribution to democratic imagination. It demands readers practise recognising 'newness', a capacity Arendt argues is central to judging the shifting common world generated and sustained in conversation. In *The Human Condition*, she writes that 'the new [. . .] always appears in the guise of a miracle' (178). True political change outpaces the concepts by which we can comprehend it, and the consequences of collective actions are never entirely predictable. She elsewhere explains that we typically react to 'newness' by neutralising its miraculous guise:

> To put it in a schematic and therefore necessarily inadequate way, it is as though, whenever we are confronted with something frighteningly new, our first impulse is to recognize it in a blind and uncontrolled reaction strong enough to coin a new word; our second impulse seems to be to regain control by denying that we saw anything new at all, by pretending that something similar is already known to us; only a third impulse can lead us back to what we saw and knew in the beginning. It is here that the effort of true understanding begins.[65]

At issue is whether we can look newness in the face, recognising genuine transformations of the many-sided world in which we live in common. We might respond initially to newness with awed mysticism, but then we are tempted, according to Arendt, to tame the experience by folding that which is new into a narrative of inevitability. Our impulse is to offer a causal explanation that is, in Arendt's words, 'altogether alien and falsifying', because 'the actual meaning of every event always transcend[s] any number of past "causes" which we may assign to it', and 'this past itself comes into being only with the event itself'.[66] Newness reveals something about the state of affairs prior to its appearance – it makes that state of affairs narratable as history, viewed anew. True understanding, for Arendt, entails learning to see the prehistory of the new event by the light it retrospectively shines, narrating the history it generates without reverting to formulas that erase contingency and human freedom. A shocking political event – such as a riot, public burnings of a novel, or an electoral result that takes pundits and the political class by surprise – demands that we judge without recourse to rules known in advance of the event, and that we interpret in ways that do not blot out the revelation. The importance of newness reinforces the case for modelling political judgement after aesthetic judgement, unmediated by concepts.

There is a striking similarity between Joshi's interpretation of Chamcha's body during the scene of the 'impromptu crisis summit' and what Arendt calls 'the hallmark of the modern historical and political sciences', which she describes as a 'confusion' whereby 'everything distinct disappears and everything that is new and shocking is (not explained but) explained away either through drawing some analogies or reducing it to a previously known chain of causes and influences'.[67] The various personal experiences that lend credence to Joshi's 'ideological view' – the undercity's familiarity with biopolitical scandals and daily abuses – are important aspects of the standpoints from which they judge, and the shadowy counterpublic is prepared to look in the face at elements of British life that the novel suggests others repress (including Chamcha, before his fall). But these experiences also cloud perception and lead to a consensus that Joshi has 'explain[ed] horns and hooves', when, really, he has explained them *away*, reducing the newness to a previously known chain of causes and addressing only the details consistent with this previously known chain. Readings of the novel that interpret the magic as a straight analogy for the operation of racism similarly miss the interpretive provocation posed by its excesses.

At the end of the riot sequence, a disagreement between Mishal Sufyan and Hanif Johnson gives voice to the tension produced by the novel's magical realist style. They are riding in an ambulance with our protagonists; Chamcha has had a heart attack, and Gibreel has collapsed into an exhausted trance after rescuing Chamcha from the burning Shaandaar café. Gibreel is murmuring, describing the trumpet that he believes blew flames (the narration is ambiguous on this point – he may have been hallucinating, or his trumpet may indeed have added to the fires consuming Brickhall). Mishal wonders if there is truth to Gibreel's description; after all, 'she remembers Chamcha as a devil, and has come to accept the possibility of many things' (484). Hanif counters, 'What has happened here in Brickhall tonight is a socio-political phenomenon. Let's not fall into the trap of some damn mysticism. We're talking about history: an event in the history of Britain. About the process of change' (484). His insistence contrasts the mystical to the political, as though we must choose if we are to remain political agents and part of a shared, material reality: '*Stay with me. The world is real. We have to live in it; we have to live here, to live on*' (484).

To this insistence, Arendt might respond that we must in fact acknowledge both – we must acknowledge the miraculous guise in which the genuinely new, socio-political phenomenon appears. We must allow ourselves to see what is shocking and unprecedented, and then seek to understand how it came into being; we must derive our judgement and historical understanding from the particulars, rather than applying concepts first. (Or as Wittgenstein might put it, we must withstand our craving for generality as long as possible.) Magical realism, then, expresses Arendt's understanding of the phenomenology of political change. This is not to say that magical-realist novels share any particular political philosophy, but where such interpretive excess occurs, it demands that a reader practise this aspect of Arendtian political thinking.

As Arendt notes, in *The Critique of Judgment* and in his more overtly political writings (about 'perpetual peace', for instance), Kant suggests that the audience is more crucial than the artist, and, in politics, the spectator is more crucial than the actor. It is through the faculty of judgement – of testing the communicability of one's estimations – that we reach public meaning. Kant posits that there is something like 'an original compact' between people, summarisable as the 'require[ment] from everyone else [that they make] reference to universal communication' when judging (§41, 139). Arendt proposes that judgement is more foundational to politics than action because it enables us to fulfil this species 'compact', and that communicability thus ought to guide action as well as judgement. That is, we ought to act in ways we believe our enlarged, imaginary community would affirm. 'The judgment of the spectator creates the space without which no such [beautiful or political] objects could appear at all', she writes. 'The public realm is constituted by the critics and the spectators, not by the actors or the makers. And this critic and spectator sit in every actor and fabricator' (*LKPP*, 63).

Interpretation is a critical part of this species compact, especially when the object at hand is the product of intentional human activity – when the object, that is, emerges in either art or politics. When we 'turn together' towards such objects of our world, we generate their shared reality by telling each other not only that the objects are *there*, in their many sides, or that they are beautiful. We also tell each other what they mean. Interpretation is internal to the activity of judgement, and it is implicitly prefaced by judgements about which objects are worthy of interpretation, but it deserves special emphasis. Emphasising interpretation suggests a tentative reconciliation between judgement, reason and mediating concepts. We offer reasons for interpretations, pointing to details in a work of art or politics and making a case – often logical – for their meaning. At the same time, we might run out of reasons and find ourselves saying, *don't you dig*? In other words, interpretations are mediated by concepts we handle by sliding in and out of the mood of the *sensus communis*. When we say what a picture, poem or policy means, we try to speak with a universal voice, but we also speak conceptually. The effort to offer a 'communicable' interpretation, which others will assent to regardless of where they stand when they are called on to say what the poem or policy means, blurs the lines between concepts, logic and judgement. We speak without 'insurance', but with conviction. It is possible, of course, to find a poem beautiful without understanding its meaning, just as it is possible to respond politically in an affective rather than articulable way. Surely, however, it is preferable to connect our judgements to interpretations we can explain by pointing to supporting details: this, at any rate, is the judgement underwriting the study of literature and other arts in the contemporary university, and it also underwrites any coherent account of democratic politics. I return to these parallels between Arendtian 'political thought' and literary studies in Chapter 5 and the afterword.

Arendt's Kantian suggestion that the spectator is more primary, and thus significant, than the actor prompts me to offer these closing thoughts about magical realism and its relation to political thinking. Newness depends on magical realism in the attitudes of political actors, and even more importantly, in the attitudes of other members of the *communis* who interpret and judge. Without a willingness to disregard the rules of what is likely, realistic or even possible according to known laws of human action, no one would launch revolutions, and even modest reforms might not be attempted. But if we follow Arendt, who follows Kant – if we draw the conclusions that Arendt's accounts of conversational worldmaking and political thinking imply – it is even more necessary for we who interpret political life to cultivate 'magical-realist' frameworks of judgement and interpretation for newness to survive. Such frameworks are necessary if we are to acknowledge, or respond articulately, when the language of the space of appearance has changed, when those deemed silent or ineligible appear and express their estimations in public, thereby altering the public realm. Without a framework by which to recognise such events *as new*, and to perceive that, as new events, they shed light on their own – our own – past and require new kinds of response, the fullness of that which is new will not last. The 'rift within the space of appearance' will be quickly sutured. If perspectives are worldmaking, as Arendt argues, then theoretical frameworks that organise perspectives are also worldmaking, or world-denying. This is one of the main reasons that framing public life via the metaphor of conversation is valuable: conversation, as I have stressed, does not presume specific rules or goals, but it does presume a shared form of life, which itself can presume nothing but continuing, transforming talk as its basis.

If we conceive of political conversation as establishing its own rules, elaborating criteria and mutual attunements that endlessly transform, we can be better prepared to look in the face at newness when the 'reality of the public realm' has transformed because new voices, claims and interpretations have been expressed.

Viewed from the conversational outlook, Rushdie's satirical representation of undercity activists has contradictory implications. On the one hand, the satire cultivates cynicism, an attitude at odds with the miraculous perception Arendt deems necessary to inaugurate and comprehend, and thereby sustain, genuinely new political conditions. On the other hand, by satirising the undercity's tendency to explain away genuine newness, *The Satanic Verses* implicitly challenges its reader to be responsive to the miraculous and shifting appearances of the world, to perceive a reality endlessly taking new shapes due to the aspects brought to bear on it. Such a public realm cannot be adequately interpreted from a dogmatic identarian standpoint, the novel suggests, nor can it be interpreted according to dominant pre-existing standards, which in both literature and politics have so often been named realism. For me this is the true ambivalence reflected by the novel's riot sequence: not its recourse to magic to evade reckoning with violence, and not even its antagonism towards identity-based counterpublics. Rather, as a participant and judge of my own political reality, I must – like the reader of the novel – have faith in miracles of Arendt's description to retain a belief in the possibility of twofold, democratically worldmaking conversation, despite the evisceration of institutions of collective life that would support such conversation. I am committed to imagining possible rather than actual worlds, and to remaining articulately responsive to that which surprises or baffles me in public life. Nonetheless, the suspension of disbelief called for by magical realism is an uneasy reflection of the implausibility of democratic conversation, supported and expanded by representative thinking, when the political economics of publicity, communication and imagination are far from auspicious. The next chapter continues to follow this ambivalent thread by considering the modes of thinking stimulated by digital social media, which, for many in the early twenty-first century, is our closest approximation to public, common conversation.

Chapter 5

# Digital vs Political Conversation: Ali Smith, Arendt and Wittgenstein

Early proponents of the Internet celebrated digital networked communication as offering solutions to the kinds of flaws in the public sphere spotlighted by *The Satanic Verses*. If the virtual equality aspired to in formulations of the liberal public sphere fails to manifest in practice, perhaps the truly virtual space of the Internet would be able to host conversations untainted by prejudice and inequality.[1] Hope for the Internet's democratising power increased with Web 2.0, the 'social' web characterised by platforms that promised to empower the average person to create and share content, bypassing or counteracting the mainstream media that 'chooses sides'.[2] Such hopes have repeatedly run aground, of course, but they persist in appeals to regulation and trust busting, and most recently (as I finish this book in 2023) in the decentralised blockchain and other 'self-certifying' Internet protocols characterised as the foundations of 'web3'.[3] For example, the blog post that announces Bluesky Public Benefit LLC, a project launched by Twitter in 2019 to develop an 'open and decentralised standard for social media', promises to 'develop and drive large-scale adoption' of new technologies like blockchain, harnessed 'for open and decentralised public conversation'.[4] With each shift in web infrastructure, boosters have promised or hoped that digital technology would free us from the limits encountered in the previous iteration, the gatekeepers of traditional media or the manipulators of attention-mining new media. Each web update is pitched, in part, as potentially restoring the conversational promise of the public sphere by enabling direct interaction between citizens, our political representatives and our wider communities.

Two different uses of the metaphor 'conversation' recur in discussions of digital social media: specific media are described as conversational when they foster discursive interchange (Twitter in contrast to blogs or email newsletters, for instance), and social media are described as a crucial thread – or threat – to the public 'conversation' vaguely conceptualised as key to liberal democracy. When social media exchanges are characterised as 'conversational', the metaphor signals that they are interactive, open-ended and experienced in the flow of time.[5] Social media exchange is also conversational in the figurative, worldmaking sense explored in this book. Through exchanging memes, hashtags and responses to online utterances, social media users 'turn together', reorganising visions of the world and in the process producing a collective that views the world in correlated terms. As Zeynep Tufekci writes of 'liking' and tweeting, such 'semi-public symbolic micro-actions can slowly reshape how people make sense of their values and their politics'.[6] Encapsulating this worldmaking sense of digital 'conversation' is the title (and central argument) of an influential study of the dynamics of meme exchange, Ryan Milner's 2016 monograph *The World Made Meme: Public Conversations and Participatory Media*. It is now widely understood that this worldmaking affordance of digital 'conversation' can bear both positive and negative political implications, empowering counterpublics like #MeToo and #BLM to insist on public acknowledgement of long-repressed aspects of our shared reality, or producing false, alternative 'realities' in digital echo chambers that imperil democratic politics.[7]

In this chapter, I take up the vexed issue of digital 'conversation' as it is obliquely reflected in Ali Smith's 2011 novel *There But For The*. The novel's plot centres on a mysterious event: a man named Miles Garth locks himself in the spare bedroom of a couple hosting a dinner party, and he remains there, without explanation, for months. This unexplained act goes viral. It inspires both the formation of a physical encampment in the alleyway behind the house he occupies and a global media phenomenon, as people claim Miles – or Milo, as they prefer to call him – as a symbol of disparate causes. I argue that this central premise allegorises the cultural ascent of memes, which I take to be exemplary of more widely shared criteria in digital conversation. Miles, I propose, transforms from an individual man into a meme, and what media scholars might call his 'producers' arrive in person.[8]

This reading takes liberties, perhaps more than any other reading in this book. I do not claim that all the allegories and hints I draw from the novel are deliberate, although I do claim their discoveries are invited. My central proposition is that we can develop the novel's hints into a clarifying critique of digital exchange by reading *There But For The* alongside new media criticism and facets of the conversational ideal, drawing the novel into conversation with ideas about language use, perception and common reality articulated in ordinary language philosophy and Hannah Arendt's political thought. I begin by outlining how the novel's explicit references to digital technology express familiar critiques of new media, linking Internet use to shallowness and distraction. I then delineate the more complicated analysis of digital media that emerges when we read the crowd outside Miles's window as a metaphor for social media communities forged through the exchange of memes. In the spirit of Wittgenstein and Cavell, I attend to the criteria by which the crowd uses 'Milo', linking this reading to Arendt's account of the 'social realm' whose conformist dynamics threaten the 'reality of the public realm'. Read thus, Smith's novel prefigures the rise of 'post-truth' conditions and links such conditions to criteria of online communication that were beginning their cultural ascent at the time of the novel's publication. Simultaneously, and most evocatively in the context of this book, *There But For The* contrasts the conventions we associate with aesthetic interpretation and creation to the tendencies of social media 'conversation' that undermine our shared sense of reality.[9] The novel's conclusion indicates that an exchange of stories and literal conversation prompts Miles into what Arendt (after Kant) calls representative thinking, the twofold conversation I elucidated in the previous chapter's account of Arendt's work on political speech and judgement. This imaginative activity inspires Miles to leave the bedroom. By tacitly contrasting memetic criteria with the criteria of thinking, interpreting and judging that stimulate him to re-join worldly reality, *There But For The* hints at a unique vision of the value of literature and conversation in an age when, to cite one of the novel's characters, 'we're forgetting how to know what's real'.

## Semblances of Plenitude and Community

*There But For The* is divided into four sections – titled 'there', 'but', 'for' and 'the' – each of which is narrated in a close third-person voice linked to one of four characters with a personal connection to Miles. The style evokes the 'tunnelling' and stream of consciousness associated with modernist texts like Woolf's *Mrs Dalloway*, unfolding a single day in each character's life and interweaving flashes of their past in dilated interruptions of the present. Anna Hardie, whose perspective focalises narration in the first section, met Miles as a teenager, when he drew her out of her shell during a trip to Europe for winners of a short story contest. They have not seen each other for decades, but Miles kept track of her contact information, and Genevieve Lee – the owner of the house he has occupied – contacts Anna hoping this woman from his past will persuade Miles to leave the spare bedroom. Mark Palmer, whose perspective filters the second section, invited Miles to the fateful dinner party after a chance meeting at a performance of Shakespeare's *A Winter's Tale*. The third section follows an elderly woman named May Young, whose daughter was friends with Miles until she died in her sleep at age fifteen; every year since then, Miles has visited May on the anniversary of the girl's death. The fourth follows the precocious (nearly) ten-year-old Brooke Bayoude, who lives near the house Miles occupies and who attended the dinner party with her parents. Between each section, the novel intersperses short texts authored by Miles, such as the story that won the contest decades earlier, a note tucked into Mark's billfold, and a postcard he sent to May the only other year he missed his annual visit.

*There But For The* never reveals a definitive motivation for Miles's act, although it suggests many reasons a person might opt out of the world of the contemporary British middle class. Smith depicts a world of borders, surveillance and wealth inequality, in which the language of human rights surfaces in advertising slogans, but not in the government agency that grants or denies asylum to migrants (in the ad in question, rights are asserted in order to be contradicted, a progressive lesson with an anti-liberal subtext: 'It's My Right To Eat Tin Cans', says a cartoon trash bin, as the audience is instructed to recycle and thus 'Deny Your Bin Its Rights' [9]). CCTVs proliferate; surveillance drones are classed as toys; and someone wonders aloud at the dinner party whether it matters if tigers go extinct, now that we have such lush digital reproductions of them. The novel additionally touches on drone warfare, Internet porn, child abuse, homophobia, loneliness, corporate propaganda (via the pun 'ethic cleansing'), casual racism and sexism, callous jokes about child labour, the neglect and erasure of elderly people, and an implicitly white supremacist media and culture. In short, the novel's backdrop is our world, scrutinised with an unsparing – and at times heavy-handed – yet also playful and occasionally joyful gaze.[10] There is no shortage of reasons a modern Bartleby-like figure might prefer not to participate in such a world.

Another object of the novel's critical scrutiny is digital technology. Mark describes the Internet as offering 'a semblance of plenitude' when it is in fact 'a new level of Dante's inferno, a zombie-filled cemetery of spurious clues, beauty, pathos, pain, the faces of puppies, women and men from all over the world tied up and wanked over in site after site, a great sea of hidden shallows' (105–106). Brooke's mother, Bernice, gives a philosophical gloss: 'The mere blowing along a road of a piece of litter, is enough to dispel the so-called truth of every single thing online. But we're forgetting how to know what's real. That's the real problem' (106). In both metaphor and substance, these criticisms echo Nicholas Carr's nearly contemporaneous book, *The Shallows: What the Internet is Doing to our Brains*, which updates Marshall McLuhan's argument that 'the medium is the message', claiming that the Internet is altering our capacities for sustained attention, the modes of private and critical thinking cultivated by print technology, which in turn also alters our sense of what it means to be a 'self'.[11] The only explicit champion of the Internet in *There But For The* is a dinner party guest depicted as racist and ignorant, who says the Internet is where she turns whenever she 'need[s] to know anything' (90). The availability of information is 'what's so great about being alive now', she continues. In the mouth of someone whose ignorance the novel demonstrates almost to excess, the words seem like confirmation of Bernice's and Mark's assessments.[12]

The familiar concern that digital connectedness has supplanted real intimacy is suggested in one of the novel's recurrent puns, in which May, the elderly filter of the third section, mishears the word 'internet' as 'intimate'. May observes that the 'intimate' seems to have damaged actual intimacy and ordinary experience: 'That was them these days, spending all their time looking up things on the intimate. The great-grandchildren, even, and them hardly past babies, spent their time on the intimate. It was all the intimate, and answer-phones and things you had to speak at rather than to' (143). This last remark about 'things you had to speak at rather than to' refers to her daughter's explanation that no one uses the phone for conversation anymore. May's second-hand assessment of the 'intimate' continues as she observes Josie Lee, the teenage daughter in the house Miles has occupied and a supporter of the encampment, who visits May after Miles sends a note to his followers requesting someone do so on the anniversary of her daughter's death:

> It was all supposed to be about how fast things were; they were always on about how fast you could get a message or how fast you could get to speak to someone or get the news or do this or that or get whatever it was they all got on it. And at the same time it was like they were all on drugs, cumbersome like cattle, heads down, not seeing where they were going.
> The girl thumbed and fingered away at her own world in her hand like it didn't matter that she was in May's hospital room, or in anyone's hospital room, on earth, in heaven, wherever. It didn't matter where in or out of the world she was. (148)

This final line, noting indifference to 'where in or out of the world' a person is, takes on complex significance when we consider that Miles is 'out of the world' at this moment, but that his withdrawal awakens among many a desire to be *in* the world, participating.

Indeed, the novel suggests that the encampment in the alleyway behind the Lees' house indexes a desire for presence, participation and meaning unmet by the networks of the digital web. One of the earliest campers calls Miles 'a wise man not found anywhere on the world wide web' (46). Another explains that he moved into the encampment after initially attending as a 'day tripper', because he had been 'worried every time I went home that I'd miss something. What if something happened and I wasn't here to see it?' (126). For the four characters whose perspectives we follow, the encampment represents a source of needed community. Anna is newly unemployed and cynically disengaged, following years working to assess claims for asylum. The only recent relationships recalled in her section are a short-lived affair with a married man and her work with the asylum seekers she feels she failed. Mark is haunted by a long-dead mother, in mourning for a more recently deceased partner, and sleeping with an unkind married man. Like Anna, the relationships he reflects on are mostly in the past. May is alone in a medical facility, awaiting transfer to a longer-term care home she has repeatedly told her adult children she wishes not to move into. She has stopped speaking in protest, and also because her speech is unreliable following a stroke. She begins speaking again when visited by Josie Lee, and at her confused but auspicious request, Josie sneaks her out of the facility and brings her to the encampment. Brooke, our fourth filter, is socially isolated and bullied by her schoolteacher, whose voice interrupts the narration repeatedly in her section with the taunt, 'YOU THINK YOU'RE SO CLEVER'. Brooke has great parents but seemingly no friends her own age, and she begins regularly skipping school and spending time at the encampment.

Yet even while the encampment offers community and belonging to people alienated in a disconnected age, it also comes to share many of the negative features ascribed by the novel to the digital world. Here is how Brooke perceives it at its height:

> The fact is, today the crowd outside Mr. Garth's room was so big that it was the kind you can get carried along with in a direction you don't really want to go in [. . .] The people sitting and standing and playing the guitars and eating their lunches on the big plastic mats that stop the grass becoming mud are back. The foodstalls are back. The Milo Merchandise stall that Mrs. Lee organized is back, with the T-shirts and badges and flags saying MILO-HIGH CLUB and SMILE-O FOR MILO;-), and the Milo Little Ponies for if people bring children. There have been flashing cameras at night for the last few nights, but the crowd has been being good because the police always move in if the crowd is too rowdy. There were TV cameras there this morning because there are two more women

who are claiming to be Mr. Garth's wives, though there are always people pretending to be Mr. Garth's wives [. . .] There are TV cameras most days now. There are cameras from America, and there were some French TV people who came for the debate they had before the last time the police moved everybody on, when France was saying that France had a person who had shut himself in first, before Mr. Garth did, so Mr. Garth wasn't the original. Also the Psychic who wears the hat and gives people the Milo Messages is back. The people who light the candles and tie ribbons and teddy bears and other things to the fences at the bottom of the gardens under Mr. Garth's windows are back. The people with the banners that say Milo for Palestine and Milo for Israel's Endangered Children and Milo for Peace and Not in Milo's Name and Milo for Troops Out of Afghanistan are back, and probably the man dressed as Batman will be back too [. . .] The lady will probably definitely be back who goes round asking everybody how much of Jesus do you need to see to believe in him. (211–212)

The Milo crowd is a site of spectacle, appropriation, commodification, an implicit debate about copyright, and political and religious proselytising. It poses a threat to individuality, the possibility of getting 'carried along [. . .] in a direction you don't really want to go in'. We see that 'Milo' is spreading worldwide via new and old media, having gained fame in Europe and the US, his originality contested in France, and his allegiance claimed by opposing sides in the conflict between Israel and advocates for Palestinian sovereignty.

The crowd is also a site of people hanging out and having fun, playing guitars, sharing meals: utopian promise mixes with ideological and economic co-optation, as well as conformity and superficiality. In short, the 'wise man not found anywhere on the world wide web' becomes the centre – or the centralising absence – of a physical web that reproduces both positive and negative aspects of the world wide web (46). When Brooke takes in the scene above, she thinks that those 'outside the house and watching YouTube and reading the papers or looking on the net' – a description that links the crowd and those following Milo through various media – are all equally unaware 'what the fact about Mr. Garth really is' (209). At this point, in the final section of the novel and roughly ten months after his initial sequestration, Miles Garth has left the room.

Indeed, most constituents of the 'Milo Masses', as Brooke's family calls them, have never known any direct 'facts' about Miles, as is underscored by their insistence on calling him Milo, since his real name is too mundane, 'wet' and 'a bit middle class', as one fan explains (127). Very few among the crowd have seen Miles apart from his hand, which emerges from the window each day to accept food delivered via a pulley system. Especially striking is the apparent indifference of the crowd about the intended meaning of his self-sequestration. No one suggests, for instance, that either the Palestinian rights group or the pro-Israeli group ought to produce evidence that his retreat has anything to do with their cause. Such a demand would reflect a misapprehension of the Milo phenomenon. It is this feature, above others, that affords the reading I develop in the next section, according to which Milo resembles a meme, and the crowd exemplifies the semi-public communities that coalesce through shared uses of digital memes. To borrow one theorist's description of digital memes, Milo has 'acquire[d] a viral character, becoming globally popular', endlessly remixed and not signifying or needing to signify any definitive 'truth'.[13]

## The Meaning of a Meme is its Use in the Language

A conversation between Brooke and her parents offers the frame I adopt for reading the crowd's uses of Milo. Brooke's father remarks that, in his view, people have joined the crowd 'because they feel so disenfranchised', adding, when Brooke seems perplexed about the connection between voting and the Milo crowd, that he means this 'metaphorically' (209). Brooke asks her mother, Bernice, to remind her what the word metaphorically means. Bernice responds first with an example ('an Alps of feeling'), then with a description of a situation in which we make use of metaphors: 'To describe something indescribable you sometimes translate it directly into something else' (210). 'Sometimes', she elaborates, metaphors are 'the only way to describe what's real, I mean because sometimes what's real is very difficult to put into words'. Brooke summarises the lesson: 'Metaphorically: another way of describing what's real' (210).

The phrasing here recalls Bernice's earlier complaint that 'we're forgetting how to know what's real' due to the influence of digital culture. If use of the Internet interferes with our understanding of how to know what's real, literary devices like metaphors do the opposite, she implies, helping us access 'what's real' when the obstacle is not forgetfulness but something closer to linguistic scepticism. When words seem likely to fail, we can draw on metaphors, and by extension make use of figurative, poetic language, rather than abandoning our efforts at expressiveness. Bernice speaks like an ordinary language philosopher: not only does she suggest accepting scepticism as the backdrop against which we improvise our communicative efforts, but she also refers, in both cases, to criteria. We are forgetting *how to know* what's real, which is a different problem than forgetting *what's real*, and rather than defining 'metaphor' she provides an example and describes the criteria for what Wittgenstein might call the language-game of using metaphors. Taking as an invitation these remarks about metaphors and differing orientations towards 'what's real', I propose reading the crowd as 'another way of describing' digitally networked community, and its uses of Milo as evocative of the criteria for using memes online. While *There But For The* does not mention memes in its assessments of digital life, the resonances between memetic exchange and the crowd's uses of Milo – and the contrast between such uses and the ideal of conversation elaborated in this book – help link memetic communication to the 'forgetting', or forgoing, of the criteria by which conversation generates what Hannah Arendt calls the reality of the public realm.

For many social media theorists, memes exemplify the participatory ethos of Web 2.0 in which, in Ryan Milner's words, 'everyday members of the public contribute their small conversational strands to the vast cultural tapestry, [. . .] memetically making their world'.[14] According to Richard Dawkins's original, pre-digital formulation, a meme is a 'unit of cultural transmission' analogous to a gene, which replicates itself in a society by provoking imitation and mixing with other memes.[15] Religion, fashion, jokes, snippets of song are all examples of memes when they 'lea[p] from brain to brain via a process which, in the broad sense, can be called imitation'.[16] A digital meme not only 'leaps from brain to brain' online but has a collective, online origination and is constitutively incomplete.[17] In an influential early definition, Limor Shifman describes Internet memes as '(a) a group of digital items sharing common characteristics [. . .] which (b) were created with awareness of each other, and (c) were circulated, imitated, and/or transformed via the Internet by many users'.[18] Whitney Phillips stresses the reflexive 'awareness' Shifman names in her study of trolling subcultures, where, she writes, memes 'compose a holistic system of meaning'.[19] They 'only make sense in relation to other memes', she continues, 'allow[ing] participants to speak clearly and coherently to other members of the collective while baffling those outside the affinity network'.[20] She further argues that the circulation of memes fortifies 'burgeoning subcultural borders', in effect generating and reinforcing the networks in which they make sense.[21] Milner, who describes meme exchange as a 'vernacular mode of public conversation', outlines 'five fundamental logics' of meme exchange: 'multimodality (their expression in multiple modes of communication)', 'reappropriation (their "poaching" of existing texts)', 'resonance (their connections to individual participants)', 'collectivism (their social creation and transformation)', and 'spread (their circulation through mass networks)'.[22]

Like a meme, Milo is a collective, 'social creation'.[23] His meanings are contingent on how fans 'poach' and remix him, attaching him to new causes. Milo signifies both support for Israel and support for Palestine, just as one of the most notorious real-world memes, Pepe the frog, has been used to signify both authoritarianism and its opposite, appropriated and reappropriated by (among others) the American alt-right, the presidential campaign of Donald Trump, the Twitter account of Russia's embassy in the UK, and pro-democracy protestors in Hong Kong.[24] The novel observes these uses of Milo without commenting on differences between Milo and Miles Garth, tracking uses of the memetic Milo without spotlighting gaps between sign and signifier. In this way, the novel's orientation towards Milo echoes the orientation towards language expressed by ordinary language philosophers, sidestepping issues of signification raised by structuralists and poststructuralists. Reading Milo as a metaphoric meme thus resonates with a strand of new media criticism that invokes Wittgenstein, whose famous description of the '*large* class of cases [. . .] in which we employ the word "meaning"' seems primed for a substitution of the word 'meme' for 'word': 'the meaning of a [meme] is its use in the language', the form of life shared and transformed by those who use memes (*PI*, §43).[25] As Wittgenstein wryly remarks of words, it is not as if 'meaning were an aura' that Milo or Pepe 'brings along with it and retains in every kind of use' (*PI*, §117).[26] What Milner calls 'fundamental logics' we might instead call, using the language of ordinary language philosophy, the 'mutual attunements or agreement in our criteria', expressed and elaborated in memetic language-games (*CR*, 168).

As introduced in the *Philosophical Investigations*, language-games like 'reporting an event' and 'making up a story' reflect features of the forms of life in which these 'games' take place at both local and broader scales (§23). Invoking ordinary language philosophy in the context of digital language use thus helps frame connections between memetic language-games and attunements expressed and elaborated on both subcultural and wider registers across many digital platforms. From the standpoint of ordinary language philosophy, studying the language-games of digital conversation can help 'bring to light the consequences of our [new, digitally enacted] agreements', 'our minds about our relations to ourselves and to others and to communities and to earth', as Cavell writes (*CR*, 32). Close readers of *The Claim of Reason* will notice that my bracketed reference to new and digitally enacted agreements replaces Cavell's original word, 'old': new agreements are replacing or retuning older ones at a rapid pace as we converse online.

In the crowd in *There But For The*, the primary agreement is to something we might call memetic performativity: to say 'Milo for Palestine' makes Milo *be* for Palestine. Yet a person who asserts 'Milo for Palestine' simultaneously implies political judgements about disputed territory, sovereignty, violence and democracy. This facet of the crowd's uses of Milo anticipates an aspect of memetic language-games that increasingly concerns theorists of digital culture. There is a difference between the literal meaning of a meme – visible to all who converse online – and the further judgements its use simultaneously requires, expresses and reinforces among those who meaningfully use it. These further judgements frequently remain opaque, or when they are visible, the sincerity or irony with which they are held is uncertain. From a person's utterance of 'Milo for Palestine' or 'Milo for Israel's Endangered Children', we cannot identify with certainty their views about specific policy questions, or about Muslim or Jewish people, although some will surely make assumptions. Likewise, a Pepe remix often does not prove a user's racism. Nonetheless, memes perform, establishing meaning with practical, worldly consequences and thus recalling the problem of intention in illocutionary utterances we first considered in Chapter 2. Theorists of online discourse have posited that this ambiguity is in fact key to the performative force of memes, rather than tangential and irrelevant, and that it fuels polarisation and the growth of extremist subcultures. Some scholars of right-wing digital communities, for instance, argue that the ambiguity of memes affords plausible deniability while simultaneously acculturating users to implied messages of racism, misogyny, transphobia, antisemitism, or other prejudice.[27] Initially ironic uses of edgy 'humour' or retweets of hastily skimmed articles transition into sincere, mutual agreements. Among left-aligned social media users, this ambiguity arguably contributes to the prevalence of outrage and moralism; if right-wing trolls routinely disavow the intentions of their utterances, left-wing observers have grown increasingly suspicious of utterances that seem to imply rather than assert views they consider hateful. So-called 'cancel culture' is a logical reaction to memetic ambiguity and irony, which is not to say that censoriousness is productive nor that it has only one point of origin.

Ordinary language philosophy reminds us that, to some extent, such ambiguous layering of judgements is simply how language works. There is always a degree of tacit, shared judgement in language: this is one implication of the phrase 'form of life', and it informs Wittgenstein's remark that, 'queer as this may sound', when we share a language, we agree 'not only in definitions but also [. . .] in judgments' (*PI*, §242). Prior to any arguments about politics, morality, culture, and so on, we must (if we are to argue verbally) already share the 'agreement in our criteria' that allows us to be mutually comprehensible. As Cavell reads Wittgenstein and reproduces in his own turns of phrase, the use of the word 'in' (rather than 'about') is 'altogether important': 'The idea of agreement here is not that of coming to or arriving at an agreement on a given occasion, but of being in agreement throughout, being in harmony, like pitches or tones, or clocks, or weighing scales, or columns of figures' (*CR*, 31–32). The 'in' reflects the depth and queerness of our agreements. Yet, especially as interpreted by Cavell (and others who challenge the view that ordinary language philosophy is inherently conservative), it is crucial to Wittgenstein's late work that criteria and forms of life are mutable and open, as speakers of a language encounter 'newcomers' or new situations, needing to 'project' words into new contexts or reassess old contexts, old agreements.[28] This is the 'lesson', Cavell remarks, of the 'recurrent silence' when the philosopher's 'explanations come to an end', the silence reached at the end of nearly every section of the *Investigations*, which Cavell reads as 'suggesting [...] a certain opening of the idea, or direction, of consent' (*PDAT*, 114; *CHU*, 76). When the philosopher falls silent, and consent to the explained criteria seems untenable to the pupil or newcomer, the latter might carry on in a new direction. Depending on how we in the philosopher's position respond, we might learn 'new meanings for words, new ways in which objects can be disclosed', as Linda Zerilli puts it, thereby 'enlarging our sense of worldly reality' (*DTJ*, 267).

It is this enlargement that is at stake in memetic language-games as described by scholars of new media and, metaphorically, the Milo crowd. Indeed, the combination of performativity and tacit, subcultural judgements makes memetic language-games remarkably well suited to the realm of life that Hannah Arendt termed the 'social', as if in naming our media we have extended her thought. For Arendt, the social realm is a space of prejudice and conformity, a threat to the twofold conversation that we have seen is central to her account of democratic public life. Her work thus clarifies how memetic and other social criteria might undermine as much as broaden political conversation. She describes the space of social life as a 'curious, somewhat hybrid realm between the political and the private', where we might expect to encounter people who express different points of view but instead find ourselves amongst people 'multiplying and prolonging the perspective of [their] neighbor[s]'.[29] Arendt did not propose combatting the existence of social life as such (and her infamous argument against mandatory school integration turned on the idea that the state must not interfere with the tribalistic dynamics of social life, which she maintained – with self-contradicting rigidity and prejudice – encompassed education). Rather, she worried that a single, dominant social order would render others silent or obsolete, as she warns occurs through totalitarianism and mass culture. We reach 'the end of the common world', Arendt writes, 'when it is seen only under one aspect and is permitted to present itself in only one perspective' (*HC*, 58).[30] In such conditions, she continues, we 'are all imprisoned in the subjectivity of [our] own singular experience, which does not cease to be singular if the same experience is multiplied innumerable times' (58).

At first glance, social media have inaugurated a situation that seems empowering to counterpublics, one which Arendt might recommend. Again, Arendt worried not about a proliferation of many social groups, but about the dominance of one singular perspective, whether enforced by the state or mass culture. For the sort of worldmaking, twofold conversation that I have argued Arendt envisions, it is less important that the perspectives expressed in public belong to individual people rather than groups, if they represent different standpoints on the same objects and issues. But if, as Arendt argues, 'incessant talk' teaches us that 'the world we have in common' is available to 'an infinite number of different standpoints, to which correspond the most diverse points of view', we cannot learn this many-sidedness of the world we have in common when our criteria foreclose conversing with those who occupy different standpoints ('Concept', 51). Whereas the common world, for Arendt, emerges and is sustained in conversation, 'rising out' of the meeting of diverse perspectives expressed publicly, the 'social' generates a mere semblance of 'reality' by proliferating the same perspective throughout a population.

On this distinction, *The Satanic Verses* offers an instructive comparison to the Milo crowd. In *The Satanic Verses*, the undercity and 'white society' (in Mishal's Arendtian phrase) operate as social groups in Arendt's sense, multiplying and prolonging perspectives on Simba and the conditions of Brickhall. Simba – and Chamcha in his devilish guise – is meme-like, used to mean entirely different things by different groups, but as we saw in the previous chapter the novel offers a glimpse of a many-sided 'reality of the public realm' when 'differing estimations' of Simba (and of racism in the UK) clash in the city streets. This newly enlarged 'common world' is quickly suppressed by a convergence of police and media power to enforce only one 'aspect', and the novel offers little reason to hope that such worldmaking encounters would 'survive' in Thatcher's Britain, against the force of state-sanctioned prejudice. But at least the undercity and 'white society' agree in a criterion that enables their differing estimations to meet: to use 'Simba' is to assert something about the common world of Britain. So, while *The Satanic Verses* reflects Arendt's concerns about threats to the common world posed by totalitarian or cultural conformity, *There But For The* reflects digital updates to these threats: 'Milo for Palestine' and 'Milo for Israel's Endangered Children' are not 'differing estimations' of Milo, although they sound as though they are, and they simultaneously imply estimations of conflict in the Middle East. Instead, they are tautological statements defining 'what's real' to those who use him thus. Encounters between the pro-Israeli and pro-Palestinian groups cannot happen within the language-games of the crowd. Viewed thus, the criteria for using Milo interfere not only with knowing what's real but also with our capacity to *make* it, in Arendt's sense of shared, common reality.

If digital conversation prompts an update to Arendt's understanding of the 'social', it also urges an update to ordinary language philosophy's understanding of convention: it is obviously untrue that 'nothing more and nothing less than shared forms of life' provide the 'shaky foundations' of mutual understanding online (*CR*, 168, 178). Not only do we communicate according to criteria programmed by digital media corporations, which treat online conversation as raw material to be mined for data, but digital platforms are populated by nonhuman 'speakers', bots 'designed to catch human attention from every crevice in the online infrastructure' by provoking 'conversation', amplifying marketing or other content, or harassing other accounts.[31] (The implications of Open AI's ChatGPT and related technologies are the subject for another book.) In short, our digital language-games are constantly retuned by engineers, algorithms and the activities of AI, which redirect our 'routes of interest and feeling' in accordance with what Shoshana Zuboff calls the 'extraction imperative' tethering the competitive survival of digital corporations to their extraction and monetisation of ever-greater quantities of data from our 'conversations'.[32] Under the economic regime variously called 'platform capitalism', 'communicative capitalism', or the 'attention' and 'surveillance economy', the objects towards which our attention is routed are irrelevant, as long as our interests keep us clicking, liking, sharing.[33] As Jodi Dean puts it, the monetisation of data has accelerated a 'shift from the use to the circulation value of communicative utterances', and 'circulation has eclipsed meaning'.[34]

This argument is by now familiar, but I want to highlight several key points of difference between our online and our ordinary 'life form of talkers'. Critical new media theorists argue that data collection is a new form of what Marxists call primitive accumulation or expropriation – in this case of data for which users are not compensated – crucial to capital's contemporary surplus.[35] The platforms and algorithms sustaining digital communication encourage us to play whatever language-games render this material easier to mine. (Let us not forget that the literal mining of minerals, metals and fossil fuels, and exploitative employment practices in factories and on the campuses and outposts of tech corporations, are also integral to this 'virtual' economy.) The 'extraction imperative' contributes to what the philosopher C. Thi Nguyen terms the 'gamification' of online conversation through the addition of features such as the 'retweet' function on Twitter, the 'like' buttons and other emojis on all platforms, algorithms that elevate 'viral' media in homepage feeds, and other designs foregrounding metrics of success that compel use.[36] Such features appear to also incentivise competitive and sectarian behaviours, 'in-group' theatrics and expressions of outrage and contempt towards outsiders, the very qualities Arendt expects of 'social' life.[37] Taking these dynamics into account, it is unsurprising that memetic language-games would strike many theorists as exemplary of communicative activities on the participatory web. Generated through participation and frequently tapping into deep, underlying judgements, they are effective game-pieces in an attention economy. Their circulation not only eclipses but to a large extent constitutes their meaning, as they at once express and subtly reconfigure the tacit 'agreements' within filter bubbles that are reinforced by algorithmic design.[38]

Read as a metaphor representing language-games that accompany our 'forgetting [of] how to know what's real', the Milo phenomenon obliquely reflects the consequences of the algorithmic retuning of virtual 'conversation' described by such theorists of platform economics. It also underscores an implication of the ideal of conversation elaborated in this book. The digital world threatens the 'world we have in common' not only through facilitating the proliferation of disinformation, misinformation and echo chambers: its very foundations incentivise modes of exchange that primarily work, that *mean*, according to criteria Arendt teaches us to call social rather than public. Milo is for Israel, and Milo is for Palestine. Milo is for peace, and Milo is a brand. These are not 'differing estimations' of Milo, and to dispute that they are all accurate – that these mantras all describe and make 'what's real' for their users – is to refer to the criteria of language-games of diminishing power in our allegedly-public discourse.

If Smith's novel complements such increasingly familiar critiques, its own, singular proposal about digital threats to the 'world we have in common' is hinted by Bernice – in the implied juxtaposition of metaphors to digital media – and developed in the novel's semi-resolution of the situation behind the crowd phenomenon, Miles's seclusion. The last section of *There But For The*, which represents the end of Miles's stay in the room from Brooke's perspective, suggestively juxtaposes memetic criteria to the criteria involved in literary experience, indicating that the latter are crucial to Miles's return to the wider world.

### 'The fact is, imagine': Reading and Representative Thinking

The novel's final section does not resolve the mysteries of Miles's behaviour. It clarifies neither his motives for locking himself in nor his reasons for leaving, for rejoining the common world, as Arendt might say. *There But For The* does offer a series of suggestive hints, however, in a sequence that links reading, writing and talking to representative thinking. For Arendt, as we have seen, representative thinking prepares us for the 'reflective judgment' that undergirds the 'world we have in common', the shaky foundations of democratic public life. The closing sequence of *There But For The* describes a scenario strikingly evocative of her accounts of the worldmaking powers of both talk and judgement, linking them not to aesthetic judgement as such, but rather to the creation and interpretation of stories. Miles leaves the spare bedroom following a conversation and exchange of stories with Brooke, which together prompt him to 'send [his] imagination visiting'. Read alongside Arendt, the exchanges between Miles and Brooke reframe the novel's concerns about the consequences of digital life, affirming a modest but potent role for both literature and conversation – understood in ordinary and figurative terms – in recovering and sustaining a common world.[39]

As we saw in Chapter 4, Arendt's turn to Kant is premised partly on the observation of similarities between aesthetic and political judgement. We universalise in each case: to say something is just or unjust is to mean that everyone ought to agree, that the justice or injustice asserted is not merely a matter of personal and idiosyncratic taste, just as there is a difference between saying 'this flower is beautiful' and 'I like this flower'. In Kant's words, we 'believe we speak with a universal voice' when passing judgements. Yet in both political and aesthetic matters, Arendt claims, we lack solid logical or conceptual justifications for our judgements: we do not reason our way to perceiving beauty or justice, and it is rare or impossible for someone to persuade another by force of facts or logic alone that they are wrong about flowers or policies. She adapts for political purposes Kant's response to this quandary as manifested in aesthetic experience, his prescription of 'representative' thinking to induce the 'enlarged mentality' – enlarged beyond personal interest – that allows reflective judgement, or judgement following reflection on what the *sensus communis* would say. In politics, Arendt writes, this means 'I [should] form an opinion by considering a given issue from different viewpoints, by making present to my mind the standpoints of those who are absent; that is, I represent them [. . .] imagin[ing] how I would feel and think if I were in their place' (TP, 241). This effort of 'sending the imagination visiting' induces disinterestedness: not the disinterestedness of abstract 'rationality', but instead the disinterestedness that allows us to test the 'communicability' of our judgements, the likelihood we speak with a voice that communicates beyond our private and social prejudices. Arendt stresses that representative thinking in politics, as in aesthetics, is not empathetic imagination or the attempt to feel as others feel; we should think in our own identities, but without clinging to contingent attachments. Like the 'incessant talk' of her exemplary Greeks, this practice affirms that 'the world we have in common is usually regarded from an infinite number of different standpoints' ('Concept', 51). And as I argued at greater length in Chapter 4, representative thinking both supplements and figuratively mirrors the conversational process through which, in Arendt's work, the common 'reality of the public realm [. . .] ris[es] out of the sum total of aspects' brought to light again and again, as we talk and turn together (HC, 57).

The consequential exchanges between Miles and Brooke begin with Brooke's discovery that the door to Miles's room has been unlocked for months. She enters and finds him sitting on a stationary bicycle. They begin talking about jokes and facts, then she asks if he wants to leave the room, observing that it is a small space in which to spend so much time. 'Could I?' he asks, and she responds, 'I don't see why not', as if he needs simple reassurance about the accessibility of ordinary life and action (226). Nonetheless, he stays behind when she goes to the kitchen to make him a cup of tea. She returns, they resume talking, and their conversation culminates with her asking, 'what is the point of a book, I mean the kinds that tell stories? If a story isn't a fact, but it is a made-up version of what happened [. . .] I mean, what is the *point* of it?' The scene continues:

> Mr. Garth leaned his head on the handlebars. Think how quiet a book is on a shelf, he said, just sitting there, unopened. Then think what happens when you open it. Yes, but what *exactly* happens? Brooke said. I have an idea, he said, I'll tell you the very beginning of a story that's not been written yet, and then you write the story for me, and we can see what happens in the process. (229)

Brooke agrees to Miles's proposal, provided he will write a story for her in return. As Wittgenstein might say, this agreement allows them to 'look and see' what happens in two different language-games, writing and reading fiction.

Miles's prompt for Brooke is to render a made-up version of his past ten months: 'There was once a man who lived in a small room and, without leaving that room, managed to cycle his bike three thousand miles' (229–230). In the story she writes, a man sits on an exercise bicycle in a bedroom. The story splits into two threads: in one, the man learns 'from frogs, who know how to develop into frogs from tadpoles, how to transform his bicycle into a Montgolfier balloon [. . .] and then he cycles into the cloudy sky over the rooftops of London', finally disappearing 'round the river bend' (235). In the other thread, the stationary bicycle transforms into an ordinary bicycle, and the man simply carries it down the stairs, out the house's front door, and onto the street on which he cycles away. In the process of writing her story – which sticks to Miles's prompt if we see the two threads as one story, representing the man's imaginative travel as he stays in place – Brooke discovers that fiction can 'be true and factual as well as a made-up thing' (233). Her mother describes her writing effort thus: 'she wants a work of the imagination that's simultaneously rigorously true' (233). These discoveries extend Brooke's education in the uses of metaphors, those imaginative translations that help us comprehend 'what's real'.

Brooke's prompt to Miles is subtly Kantian, or Arendtian: she urges him to undertake representative thinking. 'Imagine', she says, 'you were sitting there where you are, on the bike, and also here in the room with you was another version of you, like, say you but three or four days before you were ten years old, I mean if it was nearly your tenth birthday [. . .] So if that really happened in reality, what story would you tell your self and what story would your self tell you?' (230). She prompts him to imagine her standpoint, the position of a child exactly her age. He is not to empathetically project and try to see himself as Brooke herself does. Instead, he should send his imagination visiting in structural terms, to see himself from the standpoint of Brooke's literal place in the world, that of a child unencumbered by decades of experience.

There are at least four metaphors at play in the story Miles writes in response to Brooke's prompt, which opens Smith's novel as an unexplained preface. In the story, a child visits a man sitting on an exercise bike, who has bars covering his eyes and mouth, like censorship strips. The child helps pry these off the man. Once the man can see and speak again, the boy begins teaching him how to fold a paper airplane. The story includes the child's instructions in detail, and it ends after the man finishes folding the plane and sends it flying: 'it follows its flightpath exactly'. The man laughs, the boy shrugs, and the story closes with the latter's words: 'Simple, the boy says. See?' (xiii). When he leaves the room, Miles leaves the story behind for Brooke to find on a piece of paper folded like an airplane.

The most straightforward metaphor in the story is its translation of interactions between Miles and Brooke, which occurs on several registers. First, the story suggests that Brooke has helped Miles see and speak again. Incidentally, for Arendt these are the very faculties at work in the generation of the public realm, and in the novel they evidently (but opaquely) play a similar role, helping Miles make his return to the world outside the bedroom. Second, the child instructs the man to put a piece of paper to a new purpose, which reflects Brooke's literal instructions to Miles when they establish the parameters of their story exchange. Third, the interaction between the child and man can be read as a metaphor for Miles's interpretation of Brooke's story, indicating that 'what happens' to him in the process of reading her story is something analogous to instruction. Indeed, he follows the example of the man in the realistic thread of Brooke's story, the 'simple' path of walking down a flight of stairs and out a door.

Read this way, the sequence suggests that reading might prompt representative thinking in two stages. Not only does it invite us to test our judgements and interpretations against an imagined *sensus communis* via imaginatively representing alternative outlooks on the text, per Kantian theory. In addition, once we have developed an interpretation, we might treat this interpretation as another standpoint to visit, broadening our understanding of reality by encompassing this new, true as well as made-up standpoint. Insofar as it re-presents 'what happens' to him in the process of reading and reflecting on Brooke's story, Miles's story indicates that he discerns its outlook, its 'simple' point of view towards his own reality. By Arendt's account, when he sends his imagination visiting to the story's outlook as well as to the outlook Brooke urges him to take when writing his story, Miles sees his own situation in a rounder, fuller way. If the interactions between Brooke and Miles inspire him to leave the room, they do so not via deliberative persuasion, but via imaginative judgement. Speaking with Wittgenstein, we might say that Brooke prompts Miles to 'pivot' and find his 'way about', back into the world. This is the simple, yet challenging effort entailed in a transformation in outlook. Invoking Wittgenstein, I also mean to invoke Cavell's reading of Wittgenstein's *Investigations* as replete with 'scenes of instruction' that presuppose the perfectionist model of education described earlier in this book. Brooke suggestively resembles the child, the pupil or newcomer Cavell describes as consistently prompting the philosopher into a new outlook on our 'life form as talkers'.[40] In Cavell's telling, such transformations in outlook might awaken us to the necessity for change.

The story's fourth metaphoric register alludes to itself, to its instruction of its own readers. The dialogue spoken by the child tells both the man and the story's readers how to fold paper into an airplane, how to formally compose the material object Brooke finds (this was confirmed for me by a student, who delightfully arrived for our class's final discussion of the novel with a paper airplane in hand). The self-referentiality of the story also reflects the self-referentiality of the novel itself, especially in scenes in which Brooke and readers receive instruction about the uses of metaphors and 'work[s] of the imagination that [are] simultaneously rigorously true'. Moreover, when the novel closes, Brooke has just sat down to reread the story Miles left her, which, as I have mentioned, appears as the novel's preface. We now understand that the preface alludes to the ending, which in turn sends us back to the beginning. This circular structure asserts a degree of aesthetic autonomy, deriving its formal principles from within, rather than in reference to the reader or worldly reality: a 'merely formal purposiveness', as Kant puts it.

This fourth metaphor is productively paradoxical. How can the novel and Miles's story assert autonomy, alluding to formal purposes derived from within, while they also appeal pedagogically to the reader in scenes of instruction in which a character serves as a double for the reader? Read as I suggest, the novel conjoins ideas about art traditionally thought of as mutually exclusive. Is the meaning of a work of the imagination independent of its readers or viewers, or does it unfold in their uses? The novel suggests a perspective by which we might have it both ways. To the extent that it asserts its own autonomous self-legislation, the novel reminds us that any uses we derive do not wholly define its meaning. Certain formal criteria arise from within, rather than unfolding in our uses. Criteria that are autonomous from us are also, in principle, universally available: regardless of where we stand, anyone aptly attuned can notice the structure of the novel, or the metaphors at work in Miles's story. We need not use the airplane instructions to claim we have understood Miles's story, and it does not 'mean' its capacity to fly. In fact, we risk resembling the crowd if we equate the story's meaning with whatever use we make of it. Yet, if only one of my students has used Miles's story as a guide for folding paper, this speaks to the fact that the class was not mutually attuned or agreed in her criteria, whatever mix of playfulness, curiosity or procrastination prompted her to use the story thus. Other readers might agree in the relevant criteria and foreground the usefulness of the child's instructions when judging and interpreting the story. In fact, I am writing as one such reader now, striving to make the literal, tactile usefulness of the fictional instructions part of the story's public (rather than personal) meaning (I happily note that I learned this from a pupil, a newcomer to the story whose outlook and attunements differed from mine). As ever, criteria are contingent, and one thing *There But For The* proposes is that we might adopt multiple sets of criteria simultaneously, 'merely formal purposiveness' and instruction in how and why to create.

Indeed, *There But For The* explicitly recommends worldly purposes for literary devices like metaphors: above strictly formal purposiveness, such devices offer instruction in 'what's real' when 'what's real is very difficult to put into words'. The words that open Miles's story, and hence the novel, encapsulate the view that this is the 'point' not only of metaphors, but of fiction and literature more generally: 'the fact is, imagine' (xi). The first three words reflect Brooke's influence; for months, she has been slipping Miles notes that begin 'the fact is' and recount alleged facts she has newly learned. Miles, continuing with 'imagine', turns Brooke's preoccupation with facts on its head. The ensuing narrative of taking on a different position in one's own (but disinterested) identity suggests a double meaning for the line. It captures the sentiment Brooke's mother voices, in which works of the imagination may be simultaneously rigorously true, and it also captures the Kantian vision of aesthetic judgement, in which a fictional, imaginative act of representing the possible standpoints from which we might perceive an object provides the basis on which to believe we speak with a 'universal voice' when uttering judgement. We can tweak the opening words' formula slightly to align them with the terms Arendt uses in her rewriting of Kant: 'The reality is, imagine.' Imagine the facts, objectively given, from different vantage points, and you will have a more complete sense of the reality of the public and shared realm, the reality that rises out of twofold conversations as we perceive and exchange views of the facts of the world. By demanding this practice from us, self-legislating artworks – works we cannot simply use, even if we can use our interpretations of them – demand that we practise the mode of thinking and judging that Arendt deems worldmaking. They demand we exercise our best, at once ordinary and unguaranteed, chance for sharing a common world. As usually happens in aesthetic philosophy, uses are found for resistance to instrumental use.

Arendt's work helps differentiate the exchanges of talk and stories by Miles and Brooke from the crowd's uses of Milo. In aesthetics and in politics, she writes, judgement is 'one, if not the most, important activity in which [our] sharing-the-world-with-others comes to pass' ('Crisis', 221). This is because searching for universally communicable criteria behind our judgements requires that we continuously recall that the objects of our world are many-sided, and that we only share this world insofar as we can communicate about it with people who see the same world from other perspectives. I have suggested that representative thinking supports not only reflective judgement, but also what we might call reflective interpretation, assertions of meaning that aspire to universal validity, while retaining a sense that the validity sought in both aesthetic and political life is that which attends 'public' meaning: never timeless, never guaranteed, and, if not shared, apt to fall back (like judgement) on the appeal to others to keep looking. *Don't you dig?*, as Cavell writes. It is an activity in which we refer to details that others can perceive from their own standpoints, while hoping we have done sufficient, laborious imaginative travels to justify the appeal.

The difference between the criteria for reflective interpretation and memetic interpretation should be clear: the latter presupposes, while generating and sustaining, 'social' rather than 'public' objects. Consider the similarities and differences between the meaning of 'Milo' for the crowd and his meaning for readers of Smith's novel. As I have mentioned, *There But For The* never juxtaposes Milo to the 'real' Miles: we do not learn, for instance, that Miles Garth has any specific opinions about Palestinian rights, nor do we learn of any definitive meaning behind his self-sequestration. This underscores the performativity of the crowd's uses of Milo, and it establishes a parallel between the novel and the crowd, as both are held together by the absent but organising figure of Miles, whose 'essential' meaning we cannot access. But according to the criteria expressed in the language-games of literary interpretation, the meanings of Milo are not determined by performative utterance alone. Readers who wish to understand the meaning of Milo within the language of literary criticism will not claim he 'symbolises' whatever they wish; they will attend to the novel's specific ways of representing (or not) actions and character, the position of Milo and the room in relation to other events, characters and settings. I have proposed reading Milo in relation to allusions to 'what's real', which juxtapose the Internet to literary devices. A more common reading of the novel juxtaposes the Milo phenomenon to the novel's concerns about refugees and Western inhospitality to displaced persons.[41] Both readings invoke forms and details internal to the novel to invite others to see the meanings they propose. Both put their readings to further 'use', but use follows, rather than performs, the articulation of meaning.

By contrast, how does one understand the meaning of Milo in the crowd, or of Pepe or other memes online? Not by looking to formal qualities of the man or frog. Even if such qualities are occasionally pertinent, they are less crucial than circulatory use. It would be nonsense to link the meaning of Milo within the crowd to the shape of the man's arm as it extends from the window to receive lunch, or even to facts from Miles Garth's life. It would equally be nonsense to explain Pepe's use by protestors in Hong Kong by attending to the shade of green of his skin or facts about amphibian life. This is another way of saying that, in our forms of life, aesthetic judgement and interpretation invoke criteria amenable to representative thinking, whereas 'social' media do not. Brooke's initial prompt to Miles would not make sense according to the criteria of the social realm as described by Arendt, in which every perspective to which one has access is a multiplication of one's own. Nor could her story offer him a new perspective unless he willingly travelled out of his own. Milo need not be perceived or interpreted at all, let alone from different perspectives, to be 'for Israel's endangered children'.

If, as I am suggesting, Miles puts his interpretation of Brooke's story to use by sending his imagination visiting its perspective, and thereby judging his own predicament, he uses Brooke's story as I have used *There But For The* and indeed all the novels I have drawn into this book's conversations about talk, judgement, mutual responsiveness and the common world. Miles discerns an outlook through reading, which illuminates an 'aspect' of the many-sided substance that is his situation, just as I discern outlooks that help me illuminate aspects of the ideal of conversation shared by exemplary literary and philosophical texts. This analogy illuminates how representative thinking can be a route towards interpreting the meaning of a work of literature (or art more generally), independent of our uses, and simultaneously a way of *using* the interpretation without subordinating the meaning of the work to its usefulness. We can direct the work's meaning outwards, seeing how it reflects details of the world we have in common with that work, a world that is not in existence prior to such conversations involving the work. The sum total of aspects disclosed in Miles's imaginative travel is small, but he puts the effort to use. This book's sum of aspects is slightly larger, but standpoints proliferate, and the usefulness of the ideal its texts have in common is a question for individual readers.

Conversational criticism as modelled in this book thus shares the 'shaky foundations' of all language-games, some of the tremors of which are hinted in *There But For The*. At the end of the novel, Miles is a private man in a public world, having left the situation that led to his uses in a realm that resembles Arendt's social. But the crowd continues to use Milo. Genevieve Lee, who has learned to capitalise on her role as unwitting host, begins imitating Miles's hand at the window to delay or prevent the crowd's discovery that he has left. In any case, it may not matter to the crowd 'where in or out of the world' Miles is, since their uses of Milo are practically untethered from the man. At most, then, the novel suggests that the exercise of representative thinking – or of conversational reading – might be useful to the individual reader. If we follow Arendt, such individual uses have political value. As she writes when describing why 'judgment may be one of the fundamental abilities of man as a political being', it helps Miles 'orient himself in the public realm, in the common world', a world that would not exist were it not for individuals thus oriented ('Crisis', 221). The crowd carries on, however. If the novel helps us differentiate the stakes of literary-interpretative criteria from those of memetic criteria, it does not indicate that the former can counteract or transform the latter, which sustain a form of life that prevents the plural encounters through which criteria might transform. Nonetheless, I suspect Smith would urge us to continue making, sharing, interpreting and using stories, both factual and made-up, to see what happens in the process.

# Afterword

While writing and revising this book, I have frequently thought of the question Stanley Cavell poses at the end of *The Claim of Reason*, arguably the central question of his career: '[C]an philosophy', he asks, 'become literature and still know itself?' (496). A version, or inversion, of this question animates not only the present book but also much contemporary debate in literary studies: Can literary studies become philosophy – or critical theory, sociology, history, ethics, or even political action or activism – and still know itself *as* literary studies? In the 'methods wars' or 'debates' roiling the field in recent decades, dire facts about our discipline's material conditions (and those of higher education, generally) are frequently paired with charges that we inflict self-harm in our efforts to 'become' some adjacent discipline, via muddled interdisciplinarity, quests for relevance, or inflated claims of political acuity. These charges reflect an abiding tension in literary studies, which certainly appears in this book: the tension between instrumentalising our study and a view of aesthetic works as resistant to instrumentalisation, as uniquely characterised by their 'merely formal purposiveness', in Kant's formulation. This tension has been present throughout the history of the discipline in the modern university, from its Arnoldian origins as the humanising study of 'the best which has been thought or said', through today's debates about surface and depth, critique, historicism, admiration and pleasure.[1] The development of professional literary studies has arguably been propelled by the resulting dialectic, as each generation of critics grapples in different ways with the apparent friction between remaining responsive to our commitments as political, ethical and historical subjects, and remaining responsive to aesthetic pleasures, to insights and provocations that seem to exceed or rebuff efforts to render them useful.

Subgenres of literary criticism working under the banner of 'new formalism' and 'post-critique' strike me as responses to our discipline's version of Cavell's question, efforts to affirm that whatever else we do when we read literature – however much our aspirations tilt towards history, sociology, politics or ethics – we can still know ourselves as performing literary criticism when we read with attention to literary form. This is the assessment offered by Jonathan Kramnick and Anahid Nersessian, for instance, who note in a widely discussed *Critical Inquiry* essay that '[m]ore often than not, when it comes to literary criticism, form explains everything'.[2] They suggest that even as we disagree – often vehemently – about how or why literary form explains things, or what we mean by form, or what, within that deliberately pluralist 'everything', we are in fact trying to explain, attention to form is how we can continue to know ourselves as literary critics. Their intervention recalls the signature Wittgensteinian 'pivot' we have seen again and again in this book, the attempt to turn down the temperature of sceptical anxieties about our capacity to know – and truly communicate with – other people, by describing what we do with language, observing the criteria and responsibilities entailed in our uses of ordinary language (in making their case, Kramnick and Nersessian in fact draw on Wittgenstein's student, translator and literary executor, Elizabeth Anscombe). That their intervention has not assuaged our fears attests, I think, to the fact that our anxiety largely arises from an economic order untouched by explanatory criteria. This point pertains to the present afterword, and to the ways of reading adopted and advocated throughout this book, which speak partially to disciplinary doubts but which cannot alter an economic bedrock that must be addressed, if at all, by actions outside our language-games.

Cavell's question about philosophy 'becoming' literature opens a different perspective on the issues at stake, underscoring the commitments of what in this book I have called conversational reading or criticism. He does not propose that philosophy 'become' literature in the sense of obliterating the boundary between them. As Paul Standish has noted, 'the phrasing touches on an earlier sense of "becoming" as "comely" or "beautiful" and "suitable"', and the multiple valences of the question mean it 'does not collapse the distinction but reaffirms the relationship, including its mutual dependence'.[3] In other words, Cavell asks if philosophy can make itself conversable with literature, not only allowing literature to have 'a voice in what philosophy says about it', but learning to make philosophy appealing and responsive to the voice of literature (*PDAT*, 10).

Cavell poses this question after reading Shakespeare's *Othello* as expressing a better understanding of the stakes of scepticism than traditional philosophy. The play, he argues, reveals that we might be driven mad not by lack of certain knowledge (which is simply our human lot, when it comes to trusting our senses or engaging with others), but by our refusal to acknowledge what we *do* know, to 'yield' to that knowledge, as well as to the limitations and responsibilities it entails. In Cavell's reading, Othello's 'professions of skepticism over [Desdemona's] faithfulness is a cover story for a deeper conviction; a terrible doubt covering a yet more terrible certainty, an unstatable certainty', which is the certainty of his separateness from her and all the world, both of which he nonetheless needs (CR, 493). The refusal of acknowledgement here, as in other instances considered in this book, is an evasion of knowledge of the ordinary conditions of human existence, our existence 'as dependent, as partial', and the attendant responsibilities.

Philosophy can 'become' literature, in Cavell's sense, if it learns to acknowledge and respond to such revelations from works like *Othello*. Literature, he writes, can 'provide us with the knowledge of the Outsider', a suggestion that implies literature invites us into the perfectionist exchange represented so often in his work as aversive conversation with someone new or askew to our familiar ways of living and talking (CR, 476).[4] As we have seen, responsiveness in such conversation entails acknowledgement, self-disclosure. It means discovering that we are 'enchained, fixated', but also that we can 'turn (convert, revolutionize [our]self)' (CHU, 6–7). Turning in response, and finding the words for further responsiveness, a person – or a discipline, as implicit in the close of *The Claim of Reason* – can attain further selves. Such conversation, I have claimed, is for the philosophers and novelists in this book a worldmaking encounter, helping us create and continuously rejuvenate the grounds on which we (and disciplines, texts, works of art and other perspectives) meet.

In this book, I have sought to show how literary criticism can 'become' philosophy in this sense, attuning the voices of works of literature and philosophy to each other and a topic of mutual interest. My gambit has been that this way of reading allows literary criticism to aspire to worldly purposiveness, without blunt instrumentalism. I have made three interweaving arguments. First, a compelling and consistent ideal of conversation recurs in responses to scepticism offered in ordinary language, ethical, and political philosophy, most notably in work by Wittgenstein, Cavell and Hannah Arendt. Each of these philosophers recommends conversation as an alternative to sceptical withdrawal from ethical and political life. Instead of panicking about the fallibility of our perceptions, they argue, we should talk, responding to each other and the world we perceive using the conventions held in our language and broader 'forms of life'. This response shifts attention from metaphysics to ethics (in works by Cavell and Wittgenstein) and politics (in works by Arendt), turning us towards questions about what we should *do*, rather than what we can or cannot know with certainty about others, the world, and so forth. It also invokes aesthetics, suggesting that our responsiveness to each other generates our shared world, rather than merely unfolding in it. In Arendt's phrasing, a specific 'reality of the public realm' or 'world we have in common' comes into existence when and where we converse, 'rising out of the sum total of aspects' brought into relation as we talk, from our unique standpoints, about the world between us (*HC*, 57). Like aesthetic judgement, such conversation is simultaneously normative and creative, underwritten but never guaranteed by the 'shaky foundations' of our 'mutual attunement or agreement in our criteria', conventions held in our shared forms of life that themselves transform as we speak (*CR*, 168). Adapting a phrase of Cavell's, I have called this recurrent ideal the conversational outlook.

Second, I have argued that exemplary works of literature contribute insights that help clarify this outlook, as they simultaneously share and complicate the ideas about language use, aesthetic responsiveness, and community that inspire the attraction of conversation for the philosophers. The novels caution against overly idealising conversation, as they have helped illuminate limitations in the interplay between normativity and creative freedom inscribed in the conversational outlook. Moreover, they have linked these limitations to reading literature, from Anne Elliot's conversational unresponsiveness to Mrs Smith due to her literary moralism in *Persuasion*, through the restricted power of Miles's private reading, a double for Arendt's figurative conversation, at the end of *There But For The*. In varying ways, the novels have reminded us of potential alliances between literary-interpretive conventions and norms of liberal modernity that exclude, and perhaps even repress, voices through which (recalling Rushdie's phrase) newness might enter the world. Each indicates that there are aspects to 'reality' that literary texts are not only ill-suited to disclosing, but from which they might distract us, or which they might pre-emptively exclude. Neither conversation nor literature makes worlds equally hospitable to all. And in this sense, I have argued, the novels engage their readers – us – in the kind of aversive, self-critical conversation Cavell argues fosters both moral and democratic development.

Third, I have claimed that Cavell's unique 'literary-philosophical' criticism should be understood as enacting the conversational outlook, and that literary critics aspiring to worldly responsiveness might wish to read in the same spirit. Such criticism has more precise ambitions – and commitments that I have described as ethical, political and poetic – than is usually meant in rote invocations of 'conversation' to describe interdisciplinary projects. This book has tried to both elucidate and model such conversational criticism, enlisting literary works in projects that extend past their pages, without subordinating their voices to my own prior beliefs and concerns. Neither Cavell's version of conversational criticism, nor mine, theorises. I have not offered a new theory of 'the British novel', for instance – for reasons elaborated at greater length in the introduction – and I do not propose conversational criticism as a theory of how interdisciplinary literary criticism proceeds or ought to proceed. Instead, taking cues from ordinary language philosophy, I describe what I have learned to perceive about a topic of mutual interest for the novelists, philosophers and myself, through integrating the voices of literary and non-literary texts. Conversational criticism at once discovers and makes its object of study, rendering into 'reality' a 'many-sided substance', to borrow from Woolf, which is analogous to the 'reality of the public realm' Arendt describes.

In the final two chapters, I noted parallels between conversational worldmaking as described in this book and literary interpretation as it has long known itself. Interpretation, as much as judgement, both affirms and helps us judge the conversationally generated common world. As Arendt observes, 'The common element connecting art and politics is that they both are phenomena of the public world' ('Crisis', 218). In both political and artistic or cultural life, she continues, 'it is not knowledge or truth which is at stake, but rather judgment and decision, the judicious exchange of opinion about the sphere of public life and the common world, and the decision what manner of action is to be taken in it, as well as to how it is to look henceforth, what kind of things are to appear in it' ('Crisis', 223). Our individual interests (and judgements) influence our selections of texts and our responses, but by referring to a text's details, perceivable from whatever standpoint we or those with whom we converse happen to occupy, we affirm the commonality of the text. By telling one another what we think it means, and what actions might follow, we practise the judicious exchange of opinions and interpretations that reaffirms the common world. This is both invaluable and undervalued, socially and politically, at a time when world-threatening scepticism is amplified by new technologies and their manipulation by politicians, hackers and corporations. An ordinary language philosopher might phrase the point thus: the language-games we play, or ought to play, when discussing art and politics share the same criteria. In the second decade of the twenty-first century, there is an unpleasant poignancy to Cavell's remark that we might rightly feel 'terrified that maybe language (and understanding, and knowledge)' – and, Arendt would add, the 'world we have in common' – 'rests upon very shaky foundations – a thin net over an abyss' (*CR*, 178).

This is not to say that reading literature makes anyone a better subject for democratic or ethical action. Indeed, as just mentioned, the novels studied in this book themselves warn against idealising either conversation or reading itself, and many echo 'the moment of recurrent silence' Cavell discerns in the *Philosophical Investigations*, when a change in language or game must be initiated by a pupil or newcomer, because the representative of the present order runs out of explanations for why we speak and act as we do. As the novels stress, the language of literature or art, and of literary or aesthetic study, is rarefied and exclusionary. If this is the case, and if it is becoming even more intensely the case as neoliberalism erodes universities and preaches what Michael Clune calls the 'false egalitarianism' of the market over allegedly elitist aesthetic judgement, it is this exclusiveness – and its root of material inequality – we ought to contest rather than the language itself.[5] But such contestation must invoke different criteria than literary criticism, however conversational.

Conversational criticism, as I have elucidated in Cavell's work and modelled in these pages, proceeds in the same manner described above, affirming the commonality of the text, but it then turns the interpretation outwards, towards the world. The key distinction, here, is that the main object of study is not a text or tradition, but rather the world we have in common with texts, a world the texts help us perceive – and thereby inhabit – in new ways. In conversational criticism, a text's worldly purposiveness follows, rather than determines, its interpretation. We saw an example of this process in Chapter 5's reading of the closing sequence of *There But For The*, in which, I argue, Miles first interprets Brooke's story, then imaginatively inhabits its perspective, which happens to be a perspective on his own situation. The result is 'judgment and decision', his return to the common world outside the room in which he has sequestered himself for months.

Even when critics do not conceptualise their work in these terms, many implicitly turn their interests beyond the literary – and here is where charges of instrumentalism, or negligence of aesthetic form, often find their purchase. Classic works of critique, for instance, are interested less fundamentally in literature itself than in systems of power literature helps illuminate. But this does not necessarily mean they reduce literary texts to pure diagnostic instrument. A critic might find a literary text to be complicit or worse, but critique remains conversational when the ambition directs our attention beyond the text, to our world and our own positions in it, and when the critic solicits the literary text's voice in accordance with its own form of life, its purposiveness instantiated in aesthetic form. That voice will resonate differently, however, depending on the other voices to which the critic makes it respond. Works of critique are 'conversational' when they are responsive simultaneously to the literary text and to Marx, for instance, and when their primary purpose is not to expose the text's complicities and evasions, but rather to illuminate some third 'reality' of the world we have in common with the text (economic relations, racism, patriarchy, and so on). At its best, critique delights not in exposure or mastery but in discovery, often of utopian alternatives critics find within aesthetic objects, even amidst compromises with ideology.

Insofar as my account of conversational criticism does not call for a new method, but rather offers a description of agreements and ambitions informing how many of us already read, Wittgenstein might characterise this aspect of my project as 'assembling reminders for a particular purpose' (*PI*, §127). In this case, one purpose is to clarify how and why literary criticism might be put to external, worldly purposes, while still unashamedly knowing itself as literary criticism. With ordinary language philosophy, I think such 'reminders' can be crucial for understanding the grounds on which we stand, and for inviting others to stand – or playfully turn – more confidently with us. In other words, although I do not propose 'conversational criticism' as a new, general theory of interdisciplinary work, I invite others to adopt the conversational outlook as a perspective from which we can aspire for purpose or relevance outside literary studies without reducing literary texts to commodities or objects of bluntly instrumental reason.[6] For the conversational critic, the task is to interpret the text's perspective on the world we have in common, collating it with a 'sum total of aspects' the critic renders available through the work of criticism. The result is a 'reality' akin to the 'reality of the public realm' that conversation makes, according to the outlook elaborated in this book. This is neither an ontological reality nor a matter of subjective perception alone. It attests to perception collectivised and objectified – temporarily – through talk and interpretation. There are no guarantees that others will find the resulting object worth sharing. But the very shakiness of such foundations is, the critic hopes, a reason to keep talking.

# Notes

## Introduction

1. Smith, *There But For The*, 106.
2. Smith, *Autumn*, 112.
3. Cavell, *Must We Mean What We Say?* 110. Hereafter cited as *MWM*.
4. I discuss several examples of this resistance in Chapter 1.
5. For example, see Kathleen Fitzpatrick's *Generous Thinking* and a recent 'Theories & Methodologies' essay cluster in *PMLA*, 'Cultures of Argument', edited by Pardis Dabashi, *PMLA* 135.5 (2020). See Felski, *Limits of Critique*, for an influential exemplar of 'post-critique'.
6. I follow convention in referring to Cavell as an ordinary language philosopher – or a critic working in the spirit of ordinary language philosophy, as he sometimes called himself – and when I discuss ordinary language philosophy, I am referring primarily to Wittgenstein, Austin and Cavell. For further discussion of ordinary language philosophy and Cavell's relation to the work gathered under that banner, see Laugier, 'Rethinking the Ordinary', in *Contending with Stanley Cavell*, ed. Russell B. Goodman.
7. The first work to integrate Cavell and literary studies, Michael Fischer's *Stanley Cavell and Literary Skepticism*, argues that literary critique shaped by poststructuralism expresses an ethos continuous with the scepticism Cavell seeks to defuse in his philosophy. The current interest in links between ordinary language philosophy and literature is evinced by works by critics including Toril Moi, David Rudrum, Daniel Wright, Karen Zumhagen-Yekplé, Megan Quigley, Eric Lindstrom, Charles Altieri and Garry Hagberg.
8. See Kurnick, 'A Few Lies'.
9. Milton, *Doctrine and Discipline of Divorce*, 27.
10. Turkle, *Reclaiming Conversation*, 126. See McCormick, *Chattering Mind*, for a discussion of digital-age eulogies for conversation. McCormick tracks a complementary idealisation of conversation – and ambivalence towards 'chatter' – in modern European thought.
11. Quoted in Remnick, 'Obama Reckons with a Trump Presidency'.

12. Rorty, *Philosophy and the Mirror of Nature*, 394.
13. Goffman, *Forms of Talk*, 14, n8; and *Interaction Ritual*, 116–117 and 113.
14. Goffman, *Interaction Ritual*, 117.
15. Simpson, *The Academic Postmodern* and 'The Cult of "Conversation"'. Simpson particularly criticised Rorty and Michael Oakeshott, the conservative author of (among other texts) *The Voice of Poetry in the Conversation of Mankind*.
16. Tonn, 'Taking Conversation, Dialogue, and Therapy Public'. For additional critiques of vague appeals to conversation, see Walzer, 'A Critique of Philosophical Conversation' and Schudson, 'Why Conversation is Not the Soul of Democracy'.
17. Kant, 'Preface to the Second Edition', *Critique of Pure Reason*, 121.
18. Cavell, *Contesting Tears*, 221. Hereafter cited as *CT*.
19. Arendt, *Human Condition*, 283. Hereafter cited as *HC*.
20. Arendt, *The Life of the Mind*, vol. 1, *Thinking*, 49. Hereafter cited as *LMT*.
21. Wittgenstein, *Philosophical Investigations*, §108. Hereafter cited as *PI* by section number.
22. Arendt, 'The Concept of History', in *Between Past and Future*, 51. Hereafter cited as 'Concept'.
23. My language here resembles Linda Zerilli's in her argument that Arendt helps us envision political judgement as a 'world-building practice'. In Chapters 4 and 5, I build on Zerilli's readings of Arendt and ordinary language philosophy to make my related case about conversation's politically worldmaking powers, substituting 'making' for 'building' in part to stress the aesthetic component of the outlook shared across the works I discuss. See Zerilli's Conclusion in *A Democratic Theory of Judgment*, hereafter cited as *DTJ*.
24. See also Wittgenstein, *PI*, §109: 'We must do away with all explanation, and description alone must take its place. And this description gets its light, that is to say its purpose, from the philosophical problems. These are, of course, not empirical problems; they are solved, rather, by looking into the workings of our language, and that in such a way as to make us recognise those workings: in despite of an urge to misunderstand them. The problems are solved, not by giving new information, but by arranging what we have always known.'
25. Hence the title and central argument of Moi's *Revolution of the Ordinary*, a powerful appeal to literary critics to incorporate lessons from ordinary language philosophy.
26. Moi, *Revolution*, 217.
27. See also Wong, 'Late Victorian Novels, Bad Dialogue, and Talk'; the special issue of *Representations* co-edited by Lucey, McEnaney and Wolff, 'Language-in-use and the Literary Artifact'; Lucey, *Someone*; and Puckett, *Bad Form*. For a discussion of Goffman's uses of literature and their relevance to post-critique, see Love, 'Close Reading and Thin Description'; and 'Close But Not Deep'.
28. Alsop, *Making Conversation*, 4.

29. Bakhtin, 'From the Prehistory of Novelistic Discourse' in *Dialogic Imagination*.
30. As Yi-Ping Ong notes, both Lockean individualism and Descartes's doubting subject loom large in 'history of the novel' discourse, a pairing of philosophers that 'can be traced back to Ian Watt's influential account of the philosophical bases of realism in *The Rise of the Novel* (1957)' (*Art of Being*, 27). Ong argues that novel theory ought to broaden its set of philosophical interlocutors, specifically to include existentialists.
31. For arguments related to the development of bourgeois subjectivity, see Watt, Jameson and Nancy Armstrong. For analysis that links novels to the establishment of social and national ties, see Gallagher and Benedict Anderson. For claims about the moral function of realist literature and the arts generally, in training sympathy or empathy in terms beneficial to liberal democracy, see Trilling, Nussbaum (*Poetic Justice* and *Not for Profit*), Eagleton, Plotz and Keen, the latter of whom are more sceptical about the real-world consequences of empathy readers feel for characters, as well as about the virtues of liberal universalism. Others have argued that realism in the novel can have more radical political ramifications; here, see Goodlad, *Victorian Geopolitical Aesthetic*, Isobel Armstrong, *Novel Politics*, Kornbluh, *Order of Forms*, and Lesjak, *Afterlife of Enclosure*.
32. Armstrong, *How Novels Think*, 3.
33. See Barnes, *Love and Depth in the American Novel*, for a survey of approaches treating the novel 'as a technology that produced the modern liberal subject' (17). Barnes 'make[s] the case for a countertradition of novels of love that resisted the formation of the private liberal subject' (17). Paige, *Technologies of the Novel*, also offers a survey of the 'rise of the novel' narrative and its discontents, pointing to flattening generalisations, selective choices, dubious causal claims and an equally dubious understanding of historical change influenced by Foucauldian ideas of 'epistemes' and paradigm shifts, rather than (for instance) materialist analysis.
34. Postcolonial scholars have shown that when the Anglo-European tradition is not our focus, we see novels appearing in other cultures; for example, see Aravamudan, 'In the Wake of the Novel'. For complicating accounts of literary culture and liberal culture, and of the relation between the two, see Daniel Stout and Amanda Anderson.
35. Wittgenstein, *Blue and Brown Books*, 17. See also Moi's discussion of literary criticism's 'craving for generality', *Revolution*, 92–99.
36. Cavell, *MWM*, 110; *Cities of Words*, 142, hereafter cited as *Cities*. Elsewhere Cavell posits that 'at some stage the philosophical becomes, or turns into, the literary'. Cavell, *In Quest of the Ordinary*, 109, hereafter cited as *IQO*. This continues a theme first broached as a question at the end of *Claim of Reason*, where he suggests that philosophy perhaps ought to 'become literature', a provocation I revisit in the afterword.
37. *Stanley Cavell and Literary Skepticism*, 36. Fischer's purpose is less to develop a Cavellian literary criticism than to show how Cavell's influence ought to reorient criticism away from the scepticism exemplified by deconstructionist theory.

38. Cavell, *Conditions Handsome and Unhandsome*, 4. Hereafter cited as *CHU*.
39. Karen Zumhagen-Yekplé similarly reads Wittgenstein's work in terms of moral perfectionism, focusing primarily on the quest for self-discovery and improvement in the *Tractatus*, but also framing the *Investigations* and Wittgenstein's famous repudiation of the *Tractatus* as exemplary of perfectionist development through overcoming one's prior self in favour of the further self.
40. Although he frequently calls it 'Emersonian perfectionism', his range of readings makes the outlook he develops distinctly his own. I therefore join other readers of Cavell – like Alice Crary and Paul Guyer – and call it Cavellian. See Guyer, 'Examples of Perfectionism', and Crary, 'A Radical Perfectionist'.
41. For example, Cavell argues that Shakespeare's plays express ideas formalised several decades later by Descartes, and Romantics respond to Kant's (insufficient) response to scepticism by seeking to 'transcendentalize' rather than overcome 'low' and 'ordinary' experience (*IQO*, 27, 52). In Cavell's view, philosophy and poetry begin to recognise each other in the Romantic era as engaged in a struggle with scepticism, and with each other's responses to scepticism.
42. Cavell, *Claim of Reason*, 168, 178. Hereafter cited as *CR*.
43. He repeats these passages verbatim in *CHU*, 81.
44. Cavell, *A Pitch of Philosophy*, 126. Hereafter cited as *Pitch*. Cavell contrasts what we might call object-oriented scepticism to other-oriented scepticism. In the former, when the sceptic challenges your presumption of knowledge by saying, for instance, you only see the surface of that table, 'I am apt to feel bullied' by the other's argumentativeness. *Philosophy the Day After Tomorrow*, 149. He continues: 'Whereas the case of the other is too trivial almost to mention. Who doesn't know that what I go on in knowing others is [only] their outward behavior [. . .]? What is inside the other is not transparent to me. This is no news and accordingly it suggests that the problem of the other is not discovered the way the problem of the knowledge of objects is discovered' (149–150). Hereafter cited as *PDAT*.
45. Cavell, *Pursuits of Happiness*, 87. Hereafter cited as *Pursuits*.
46. Arendt, like Cavell, is an interdisciplinary thinker who refused the label of 'philosopher', preferring theorist or political scientist. This stemmed in part, she explained, from her sense of an enmity between philosophy (thinking) and politics (acting). To call herself a political theorist was to sidestep the 'burden' of that traditional enmity. I refer to her as a philosopher nonetheless. Yet, I see her foremost as another exemplar of conversational criticism: a 'pearl diver,' as she called Walter Benjamin, gathering reminders from as promiscuous a set of sources as Cavell. For her distinction between 'political theorist' and 'political philosopher', see the first four minutes of the interview by Günter Gaus, *Zur Person: Hannah Arendt*.
47. Ngai, *Theory of the Gimmick*, 20.
48. Kant, *Critique of Judgment*, §40, 138. Hereafter cited as *CJ* by numbered section and page.

49. The earliest uses of conversation to denote verbal communication, according to the *Oxford English Dictionary*, occur in the late sixteenth century (roughly half a century before Milton's *Doctrine*). See 'conversation, n. 7a'. *OED Online*.
50. As Wittgenstein's famous claim in *Philosophical Investigations* goes, 'For a *large* class of cases – though not for all – in which we employ the word "meaning" it can be defined thus: the meaning of a word is its use in the language' (§43). See also *PI*, §340 and §109.
51. Andrew Norris and Aletta Norval both make Cavell's 'aversive conversation' central to their discussions of his work's resources for political theory.
52. s.v. 'converse', *OED Online*. See also the etymology for 'convert'.
53. See Plotz, *The Crowd*, for analysis of representations of public discord in nineteenth-century British fiction and nonfiction.
54. In 'A Matter of Meaning It', Cavell writes that there are cases in which 'the appeal to intention can *in fact* be inappropriate or distracting or evasive, as it can in moral contexts', but that altogether denying the importance of intention amounts to denying that 'the first fact of works art is that they are meant, meant to be understood. A poem, whatever else it is, is an *utteranc* (outer-ance)' (*MWM*, 225, 228). Contemporary critics with whom I am a wayward fellow traveller regarding the question of intentionalism – wayward because I join Cavell in describing conversations that the works of art themselves do not directly engage – build largely on the influential essay 'Against Theory' by Steven Knapp and Walter Benn Michaels, and include Nicholas Brown, Lisa Siraganian and Charles Hatfield.
55. Cavell, *PDAT*, 10.
56. Rudrum, *Stanley Cavell and the Claim of Literature*, 5. Hereafter cited as *Claim of Literature*. For related warnings against the idea of an 'approach' to texts, see also Mulhall, 'On Refusing to Begin' in *Contending with Stanley Cavell*, ed. Russell B. Goodman.
57. For Norris, this link between tentative, provisional community and ordinary language philosophy points to one of the primary contributions Cavell offers to political thought. As Norris notes, Cavell implies that aesthetic criticism offers another model of such work.
58. Chodat, 'Experts and Encounters', 994.
59. Miller, *Burdens of Perfection*, 30. See also Miller, 'Implicative Criticism, or The Display of Thinking'.
60. See Mulhall, 'Inner Constancy', in *Varieties of Skepticism*, for a helpful discussion of this interrelation between normativity and openness in ordinary language philosophy.

## Chapter 1

1. Mee, *Conversable Worlds*, 201.
2. As I discuss, this aspect of my reading extends analysis first developed by Adela Pinch, Deidre Lynch and Andrew H. Miller.

3. For more on links between Cavell's thought and education, see Standish and Sato, eds, *Stanley Cavell and the Education of Grownups*.
4. See Miller, *Burdens of Perfection*, 3.
5. The examples he provides are 1990s-era self-help and military recruitment slogans urging, 'Be all that you can be' (*CHU*, 16). Such perfectionisms are 'debased', he writes, because they advance an image of the perfected (and 'mercenary') self.
6. Milton, *Doctrine*, 27.
7. For further discussion of Cavell's engagement with Austen and Austen's additional resources for ordinary language philosophy, see Lindstrom, *Jane Austen and Other Minds*, and Walker, 'Austen and Cavell'.
8. Quoted in *PDAT*, 127.
9. Austen, *Pride and Prejudice*, 225. Hereafter cited as *PP*.
10. Austen, *Emma*, 20.
11. Commentary on Austen's ambivalent depiction of marriage is ample, of course. See Walker, *Marriage, Writing, and Romanticism*, for a compelling argument that Austen's novels display an attitude towards marriage neither celebratory nor condemnatory, but instead 'indifferent'. Hereafter cited as *Marriage*.
12. In outline, the novel resembles Shakespeare's *The Winter's Tale*, which Cavell calls a 'relative[e] of [. . .] the comedy of remarriage' (*Cities*, 421).
13. Austen, *Persuasion*, 35.
14. Lynch, *Economy of Character*, 218.
15. See Pinch, 'Lost in a Book: Jane Austen's *Persuasion*'.
16. Gloria Sybil Gross has declared her a 'mercenary' with a 'greedy, grasping rage for power'. Gross, 'Flights Into Illness', in *Literature and Medicine During the Eighteenth Century*, 190. See also Gevirtz, *Life after Death*. In their classic, *Madwoman in the Attic*, Sandra Gilbert and Susan Gubar read Mrs Smith as symptomatic of more collective ills. The West Indian connection means that she can also be read, as Walker summarises, as 'a self-interested cog in colonialist machinery', which notably still encompassed slavery (*Marriage*, 174).
17. Monica Cohen has proposed that, ethical and political implications aside, the fact that the widowed Mrs Smith ultimately obtains colonial property for herself (with Wentworth's help) is a 'radical *tour de force* buried in an ostensibly incidental subplot'. Cohen, 'Persuading the Navy Home', 348.
18. Brodie, 'Society and the Superfluous Female', 716.
19. Ibid.
20. In *Marriage*, Walker suggests that the final lines of the novel might even be narrated from Mrs Smith's point of view, or at least from the point of view of Anne's only 'two friends in the world', Mrs Smith and Lady Russell.
21. Walker, *Marriage*, 175–176.
22. There is something transgressive in Mrs Smith's friendship with a nurse, given the low moral estimation of nurses at the time. It is, at least, a sign of her downward mobility. As Susan Jones describes, nursing was then extremely difficult and undervalued, 'few would willingly undertake

the profession', and those who did 'were associated with transgressive sexuality and with a working class held in high distrust'. See Jones, 'Thread-cases, Pin-cushions, and Card-racks'.
23. Anne's phrasing echoes Austen's contemporary, Thomas Gisborne, who wrote that 'Fortitude is not to be sought merely on the rampart, on the deck, on the field of battle. Its place is no less in the chamber of sickness and pain, in the retirements of anxiety, of grief, and of disappointment.' Quoted in Knox-Shaw, *Jane Austen and the Enlightenment*, 239. Shaw remarks that the mismatch between Anne's Gisborne-echoing loftiness and Mrs Smith's responses suggests a 'touch of skeptical materialism', but this only scratches the surface of the scene's complex critique (ibid.).
24. Both are also, of course, media tasked with the globalisation of English (literary) culture. For an argument that *Persuasion* endorses the globalisation of English culture by transforming Kantian cosmopolitan tolerance into a nationalist cultural pride, see Rogers, 'Philosophy in Austen's Pump Room'.
25. See Taylor, *A Secular Age*.
26. Hadley, *Liberal Cognition*, 9. Hadley argues that the eighteenth- and early nineteenth-century self-fashioning that Lynch describes in authors such as Austen is the precursor to 'liberal cognition' modelled in later nineteenth-century fiction, which trades sensibility for the more abstract, impersonal 'mental space realised in the balloting booth' (ibid., 87, n40).
27. See Jones, *Consensual Fictions*, for a fuller consideration of the interweaving of liberalism and courtship in Romantic and Victorian novels.
28. Rawls, *A Theory of Justice*, 266. Hereafter cited as *ToJ*.
29. See Mills, *Black Rights, White Wrongs*, especially chapter 5, '"Ideal Theory" as Ideology'. As critics sometimes complain, Mills wishes to transform rather than refute liberalism; in this sense, he makes a perfectionist, aversive continuation of liberalism. For arguments regarding the limits of Mills's project, see Darby, 'Charles Mills's Liberal Redemption Song', and Hughey, 'Four Thoughts on Charles Mills – *Black Rights/White Wrongs: The Critique of Racial Liberalism*'. For an argument, contra Mills, that ideal theory can be useful combatting racism and other injustices in non-ideal societies, see Shelby, 'Racial Realities and Corrective Justice'. See also Mills, 'Retrieving Rawls for Racial Justice?' and Shelby, 'Race and Social Justice'.
30. Aware of this objection, Rawls argues that thinking with ideals is useful and should not be taken to exclude thinking about the non-ideal world. Countless essays and books examine the cases for and against ideal theory. For further discussion, see Valentini, 'Ideal vs. Non Ideal Theory'; Farrelly, 'Justice in Ideal Theory'; Simmons, 'Ideal and Nonideal Theory'; Hamlin and Stemplowska, 'Theory, Ideal Theory and the Theory of Ideals'; and Sen, 'What Do We Want from a Theory of Justice?'.
31. A person awakening to injustice might find society 'still habitable', Cavell writes, for reasons ranging from a sense of 'oppressive helplessness' or cynicism, to faith in procedures of reform and society's longer-term arc towards justice. We might consider our society's present degree of justice 'good

enough', appropriately open to reform, 'better than any other [society] with comparable resources', or better than 'the human cost of changing it' would be (*CHU*, 184). If such considerations are part of the conversation of justice, we must recognise them to be judgements rather than rules, hence open to revision. How to judge *well* in a democratic context is the subject of this book's final chapters, but here I note, with Cavell, that politics entails judgement, and no thought experiments or rational procedure can move political life onto firmer ground.

32. His treatment of 'consent from above' as compatible with the pursuit of justice is one indication of distance between his perfectionism and Marxist or otherwise more radical critiques of liberalism. Yet it also continues the subtle differentiation between his orientation and a conventionally liberal one, his emphasis on responsiveness and self-reproach in a non-ideal, never-perfected democracy. If change is to take place by means other than violence, those 'above' must discover its necessity.
33. See also Norval, *Aversive Democracy*, 177.
34. We might see Victorian novels dedicated to class conflict and the 'condition of England' by authors such as Charles Dickens, Elizabeth Gaskell and George Eliot as testing the capacity for the conversations of literature and liberalising Britain to encompass working-class voices. These novels largely suggest that the path towards inclusion is one of assimilation. *Persuasion* reminds us that assimilation to a liberal/literary form of life might limit mutual education.
35. Relatedly, in 'Politics As Opposed to What?', Cavell likens reading to psychoanalytic conversation, a 'paradoxical' encounter in which the reader is at once reading and allowing herself to be read by the text, 'turning the picture of interpreting a text into one of being interpreted by it' (176). See Rudrum for a discussion of Cavell's vision of reciprocity between reader and text, which distinguishes Cavell's vision from Derridean and poststructuralist formulations of the paradoxes of textuality, as well as from Harold Bloom's account of 'being read' by great works of literature (*Claim of Literature*, 31).
36. Rudrum, *Claim of Literature*, 165. Rudrum and Norval both recommend supplementing Cavell's conversational ideal with Jacques Rancière's attention to *dissensus*, moments when the 'part that has no part' in political 'conversation' disrupts the existing 'language' and transforms the political realm. I revisit Rancière in Chapter 4.

## Chapter 2

1. Austin, *How To Do Things With Words*, 6. Hereafter cited as *How to Do*.
2. See Lorenzini, 'From Recognition to Acknowledgement', for a complementary analysis of Cavell's account of conversation as a 'mode of association' and 'form of life' in which passionate utterances are crucial.
3. Divorce was exceptionally rare at the time of the publication of *The Egoist*, although the Matrimonial Causes Act of 1857 had enabled a broader

population to divorce by establishing a Divorce Court that was not overseen by the Church and allowed people to divorce without a parliamentary bill. For discussion of this Act, see Shanley, '"One Must Ride Behind"', and Hammerton, 'Victorian Marriage and the Law of Matrimonial Cruelty'.
4. Meredith, *The Egoist*, 92. Hereafter cited as *Egoist*.
5. In the passage Freud cites, Clara inadvertently swaps the last name of the man she loves, Vernon Whitford, for that of the man Willoughby's first fiancée eloped with, Harry Oxford. Later, Meredith's narrator remarks that 'all the doors are not open in a young lady's consciousness' (335). For discussion of the novel's relation to psychoanalytic theory, see O'Toole, 'Meredithian Slips'.
6. Craig, 'Promising Marriage', 907.
7. Toner, *Ellipsis in English Literature*, 147, 139.
8. See Wright, *Bad Logic*. For a different angle on the novel's implicit philosophy of language, focusing on its 'granular descriptions', see Bartlett, *Object Lessons*, chapter 1.
9. Butler, *Excitable Speech*, 11. Butler invokes the figure of chiasmus to describe the relation between the commissive utterance, in her example a threat, and 'the act that is threatened': both depend on the other, or the idea of the other, to make full sense.
10. Oliphant, [Review of *The Egoist*], in *George Meredith: The Critical Heritage*, 240.
11. See Gray, 'Metaphors and Marriage Plots'.
12. An example of this strategy employed to try to trap a different woman, Laetitia, occurs at the end of the novel when Willoughby attempts to swap fiancées. Laetitia responds to a knock on the door, thinking it is Clara, with the invitation, 'come in, dear'. Willoughby enters, 'seize[s] her hands', and exclaims, 'Dear! [. . .] You cannot withdraw that. You call me dear. I am, I must be dear to you. The word is out, by accident or not, but, by heaven, I have it and I give it up to no one' (593). Not only does he treat an utterance not meant to be performative as though it is, but he leans on the separability of illocution from intention.
13. Derrida, *Limited Inc*, 18.
14. Ibid., 14.
15. Ordinary language philosophy does not entail imagining, as Derrida indicates, a metaphysical 'force' projected from the liberal subject into the world, via speech. As Cavell argues in *A Pitch of Philosophy*, Derrida correctly sees 'voice' as important to ordinary language philosophy, but incorrectly conflates its meaning for Austin with metaphysical presence. For Searle's response to Derrida, see 'Reiterating the Differences: A Reply to Derrida', and for Derrida's scornful reply, see 'Afterword' in *Limited, Inc*. For a comparison of their exchange to the interests of ordinary language philosophers, see Moi, *Revolution*, 65–72.
16. Culler, 'Philosophy and Literature', 507.
17. When Wittgenstein poses the question of whether we can 'imagine a language' developed by a person 'for his private use', he is prompting

an ordinary language (rather than ontological) observation about language, about what we mean when we say (or imagine) 'language': language is something we understand to be fundamentally shared, and thus we struggle to make sense of the concept of 'private language' (*PI*, §243). By Cavell's reading, the purpose of Wittgenstein's discussion of private language is therapeutic: 'its point is to release the fantasy expressed in the denial that language is something essentially shared' (*CR*, 343). In the process it also 'illuminate[s] something about the publicness of language, the *depth* to which language is agreed in' (*CR*, 343).
18. See *CT*, 98–104, for Cavell's discussion of the 'gender asymmetry' of scepticism as expressed in Western philosophy and culture, including psychoanalysis. For further discussion of Cavell's treatment of gender, including an overview of feminist responses to his work, see Wheatley, *Stanley Cavell and Film*.
19. Meredith, *Egoist*, 194; Wright, *Bad Logic*, 88.
20. Cavell links inflexible approaches to promising to his critique of Rawls's *Theory of Justice*, discussed in Chapter 1, arguing that Rawls's comments about resentment extend his view of society as founded on an implicit promise. Cavell connects this to an early essay by Rawls, 'Two Concepts of Rules', in which Rawls appears to advocate an inflexible approach to 'bona fide' promises. See *CHU*, 113–114, and *Cities*, 174–189.
21. We can imagine that in the terms of Meredith's novel, political changes could empower women in tangible ways. It thus invites us to question the criteria of its form of life, without necessarily fantasising that an alternative form of life might defeat scepticism.
22. Besant, *Marriage: As It Was, As it Is, and As It Should Be*, 10.
23. The English jurist William Blackstone noted in his 1838 *Commentaries on the Laws of England* that this implies 'a husband cannot covenant or contract with his wife', because people cannot legally contract with themselves. Quoted in Besant, *Marriage*, 9.
24. Wright, *Bad Logic*, 88.
25. Craig, 'Promising Marriage', 907.
26. Sandra Laugier's treatment of this element of Cavell and Wittgenstein is helpful. She writes: 'for Cavell it is crucial that Wittgenstein says that we agree in and not on language. This means that we are not agents of the agreement; that language precedes this agreement as much as it is produced by it and that this circularity constitutes an irreducible element of scepticism'. Laugier, 'The Ethics of Care as a Politics of the Ordinary', 230.
27. For further discussion of how novels have taken up the philosophical problem of vagueness, see Wright, *Bad Logic*, and Quigley, 'Modern Novels and Vagueness'. Quigley focuses on the 'linguistic turn' evident in modernist art and coinciding with modernist works of philosophy, like Wittgenstein's *Tractatus*. Wright argues that nineteenth-century literary realists were already investigating linguistic vagueness.
28. See Sainsbury and Williamson, 'Sorites' in *A Companion to the Philosophy of Language*, 734–764; Wright, *Bad Logic*, 111–112.

29. Sainsbury and Williamson, 'Sorites', 741.
30. Ibid.
31. Quantum theory holds that atoms can be in two states at the same time: when *unobserved*, electrons passing through an experiment leave traces indicating they behave like a wave, distributing their tiny mass across a spectrum of positions. But when *observed*, they behave like particles, each following a singular path through the system. In Schrödinger's translation of this theory from the 'micro' scale of quantum particles to the 'macro' scale of cats, a cat's life hinges on the position of a quantum particle that, until observed, behaves in a way represented by a wave function. Before we peek into that box, the cat is – theoretically speaking – both alive and dead: the quantum particle is simultaneously in the position that would release a poisonous acid and the position that would leave it untouched. As soon as we peek into the box, the particle has a position, and the cat proves to be either alive or dead. See Schrödinger, 'The Present Situation in Quantum Mechanics'.
32. I take the phrase 'scene of instruction' and the word 'newcomer' from Cavell. See *CHU*, 64–100, and the title chapter of *Philosophy the Day After Tomorrow*.

## Chapter 3

1. Woolf, 'Walter Sickert: A Conversation'.
2. Woolf, *A Room of One's Own*, 110.
3. Woolf, *The Voyage Out*, 63.
4. Woolf, *Mrs Dalloway*, 118.
5. Woolf, *To the Lighthouse*, 123–124.
6. Woolf, *The Waves*, 276, 138, 77.
7. In scenes of literal conversation, her narrative voice often focuses on the non-verbal attunement or divergence of thoughts rather than on the actual words exchanged, the 'conversation behind the conversation', in Julia Briggs's apt phrase. Briggs focuses on Woolf's treatment of taboo subjects including sexuality, trauma, war, same-sex love, and even friendships between women, directing attention to Woolf's thematic and stylistic subversion of conventions obscuring open discussion. See Briggs, 'The Conversation Behind the Conversation'. Martha Nussbaum provides an implausibly romantic reading of the Ramsays' non-verbal communication. See Nussbaum, 'The Window'. For the historical importance of conversation for the Bloomsbury Group, see Banfield, *Phantom Table*, especially 16–17.
8. Woolf, *The Diary of Virginia Woolf*, vol. 3, 203.
9. This history is traced in numerous studies. See Banfield, *Phantom Table*, 30–36, for an account of the conversations of 'Thursday Evenings' in Bloomsbury in relation to Woolf's philosophical development.
10. She describes the 'Angel in the House' in 'Professions for Women': 'She was intensely sympathetic. She was immensely charming. She was utterly

unselfish. She excelled in the difficult arts of family life. She sacrificed herself daily.' See *Selected Essays of Virginia Woolf*, ed. David Bradshaw, 141. This figure, she explains, haunts a woman who wishes to write truthfully, for the ideal of femininity expressed in the Angel is one that does not criticise or think independently. 'Killing the Angel in the House', she states, 'was part of the occupation of a woman writer' (ibid., 142).
11. In a reading with affinity, but not much overlap, to mine, Zumhagen-Yekplé places this passage in dialogue with Wittgenstein and Cora Diamond to show Woolf testing the language-games available for secular expressions of mystical desire.
12. Woolf, *Room*, 87–88.
13. As Elizabeth Alsop points out, most critics have either treated the utterances as more plausible and thus realistic than they are, or denied realism altogether, going so far as to deny there are six characters at all.
14. Alsop, *Making Conversation*, 123.
15. Banfield, *Phantom Table*, ix. As Banfield tracks, early twentieth-century advances such as 'Max Plank's discovery of the quantum in 1900, the confirmation and application of Niels Bohr's theory of the atom between 1913 and 1925, [and] Einstein's formulation of the special theory of relativity in 1905' prompted philosophers such as Russell and G. E. Moore to grapple with 'two versions of a knowledge of the external world, one direct apprehension of it through the senses and the other scientific knowledge, chiefly modern physics' (ibid., 5–6). In Alfred North Whitehead's words, 'the new situation in the thought of today arises from the fact that scientific theory is outrunning common sense' (quoted in ibid., 6).
16. Russell, *An Outline of Philosophy*, 225.
17. See Marcus, 'Britannia Rules The Waves'; McGee, 'The Politics of Modernist Form'; and Purifoy, 'Melancholic Patriotism and *The Waves*'.
18. Russell, *Problems of Philosophy*, 21. Hereafter cited as *Problems*.
19. Russell, *Our Knowledge of the External World*, 70. Hereafter cited as *Our Knowledge*.
20. Banfield, *Phantom Table*, 72.
21. For a definitive study of the influence of Kantian aesthetic and ethical theory on Woolf and others in the Bloomsbury Group, see Froula, *Virginia Woolf and the Bloomsbury Avant-Garde*. Banfield notes that Woolf's narrative aesthetic in *The Waves* and other novels enacts Russell's theory, as the narrative perspective shifts between subjective points of view, emphasising that 'reality' is never perceived in its entirety from these private windows, that its existence is attested to, but never encompassed by, consistencies between limited points of view.
22. Ngai, *Gimmick*, 19.
23. See Terada, *Looking Away*.
24. Kant, 'Preface to the Second Edition', *Critique of Pure Reason*, 115.
25. Rhoda's fantasising manifests what Terada has called 'phenomenophilia', an impulse of 'looking away' from the given world, which Terada argues emerged in Western culture as a response to scepticism, specifically as

outlined in Kant's work (*Looking Away*, 4). Terada traces this trope of 'looking away' through works of literature and philosophy following Kant, proposing it turns from a reality that is neither chosen nor guaranteed to correspond to the concepts our minds construct from sense data. A 'phenomenophile' withdraws from this 'nonoptional' and uncertain reality into private, idiosyncratic fantasy (75). This withdrawal comes at the cost of community. Terada argues that Kant's *Critique of Judgment* offers aesthetic judgement as an alternative to the phenomenophile's response to his earlier *Critique of Pure Reason*. Aesthetic judgement affirms community in a way that sense perception alone cannot, and the universalising conviction of aesthetic judgement, Terada argues, gives us 'a glimpse of a basis for spontaneous community' (99). In this light, Rhoda's vision of a dwelling-place is even more stirring: the phenomenophile is reconciled to non-optional reality and the chance for common ground by conversation undertaken in a Kantian, disembodied frame of mind.

26. Froula has argued that the Bloomsbury circle took from Kant the idea that the 'escape from personality' that a person experiences in artistic contemplation is a form of 'freedom that mediates sociability and community [. . .] by transposing its beholders beyond egotism into (possible) disinterested pleasure'. For Froula, this 'disinterestedness' enables a 'noncoercive dialogue about the *sensus communis*, or common values'. I largely agree, but the form of *The Waves*, and dinner scenes in that novel and *To the Lighthouse*, link this feeling to literal conversation, suggesting that Woolf's characters are not exactly in 'dialogue about the *sensus communis*' but are instead *building* it in dialogue, as they speak, as though this sense of commonness is itself a product of conversation undertaken in a state of aesthetic disinterestedness. Froula, *Virginia Woolf and the Bloomsbury Avant-Garde*, 13–14.

## Chapter 4

1. Infamously, Arendt opposed mandatory school integration in the US, because she claimed that prejudice in social life (a category in which she included public education) is inevitable and non-political, and therefore not subject to political intervention. I share Linda Zerilli's view that Arendt's account of political judgement describes a *mode* of judgement that we can apply to anything we deem political, her own definitions notwithstanding. See Zerilli, *DTJ*, and Arendt, 'Reflections on Little Rock'. See Allen, *Talking to Strangers*, for an excellent analysis of Arendt's views on school integration, which includes an account of Arendt's exchanges with Ralph Ellison, who prompted Arendt to revise some of her views on civil rights politics.
2. Magical realism stands charged of reinforcing colonialist stereotypes of 'third world' cultures or participating in the commodification of these cultures. See Taussig, *Shamanism, Colonialism, and the Wild Man*, and

Moses, 'Magical Realism at World's End'. Against these critiques are those who maintain that, as Wendy Faris writes, 'the narrative strategies of magical realism [may be seen] as a decolonizing poetics'. Faris, 'The Question of the Other', 106. See also Hegerfeldt, *Lies that Tell the Truth*, and Moreillas, *The Exhaustion of Difference*.

3. It is in Farishta's storyline that the depiction of Islam and the Prophet takes place, and my analysis focuses on Chamcha's storyline. However, I want to acknowledge the complex issues at play: 'Mahound' is a fundamentalist and hypocrite, and the very name is an allusion to a history of demonising Islam (the narrator claims to be 'reclaiming' and transforming the epithet, but many readers were not persuaded). Mahound is also an outsider whose ascent to power challenges an oppressive government that resembles the discriminatory state of 1980s Britain. Moreover, Mahound's fundamentalism is represented ambivalently, as both passionate dedication capable of changing the world, and as bloody, unyielding extremism. As Janice Ho argues, 'We cannot read the sociopolitical structures of Islam in *The Satanic Verses* as mere mimetic representations of a historical referent. Instead, Rushdie has grafted these structures onto contemporary versions of social marginality, effecting a bifurcation that asks us to draw historical parallels between the persecution of the prophet Muhammad and his followers and the present-day exclusions of immigrant communities in white Britain.' Ho, *Nation and Citizenship in the Twentieth-Century British Novel*, 213.

4. In Stuart Hall's words, '[There was a] moment when the term "black" was coined as a way of referencing the common experience of racism and marginalization in Britain and came to provide the organizing category of a new politics of resistance, among groups and communities with, in fact, very different histories, traditions and ethnic identities.' Hall, 'New Ethnicities', in *Stuart Hall: Critical Dialogues in Cultural Studies*, 442.

5. Hate crimes against people of colour in Britain increased in frequency in the 1970s and 1980s, bolstered by the increasing prominence of the fascist party, the National Front, as well as the rhetoric of mainstream conservatives and major press outlets. A struggling economy and high rates of unemployment were contributors.

6. Interest in the concept of the counterpublic was gaining currency in critical theory at the time *The Satanic Verses* appeared – a synchrony I cannot explore further here, other than to observe that an opportunity was missed to draw the novel (and its controversial reception) into then-emergent debates. Nancy Fraser's hugely influential 'Rethinking the Public Sphere' was published two years after the novel. An early adoption of the term within literary studies appears in Felski, *Beyond Feminist Aesthetics*, which includes discussion of feminist 'oppositional discursive space' under the rubric of counterpublics (171).

7. Fraser, 'Rethinking the Public Sphere', 61.

8. The book is rooted in Marxist class analysis. Nonetheless, according to Miriam Hansen, the concept of a 'counterpublic' enabled 'a whole spectrum

of groups and movements [...] to think of their work as at once oppositional and public'. Hansen, 'Unstable Mixtures, Dilated Spheres', 186. This essay also served as the foreword to the English translation of Negt and Kluge's book.
9. Fraser cites 'revisionist historiography' by Joan Landes, Geoff Eley and Mary Ryan, who document the exclusions constitutive of the bourgeois public sphere (focusing on gender and class) and describe the efforts by excluded groups to forge their own counterpublics.
10. Negt and Kluge, *Public Sphere and Experience*, 2.
11. Habermas has acknowledged that 'the exclusion of women had a structuring significance' in the development of the bourgeois public sphere. See Habermas, 'Some Further Reflections on the Public Sphere', in Calhoun, *Habermas and the Public Sphere*.
12. Kalliney, *Cities of Affluence and Anger*, and 'Globalization, Postcoloniality, and the Problem of Literary Studies in *The Satanic Verses*'.
13. Not all liberal theories of the public sphere are equal in this regard; see Benhabib, *Situating the Self*, for an account of communicative ethics that is largely consistent with Habermas's, while also striving to acknowledge the relevance of embodied experience.
14. This is the originally reported height of Mt Everest; British surveyors had calculated a height of 29,000 feet and added two feet to make it less implausibly round – one of many details in the novel mocking colonial pretences. See Stegman, 'The Problem of Numeracy'.
15. Even critics whose readings are nuanced and otherwise impressive – such as Peter Kalliney, Brian Finney and Josie Gill – often overlook the significance of the metamorphosis's beginning during the fall.
16. See Dawson for an analysis of how the novel (and the surrounding Rushdie Affair) 'dramatizes the way in which women's identity and rights have frequently been displaced in the internecine struggles of racialized communities within both Britain and India over the course of the last decades'. Dawson, *Mongrel Nation*, 125.
17. Mouffe redescribes democratic politics as consisting of 'agonistic pluralism', a concept through which she strives to replace Schmitt's 'antagonism', conceptualising disagreement as divergence between adversaries who share common values but differing interpretations about how they manifest. See Mouffe, 'Which Public Sphere for a Democratic Society?' Her critiques of the liberal vision of politics have developed over decades, initially through collaboration with her partner Ernesto Laclau in (most prominently) *Hegemony and Socialist Strategy*.
18. Baucom, *Out of Place*, 218.
19. Hall, 'From Scarman to Stephen Lawrence', 183.
20. Ibid., 190.
21. Solomos et al., 'The Organic Crisis of British Capitalism and Race', in Centre for Contemporary Cultural Studies, *The Empire Strikes Back*, 27. The CCCS authors allege that 'research on race relations in Britain' is dominated by a 'liberal-democratic pluralist framework' that insufficiently

contextualises racial politics in relation to the wider disintegration of the postwar 'consensus' (12).
22. *Financial Times*, 'Outbreak of an Alien Disease'.
23. *Financial Times*, 'Searching for Consensus'.
24. Quoted in Solomos et al., 'The Organic Crisis of British Capitalism and Race', 25. According to the CCCS authors, rhetoric originating in the Conservative Party and repeated in the media made race a scapegoat for economic problems and the denial of Britain's post-imperial demotion in the global capitalist economy. See *The Empire Strikes Back*, and Hall et al., *Policing the Crisis*.
25. The rhetoric of infection resurfaced in responses to protests against *The Satanic Verses*. The day after tens of thousands of people marched against the novel, *The Sunday Times* ran a story warning that 'Islamic militancy' is no longer restricted to 'far-off countries of which we know nothing' and 'is now a potent, living organism in the body of Britain itself, impossible to wish away or assimilate or suppress' (quoted in Dawson, *Mongrel Nation*, 122–123).
26. For discussion of the significance of the cinematic language, see Rombes, Jr., '*The Satanic Verses* as a Cinematic Narrative'.
27. Habermas, *Structural Transformation of the Public Sphere*, 31. Habermas describes the early co-evolution of literary and political public spheres in chapters 1 and 2.
28. Zerilli, '"We Feel Our Freedom"', 166.
29. If people assemble to talk about the reality of education and its links to citizenship, it becomes political by Arendt's own account of the performatively generated public realm.
30. Butler, *Notes Toward a Performative Theory of Assembly*, 5.
31. Rancière, *Disagreement*, 50.
32. Rancière, *Dissensus*, 152.
33. Rancière, *Disagreement*, 58.
34. Ibid., 27.
35. Rancière, *Dissensus*, 31–32.
36. Baucom, *Out of Place*, 213.
37. Ibid.
38. As I mentioned, Baucom argues that the novel advocates the hybridity signified in the trope of tropicalisation.
39. Kalliney, 'Globalization, Postcoloniality, and the Problem of Literary Studies in *The Satanic Verses*', 76.
40. Norval, '"Writing"', 813.
41. Zerilli contrasts Arendt's thought to relativism in chapter 6 of *DTJ*.
42. Arendt, 'Truth and Politics', in *Between Past and Future*, 241–242. Hereafter cited as TP.
43. Arendt, 'Crisis in Culture', in *Between Past and Present*, 220. Hereafter cited as 'Crisis'.
44. Here, note both continuity and divergence from her Platonic account of rational thinking as a 'soundless dialogue we carry on with ourselves'

(Arendt, *LMT*, 6). In rational thinking, one's goal is to be consistent with oneself, to determine something like a categorical imperative to guide understanding. When judging, we seek agreement not with ourselves, but with our communities.
45. Habermas, 'Concluding Comments on Empirical Approaches to Deliberative Politics', 384.
46. Whereas Rawls proposes barring or seriously discouraging 'comprehensive doctrines' from the discourse of the 'political public sphere', Arendt suggests treating them as opinions, rather than truths, and thus inviting them into the talk that constitutes public life while also subjecting them to judgement. Insofar as we are considering political life, she writes, we must allow for conflicting opinions; the claims treated as 'truth' by religious or philosophical doctrine must be treated as 'opinion' in public life.
47. Habermas, 'Hannah Arendt's Communications Concept of Power', 23.
48. Habermas, 'Concluding Remarks', 477.
49. Arendt remarks: 'nothing, indeed, is more common, even among highly sophisticated people, than the blind obstinacy that becomes manifest in lack of imagination and failure to judge. But the very quality of an opinion, as of a judgment, depends upon the degree of its impartiality' (TP, 242). In other words, people may have a low-quality opinion or judgement because they lack or withhold imagination.
50. As Zerilli shows, misreadings of Arendt result from failing to track her distinction between moral and political judgement.
51. Arendt, 'Introduction *Into* Politics', 101.
52. Arendt, *Eichmann in Jerusalem*, 295.
53. May, 'Theresa May's Conference Speech in Full'.
54. See Benhabib, *Exile, Migration, and Statelessness*; and Stonebridge, *Writing and Righting*, and *Placeless People*.
55. See the conclusion of Zerilli's *DTJ*.
56. This phrase is similar in narrative function to 'once upon a time', and it is found in the Quran, where, Vijay Mishra remarks, 'its appearance has sparked a theological debate'. Mishra, 'Rushdie-Wushdie', 400.
57. Rushdie, 'In Good Faith', 4.
58. Rushdie, 'Is Nothing Sacred?'
59. Ibid.
60. Talal Asad's 'Ethnography, Literature, and Politics' remains an important critique of the 'liberal' adoption of the book as a flag for free speech. See also Brennan, *Wars of Position*, particularly 76–80, for a detailed account of the reception history of *The Satanic Verses* that tracks parallels between the 'illiberal' response to the novel among those offended by its portrayal of the Prophet and the anti-Islamic uses that 'Western' states made of the 'Rushdie affair'.
61. See Allan, *In the Shadow of World Literature*.
62. Modood, 'Muslims, Race and Equality in Britain', 129.
63. As Asad points out, secular and liberal England had, at the time, a law outlawing blasphemous representations of Jesus Christ, a law used against

a satirical gay publication less than a decade before the controversies surrounding *The Satanic Verses*. In other words, one of the central demands of the protestors was effectively liberal: they wanted their faith to receive equal consideration under the anti-blasphemy law. See Dawson, *Mongrel Nation*, 124.
64. Bhabha, 'Introduction', in *Nation and Narration*, 7. See note 2 above for discussion of the critiques of magical realism.
65. Arendt, 'Understanding and Politics (The Difficulties of Understanding)', in *Essays in Understanding*, 325, n7.
66. Ibid., 319.
67. Arendt, 'A reply to Eric Voegelin', in *Essays in Understanding*, 407.

## Chapter 5

1. As Wendy H. K. Chun has pointed out in *Control and Freedom*, much net-utopianism implicitly invoked narratives of racial passing, privatising civil rights by making the latter available to Internet consumers whose race is allegedly invisible.
2. In the paper that provided an early definition of Web 2.0, computer scientists emphasise what they call the 'democratic nature' of the 'technological aids [. . .] to maximize the potential for content creation'. Cormode and Krishnamurthy, 'Key Differences Between Web 1.0 and Web 2.0'.
3. See Graber, 'Web3 is Self-Certifying'.
4. Graber, 'Announcing Bluesky PBLCC'.
5. Tufekci, for instance, has criticised a tendency of the news media (especially in the early years of social media) to refer to 'snapshots' of social media, such as specific tweets or Facebook updates, because 'social media is not a snapshot that can be understood in one moment, or through back-scrolling. It's a lively conversation, a community, an interaction with implicit and explicit conversations and channels of signaling, communication and impression'. Tufekci, 'Social Media Is a Conversation, Not a Press Release'.
6. See Tufekci, 'Capabilities of Movements and Affordances of Digital Media: Paradoxes of Empowerment'.
7. For analysis of the role of digital media in recent political movements such as Black Lives Matter, see Freelon, McIlwain and Clark, 'Quantifying the Power and Consequences of Social Media Protest', and Tufekci, *Twitter and Tear Gas*.
8. Some new media critics have adopted the portmanteau 'produser' to describe digital content creators; another common term is 'prosumer'. Both reference the fact that users of Web 2.0 new media are essential to the production of value on these platforms. See Bruns, *Blogs, Wikipedia, Second Life, and Beyond*, and Ritzer and Jurgenson, 'Production, Consumption, Prosumption', especially 17–20. I have elsewhere argued that the 'social' behaviour we undertake online constitutes a form of reproductive labour, and that the materialist feminist analysis of reproductive labour yields

valuable theoretical as well as political insights for critics of digital social media. See Greer, 'Wages For Facework'.
9. Focusing on memes, I bracket other forms that 'conversation' takes on digital platforms, such as interpersonal chat, wikis, discussion boards, and chatbots that facilitate what computer scientist Kris Hammond termed 'conversation as an interface' between consumers and companies. See Hammond, 'Conversation as Interface'.
10. Readings of *There But For The* have tended to focus on its critiques of middle-class complacency in an unequal world. See Bennett, 'This Ridiculous Thing That Passes for a Passport', and Davies, 'The Complexities of Dwelling in Ali Smith's *There but for the*'.
11. McLuhan argues that private reading and thinking not only loosened our ancestors' reliance on mediating authorities, but also rewired their brains and transformed society, partly through strengthening individualism. In his arguments about links between reading and cognition, Carr draws heavily from the education and neuroscience researcher Maryann Wolf.
12. For sharp criticism of the novel's caricaturing of unlikeable representatives of the British middle and upper class, see Tait, 'The Absolute End'. I offer a defence of Smith's use of caricature in '"Going to Collage"'.
13. Goriunova, 'The Force of Digital Aesthetics', 55.
14. Milner, *World Made Meme*, 2.
15. Dawkins, *The Selfish Gene*, 192.
16. Ibid.
17. See Milner's introduction for an account of the term's trajectory from Dawkins's work to contemporary popular media.
18. Shifman, *Memes in Digital Culture*, 41.
19. Phillips, *This is Why We Can't Have Nice Things*, 22.
20. Ibid.
21. Ibid., 62.
22. Milner, *World Made Meme*, 5.
23. Milo in this sense resembles a celebrity, whose public persona is also a quasi-fictional social creation. But, as Goriunova writes, a celebrity is more like an icon, which 'bears a constant relation to its subject and has some shared quality with it that it comes to represent, whereas a meme stands in a significantly weaker position in relation to such tight symbolism' ('The Force of Digital Aesthetics', 57).
24. See Ko, 'How Pepe the Frog Became Face of Hong Kong Protests – Despite Cartoon Being a Symbol of Hate in US'.
25. When new media scholars have drawn on Wittgenstein's account of language-in-use to discuss memes, they have typically done so in a cursory manner, as a preface to empirical study. See, for instance, Tuters and Hagen, '(((They))) Rule', and Denisova, *Internet Memes and Society*. See also Grundlingh, 'Memes as Speech Acts'.
26. Notice that in the famous passage about 'meaning', Wittgenstein does not define the word 'meaning' but instead demonstrates the practice he advocates, describing our uses of the word. This description alludes to the

significance of shared criteria; a word, bearing no aura of its own, does not mean whatever it is used to mean unless fellow speakers of the language agree.
27. For discussions of this dynamic in right-wing online discourse, see Tuters, 'LARPing', Tuters and Hagen, '(((They))) Rule', and Weatherby, 'Irony and Redundancy'.
28. For discussion of competing interpretations of Wittgenstein's work's conservatism, see Zerilli, *DTJ*, chapter 8.
29. Arendt, 'Reflections on Little Rock', 51; *HC*, 58.
30. Arendt partly blamed labour unions (and Marxism) for politicising the private (in her view) activity of labour. I disagree with her equation of labour with privacy and class solidarity with 'social' logic, as well as her insistence that we distinguish politics, as a realm of freedom, from economics, the realm of material necessity. My previous chapter sought to show that Arendt's model of political judgement can transcend the categories she established; here, I similarly maintain that we can undertake the mode of thinking she described as political in relation to material necessity.
31. Slater, 'Chatbots', 182.
32. Zuboff, *The Age of Surveillance Capitalism*.
33. See Dean, 'Big Data', and 'Communicative Capitalism and Revolutionary Form'; Zuboff, *Surveillance Capitalism*; Srnicek, *Platform Capitalism*; Fuchs and Dyer-Witheford, 'Karl Marx @ Internet Studies'; Andrejevic, *iSpy*, and 'Critical Media Studies 2.0'; and Crawford and Joler, 'Anatomy of an AI System'.
34. Dean, 'Communicative Capitalism and Revolutionary Form', 331–332.
35. See Marx, *Capital*, VIII. There is debate among critics as to whether the new media economy should be understood as a 'mutation' of capitalism demanding a departure from Marxist theory, or whether the work of Marx and Engels remains the best framework for analysis. For an account of this debate, see Kivotidis, 'Break or Continuity?'
36. Nguyen, 'How Twitter Gamifies Communication'.
37. Social media sociologist Brady Robards calls this 'neo-tribalism', borrowing the term from Michel Maffesoli. Robards, 'Belonging and Neo-Tribalism on Social Media Site Reddit', in *Neo-Tribes*, eds Anne Hardy, Andy Bennett and Brady Robards. See also Bucher and Helmond, 'The Affordances of Social Media Platforms', in *The SAGE Handbook of Social Media*, eds Jean Burgess, Alice Marwick and Thomas Poell. These ideas are empirically supported by cognitive and data scientists, who argue that 'gamification' exploits a process known as 'reinforcement learning'. They find correlation between intensifying tribalistic behaviours, such as the expression of moral outrage or demonising political enemies, and gamification in platform design. As the authors of one study note, 'outrage-provoking content draws high engagement'. Brady et al., 'How Social Learning Amplifies Moral Outrage Expression in Online Social Networks', 9. See also Lindström et al., 'A Computational Reward Learning Account of Social Media Engagement', and Rathje, Van Bavel and van der Linden, 'Out-Group Animosity Drives Engagement on Social Media'.

38. Pariser, in *The Filter Bubble*, coined 'filter bubble' to describe an effect of Google's individually tailored search results. This effect is surely intensified on social media platforms whose algorithms personalise feeds.
39. It is common among scholars of Smith's work to link her formal experiments to ideas about reading and interpretation. Whereas other critics tend to elaborate an ethics of reading in Smith's demands on the reader, I focus less on the reader's experience than on the modes of interpretation staged in the novel. See Currie, 'Ali Smith and the Philosophy of Grammar', in *Ali Smith: Contemporary Critical Perspectives*, eds Monica Germanà and Emily Horton, and McNeill, 'Ali Smith and the Art of the Epigraph'.
40. The sequence under consideration thus evokes one of Cavell's recurrent characterisations of philosophy as the 'education of grown-ups' (*CR*, 125). Cavell suggests that the activity of philosophical enquiry is a continuous re-discovery of *oneself* as a child, as we rediscover and reformulate our ordinary attunements. Philosophy becomes a matter of learning to think in one's own position from the standpoint of a child, with the curiosity, openness and senses of possibility and imagination that entails. As the Cavellian philosopher of education Viktor Johansson writes, 'philosophy needs to turn to children, to think with children, like children, in encounters with children', because children's questions and imaginative play can reorient our perceptions of ordinary life (Johansson, 'Unserious but Serious Pilgrimages', 323). The closing exchange of stories and conversation between Brooke and Miles puts the idea of the 'education of grown-ups' in both literal and figurative terms: by talking and exchanging imaginative works with a child, who in turn urges him to imaginatively converse with the child version of himself, Miles sees his life and the grounds he occupies from a new standpoint.
41. See also Campos, 'Ali Smith's Parasitic Poetics'.

## Afterword

1. Arnold, *Culture and Anarchy*, 6. Histories of literary studies such as Eagleton's *Literary Theory: An Introduction* and Graff's *Professing Literature* name Arnold as a key influence in the formal development of the discipline.
2. Kramnick and Nersessian, 'Form and Explanation', 650.
3. Standish, 'Rigour and Recoil', 624.
4. *The Claim of Reason* does not yet develop this idea in terms of perfectionism, but Cavell's way of describing the relation between literature and philosophy, and the terms of acknowledgement required in such a relation, anticipates many themes he later develops under the rubric of perfectionism.
5. See Clune's *A Defense of Judgment*, which draws a firm distinction between Rancière's claims regarding the egalitarian freedom of aesthetic forms and Clune's view that judgement founded on unequal expertise is necessary in order to distinguish aesthetic objects that promise freedom from the marketplace.

6. Champions of literary autonomy typically ascribe worldly purposes to autonomy, sometimes quite minimally, as in the closing words of Nicholas Brown's *Autonomy*: 'Art opposes capitalism, but it is powerless. Meanings compel through freedom: there is no line that leads from this to that. The power of an argument is of an entirely different order from the power of a union. But you can't have a union without an argument' (182).

# *Bibliography*

Allan, Michael. *In the Shadow of World Literature: Sites of Reading in Colonial Egypt*. Princeton, NJ: Princeton University Press, 2016.
Allen, Danielle. *Talking to Strangers: Anxieties of Citizenship Since Brown v. Board of Education*. Chicago: University of Chicago Press, 2004.
Alsop, Elizabeth. *Making Conversation in Modernist Fiction*. Columbus: Ohio State University Press, 2019.
Altieri, Charles. *Reckoning With the Imagination: Wittgenstein and the Aesthetics of Literary Experience*. Ithaca, NY: Cornell University Press, 2015.
Anderson, Amanda. *Bleak Liberalism*. Chicago: University of Chicago Press, 2016.
Anderson, Benedict. *Imagined Communities*. New York: Verso, 1983.
Andrejevic, Mark. 'Critical Media Studies 2.0'. *Interactions: Studies in Communication & Culture* 1, no. 1 (2009): 35–51.
Andrejevic, Mark. *iSpy: Surveillance and Power in the Interactive Era*. Lawrence: University Press of Kansas, 2007.
Aravamudan, Srinivas. 'In the Wake of the Novel: The Oriental Tale as National Allegory'. *Novel: A Forum on Fiction* 33, no. 1 (1999): 5–31.
Arendt, Hannah. 'A Reply to Eric Voegelin'. In *Essays in Understanding, 1930–1954: Formation, Exile, and Totalitarianism*. Edited by Jerome Kohn, 401–408. New York: Harcourt Brace, 1994.
——. *Between Past and Future: Eight Exercises in Political Thought*. New York: Viking Press, 1968.
——. *Eichmann in Jerusalem*. Rev. ed. New York: Penguin, 2006.
——. 'Introduction *Into* Politics'. In *The Promise of Politics*. Edited by Jerome Kohn, 93–200. New York: Schocken, 2005.
——. *Lectures on Kant's Political Philosophy*. Chicago: University of Chicago Press, 1989.
——. 'Reflections on Little Rock'. *Dissent* 6, no. 1 (1959): 45–56.
——. *The Human Condition*. Chicago: University of Chicago Press, 1958.
——. *The Life of the Mind*, vol. 1, *Thinking*. New York: Harcourt, 1978.
——. 'Understanding and Politics (The Difficulties of Understanding)'. In *Essays in Understanding*, 307–327.

Arendt, Hannah, interview by Günter Gaus. *Zur Person: Hannah Arendt*. Zweites Deutsches Fernsehen. 26 October 1964. https://www.youtube.com/watch?v=dsoImQfVsO4

Armstrong, Isobel. *Novel Politics: Democratic Imaginations in Nineteenth-Century Fiction*. Oxford, UK: Oxford University Press, 2016.

Armstrong, Nancy. *How Novels Think: The Limits of British Individualism from 1719–1900*. New York: Columbia University Press, 2005.

Arnold, Matthew. *Culture and Anarchy*. Cambridge, UK: Cambridge University Press, 1932.

Asad, Talal. 'Ethnography, Literature, and Politics: Some Readings and Uses of Salman Rushdie's *The Satanic Verses*'. *Cultural Anthropology* 5, no. 3 (1990): 239–269.

Austen, Jane. *Emma*. London: Collins, 1965.

———. *Persuasion*. Hertfordshire: Wordsworth Editions, 1998.

———. *Pride and Prejudice*. New York: Barnes and Noble Books, 2003.

Austin, J. L. *How To Do Things With Words: The William James Lectures Delivered at Harvard University in 1955*. Oxford, UK: Clarendon Press, 1962.

Bakhtin, Mikhail. *The Dialogic Imagination: Four Essays*. Edited by Michael Holquist. Translated by Caryl Emerson and Michael Holquist. Austin: University of Texas Press, 1981.

Banfield, Ann. *The Phantom Table*. Cambridge, UK: Cambridge University Press, 2000.

Barnes, Ashley. *Love and Depth in the American Novel*. Charlottesville: University of Virginia Press, 2020.

Bartlett, Jami. *Object Lessons*. Chicago: University of Chicago Press, 2016.

Baucom, Ian. *Out of Place: Englishness, Empire, and the Locations of Identity*. Princeton, NJ: Princeton University Press, 1999.

Benhabib, Seyla. *Exile, Migration, and Statelessness: Playing Chess with History from Hannah Arendt to Isiah Berlin*. Princeton, NJ: Princeton University Press, 2018.

———. *Situating the Self: Gender, Community, and Postmodernism in Contemporary Ethics*. New York: Routledge, 1992.

Bennett, Alice. '"This Ridiculous Thing That Passes for a Passport": Seeking Asylum in Ali Smith's Fiction'. *Contemporary Women's Writing* 12, no. 3 (2018): 322–337.

Besant, Annie. *Marriage: As It Was, As it Is, and As It Should Be*. 2nd ed. London: Freethought Publishing Company, 1882.

Bhabha, Homi. 'Introduction: Narrating the Nation'. In *Nation and Narration*. Edited by Homi Bhabha, 1–7. New York: Routledge, 1990.

Brady, William J., Killian McLoughlin, Tuan N. Doan and Molly J. Crockett. 'How Social Learning Amplifies Moral Outrage Expression in Online Social Networks'. *Science Advances* 7, no. 33 (2021): eabe5641.

Brennan, Timothy. *Wars of Position: The Cultural Politics of Left and Right*. New York: Columbia University Press, 2006.

Briggs, Julia. 'The Conversation Behind the Conversation: Speaking the Unspeakable in Virginia Woolf'. *Etudes Anglaises* 58, no. 1 (2005): 6–14.

Brodie, Laura Fairchild. 'Society and the Superfluous Female: Jane Austen's Treatment of Widowhood'. *Studies in English Literature, 1500–1900* 34, no. 4 (1994): 697–718.

Brown, Nicholas. *Autonomy: The Social Ontology of Art Under Capitalism*. Durham, NC: Duke University Press, 2019.

Bruns, Axel. *Blogs, Wikipedia, Second life, and Beyond: From Production to Produsage*. New York: Peter Lang, 2008.

Bucher, Taina and Anne Helmond. 'The Affordances of Social Media Platforms'. In *The SAGE Handbook of Social Media*. Edited by Jean Burgess, Alice Marwick and Thomas Poell, 233–254. London: SAGE, 2017.

Butler, Judith. *Excitable Speech: A Politics of the Performative*. New York: Routledge, 1997.

—. *Notes Toward a Performative Theory of Assembly*. Cambridge, MA: Harvard University Press, 2015.

Calhoun, Craig, ed. *Habermas and the Public Sphere*. Cambridge, MA: The MIT Press, 1992.

Campos, Liliane. 'Ali Smith's Parasitic Poetics'. *MFS Modern Fiction Studies* 68, no. 2 (2022): 346–369.

Carr, Nicholas. *The Shallows: What the Internet is Doing to Our Brains*. New York: Norton, 2010.

Cavell, Stanley. *A Pitch of Philosophy: Autobiographical Exercises*. Cambridge, MA: Harvard University Press, 1994.

—. *Cities of Words: Pedagogical Letters on a Register of the Moral Life*. Cambridge, MA: Harvard University Press, 2005.

—. *Conditions Handsome and Unhandsome: The Constitution of Emersonian Perfectionism, The Carus Lectures, 1988*. Chicago: University of Chicago Press, 1990.

—. *Contesting Tears: The Hollywood Melodrama of the Unknown Woman*. Chicago: University of Chicago Press, 1996.

—. *In Quest of the Ordinary: Lines of Skepticism and Romanticism*. Chicago: University of Chicago Press, 1994.

—. *Must We Mean What We Say?* Cambridge, UK: Cambridge University Press, 1976.

—. *Philosophy the Day After Tomorrow*. Cambridge, MA: Harvard University Press, 2006.

—. 'Politics as Opposed to What?' *Critical Inquiry* 9, no. 1 (1982): 157–178.

—. *Pursuits of Happiness: The Hollywood Comedy of Remarriage*. Cambridge, MA: Harvard University Press, 1981.

—. *The Claim of Reason: Wittgenstein, Skepticism, Morality, and Tragedy*. New York: Oxford University Press, 1979.

Chodat, Robert. 'Experts and Encounters'. *PMLA* 135, no. 5 (2020): 989–994.

Chun, Wendy H. K. *Control and Freedom: Power and Paranoia in the Age of Fiber Optics*. Cambridge, MA: The MIT Press, 2008.

Clune, Michael W. *A Defense of Judgment*. Chicago: University of Chicago Press, 2021.

Cohen, Monica F. 'Persuading the Navy Home: Austen and Married Women's Professional Property'. *Novel: A Forum on Fiction* 29, no. 3. (1996): 346–366.

'conversation, n. 7a'. *OED Online*. December 2022. New York: Oxford University Press. www.oed.com/view/Entry/40748

'converse, v'. *OED Online*. December 2022. New York: Oxford University Press. www.oed.com/view/Entry/40763

'convert, v'. *OED Online*. December 2022. New York: Oxford University Press. www.oed.com/view/Entry/40777

Cormode, Graham and Balachander Krishnamurthy. 'Key Differences Between Web 1.0 and Web 2.0'. *First Monday* 13, no. 6 (2008). http://www.ojphi.org/ojs/index.php/fm/article/view/2125/1972

Craig, Randall. 'Promising Marriage: *The Egoist, Don Juan*, and the Problem of Language'. *ELH* 56, no. 4 (1989): 897–921.

Crary, Alice. 'A Radical Perfectionist: Revisiting Cavell in the Light of Kant'. *Journal of Aesthetic Education* 48, no. 3 (2014): 87–98.

Crawford, Kate and Vladan Joler. 'Anatomy of an AI System'. White Paper. 2018. https://cache.fluxo.info/data/4c/ab/4cab5c66a9e44e27f58dd79918f489d7ed08da09/screenshot.pdf

Culler, Jonathan. 'Philosophy and Literature: The Fortunes of the Performative'. *Poetics Today* 21, no. 3 (2000): 503–519.

Currie, Mark. 'Ali Smith and the Philosophy of Grammar'. In *Ali Smith: Contemporary Critical Perspectives*. Edited by Monica Germanà and Emily Horton, 48–60. London: Bloomsbury, 2013.

Dabashi, Pardis, ed. 'Theories & Methodologies: Cultures of Argument'. *PMLA* 135, no. 5 (2020): 946–1020.

Darby, Derrick. 'Charles Mills's Liberal Redemption Song'. *Ethics* 129, no. 2 (2019): 370–397.

Davies, Ben. 'The Complexities of Dwelling in Ali Smith's *There but for the*'. *Critique: Studies in Contemporary Fiction* 58, no. 5 (2017): 509–550.

Dawkins, Richard. *The Selfish Gene*. New York: Oxford University Press, 1976.

Dawson, Ashley. *Mongrel Nation: Diasporic Culture and the Making of Postcolonial Britain*. Ann Arbor: University of Michigan Press, 2007.

Dean, Jodi. 'Big Data: Accumulation and Enclosure'. *Theory & Event* 19, no. 3 (2016).

——. 'Communicative Capitalism and Revolutionary Form'. *Millennium: Journal of International Studies* 47, no. 3 (2019): 326–340.

Denisova, Anastasia. *Internet Memes and Society*. New York: Routledge, 2019.

Derrida, Jacques. *Limited Inc*. Translated by Samuel Weber and Jeffrey Mehlman. Evanston, IL: Northwestern University Press, 1988.

Eagleton, Terry. *Literary Theory: An Introduction*. 2nd ed. Minneapolis: University of Minnesota Press, 1996.
Faris, Wendy B. 'The Question of the Other: Cultural Critiques of Magical Realism'. *Janus Head* 5, no. 2 (2002): 101–119.
Farrelly, Colin. 'Justice in Ideal Theory: A Refutation'. *Political Studies* 55, no. 4 (2007): 844–864.
Felski, Rita. *Beyond Feminist Aesthetics: Feminist Literature and Social Change*. Cambridge, MA: Harvard University Press, 1989.
—. *The Limits of Critique*. Chicago: University of Chicago Press, 2015.
*Financial Times*. 'Outbreak of an Alien Disease'. 11 July 1981.
*Financial Times*. 'Searching for Consensus'. 11 July 1981.
Finney, Brian. 'Demonizing Discourse in Salman Rushdie's "The Satanic Verses"'. *ARIEL: A Review of International English Literature* 29, no. 3 (1998): 67–93.
Fischer, Michael. *Stanley Cavell and Literary Skepticism*. Chicago: University of Chicago Press, 1989.
Fitzpatrick, Kathleen. *Generous Thinking: A Radical Approach to Saving the University*. Baltimore, MD: Johns Hopkins University Press, 2021.
Fraser, Nancy. 'Rethinking the Public Sphere: A Contribution to the Critique of Actually Existing Democracy'. *Social Text* 25/26 (1990): 56–80.
Freelon, Deen, Charlton McIlwain and Meredith Clark. 'Quantifying the Power and Consequences of Social Media Protest'. *New Media & Society* 20, no. 3 (2018): 990–1011.
Froula, Christine. *Virginia Woolf and the Bloomsbury Avant-Garde*. New York: Columbia University Press, 2005.
Fuchs, Christian and Nick Dyer-Witheford. 'Karl Marx @ Internet Studies'. *New Media & Society* 15, no. 5 (2013): 782–796.
Gallagher, Catherine. *The Industrial Reformation of English Fiction: Social Discourse and Narrative Form, 1832–1867*. Chicago: University of Chicago Press, 1985.
Gevirtz, Karen Bloom. *Life After Death: Widows and the English Novel, Defoe to Austen*. Cranbury, NJ: Associated University Press, 2005.
Gilbert, Sandra and Susan Gubar. *Madwoman in the Attic: The Woman Writer and the Nineteenth-Century Literary Imagination*. New Haven, CT: Yale University Press, 1979.
Gill, Josie. '"Under Extreme Environmental Pressure, Characteristics Were Acquired": Epigenetics, Race and Salman Rushdie's *The Satanic Verses*'. *Textual Practice* 29, no. 3 (2015): 479–498.
Goffman, Erving. *Forms of Talk*. Philadelphia: University of Pennsylvania Press, 1981.
—. *Interaction Ritual*. New Brunswick, NJ: Transaction Publishers, 2005.
Goodlad, Lauren. *The Victorian Geopolitical Aesthetic: Realism, Sovereignty, and Transnational Experience*. Oxford, UK: Oxford University Press, 2015.

Goriunova, Olga. 'The Force of Digital Aesthetics. On Memes, Hacking, and Individuation'. *The Nordic Journal of Aesthetics*, no. 47 (2014): 54–75.

Graber, Jay. 'Announcing Bluesky PBLCC'. *The Latest from Bluesky* (blog). 7 February 2022. https://blueskyweb.org/blog/2-7-2022-overview

——. 'Web3 is Self-Certifying'. *Medium* (blog). 23 December 2021. https://jaygraber.medium.com/web3-is-self-certifying-9dad77fd8d81

Graff, Gerald. *Professing Literature: An Institutional History*. Chicago: University of Chicago Press, 1987.

Gray, Erik. 'Metaphors and Marriage Plots'. *Partial Answers: Journal of Literature and the History of Ideas* 12, no. 2 (2014): 267–286.

Greer, Erin. '"Going to Collage": Ali Smith's *Autumn* and Post-Liberal Democratic Imagination'. *C21: Journal of 21st Century Writings* (forthcoming).

——. 'Wages For Facework: Black Mirror's "Nosedive" and Digital Reproductive Labor'. *Camera Obscura* 35, no. 3 (2020): 87–115.

Gross, Gloria Sybil. 'Flights into Illness: Some Characters in Jane Austen'. In *Literature and Medicine during the Eighteenth Century*. Edited by Marie Mulvey Roberts and Roy Porter, 188–199. London: Routledge, 1993.

Grundlingh, L. 'Memes as Speech Acts'. *Social Semiotics* 28, no. 2 (2018): 147–168.

Guyer, Paul. 'Examples of Perfectionism'. *Journal of Aesthetic Education* 48, no. 3 (2014): 5–27.

Habermas, Jürgen. 'Concluding Comments on Empirical Approaches to Deliberative Politics'. *Acta Politica* 40, no. 3 (2005): 384–392.

——. 'Concluding Remarks'. In Calhoun, *Habermas and the Public Sphere*, 462–479.

——. 'Hannah Arendt's Communications Concept of Power'. Translated by Thomas McCarthy. *Social Research* 44, no. 1 (1977): 3–24.

——. 'Some Further Reflections on the Public Sphere'. In Calhoun, *Habermas and the Public Sphere*, 421–461.

——. *The Structural Transformation of the Public Sphere: An Inquiry into a Category of Bourgeois Society*. Translated by Thomas Burger with Frederick Lawrence. Cambridge, MA: The MIT Press, 1991.

Hadley, Elaine. *Liberal Cognition: Practical Citizenship in Mid-Victorian Britain*. Chicago: University of Chicago Press. 2010.

Hagberg, Garry L. *Meaning and Interpretation: Wittgenstein, Henry James, and Literary Knowledge*. Ithaca, NY: Cornell University Press, 2018.

Hall, Stuart. 'From Scarman to Stephen Lawrence'. *History Workshop Journal* 48 (1999): 187–197.

——. 'New ethnicities'. In *Stuart Hall: Critical Dialogues in Cultural Studies*. Edited by David Morley and Kuan-Hsing Chen, 442–451. London: Routledge, 1996.

Hall, Stuart, Chas Critcher, Tony Jefferson, John Clarke and Brian Roberts. *Policing the Crisis: Mugging, the State and Law and Order*. 2nd ed. Basingstroke, UK: Palgrave Macmillan, 2013.

Hamlin, Alan and Zofia Stemplowska. 'Theory, Ideal Theory and the Theory of Ideals'. *Political Studies Review* 10, no. 1 (2012): 48–62.

Hammerton, A. James. 'Victorian Marriage and the Law of Matrimonial Cruelty'. *Victorian Studies* 33, no. 2 (1990): 269–292.

Hammond, Kris. 'Conversation as Interface: The 5 Types of Chatbots'. *Computerworld*. 13 July 2016. https://www.computerworld.com/article/3094300/emerging-technology/conversation-as-interface-the-5-types-of-chatbots.html

Hansen, Miriam. 'Unstable Mixtures, Dilated Spheres: Negt and Kluge's *The Public Sphere and Experience*, Twenty Years Later'. *Public Culture* 5, no. 2 (1993): 179–212.

Hatfield, Charles. *The Limits of Identity: Politics and Poetics in Latin America*. Austin: University of Texas Press, 2015.

Hegerfeldt, Anne C. *Lies That Tell the Truth: Magic Realism Seen Through Contemporary Fiction from Britain*. New York: Rodopi, 2005.

Ho, Janice. *Nation and Citizenship in the Twentieth-Century British Novel*. New York: Cambridge University Press, 2015.

Hughey, Matthew W. 'Four Thoughts on Charles Mills – *Black Rights/ White Wrongs: The Critique of Racial Liberalism*'. *Ethnic and Racial Studies* 41, no. 3 (2018): 523–531.

Jameson, Frederic. *The Political Unconscious: Narrative as a Socially Symbolic Act*. London: Routledge, 1983.

Johansson, Viktor. 'Unserious but Serious Pilgrimages: What Educational Philosophy Can Learn about Fiction and Reality from Children's Artful Play'. *Educational Theory* 67, no. 3 (2017): 309–326.

Jones, Susan E. 'Thread-cases, Pin-cushions, and Card-racks: Women's Work in the City in Jane Austen's Persuasion'. *Persuasions On-line* 25, no.1 (Winter 2004). http://www.jasna.org/persuasions/on-line/vol25no1/jones.html

Jones, Wendy S. *Consensual Fictions: Women, Liberalism, and the English Novel*. Toronto: University of Toronto Press, 2005.

Kalliney, Peter J. *Cities of Affluence and Anger: A Literary Geography of Modern Englishness*. Charlottesville: University of Virginia Press, 2007.

——. 'Globalization, Postcoloniality, and the Problem of Literary Studies in *The Satanic Verses*'. *MFS Modern Fiction Studies* 48, no. 1 (2002): 50–82.

Kant, Immanuel. *Critique of Pure Reason*. Translated by P. Guyer and A. Wood. New York: Cambridge University Press, 1998.

——. *The Critique of Judgment*. Translated by J. H. Bernard. New York: Free Press, 1951.

Keen, Suzanne. *Empathy and the Novel*. New York: Oxford University Press, 2007.

Kivotidis, Dimitrios. 'Break or Continuity? Friedrich Engels and the Critique of Digital Surveillance'. *tripleC: Communication, Capitalism & Critique. Open Access Journal for a Global Sustainable Information Society* 19, no. 1 (2021): 97–112.

Knapp, Steven and Walter Benn Michaels. 'Against Theory'. *Critical Inquiry* 8, no. 4 (1982): 723–742.
Knox-Shaw, Peter. *Jane Austen and the Enlightenment*. New York: Cambridge University Press, 2004.
Ko, Christina. 'How Pepe the Frog Became Face of Hong Kong Protests – Despite Cartoon Being a Symbol of Hate in US'. *South China Morning Post*. 17 August 2019. https://www.scmp.com/lifestyle/arts-culture/article/3023060/how-pepe-frog-became-face-hong-kong-protests-despite-cartoon
Kornbluh, Anna. *The Order of Forms: Realism, Formalism, and Social Space*. Chicago: University of Chicago Press, 2019.
Kramnick, Jonathan and Anahid Nersessian. 'Form and Explanation'. *Critical Inquiry* 43, no. 3 (2017): 650–669.
Kurnick, David. 'A Few Lies'. *ELH* 87, no. 2 (Summer 2020): 349–374.
Laugier, Sandra. 'Rethinking the Ordinary: Austin *after* Cavell'. In *Contending with Stanley Cavell*. Edited by Russell B. Goodman. New York: Oxford University Press, 2005.
——. 'The Ethics of Care as a Politics of the Ordinary'. *New Literary History* 46, no. 2 (2015): 217–240.
Lesjak, Carolyn. *The Afterlife of Enclosure*. Palo Alto, CA: Stanford University Press, 2021.
Lindström, Björn, Martin Bellander, David T. Schultner, Allen Chang, Philippe N. Tobler and David M. Amodio. 'A Computational Reward Learning Account of Social Media Engagement'. *Nature Communications* 12, no. 1 (2021): 1–10.
Lindstrom, Eric Reid. *Jane Austen and Other Minds*: Ordinary Language Philosophy in Literary Fiction. New York: Cambridge University Press, 2022.
Lorenzini, Daniele. 'From Recognition to Acknowledgement: Rethinking the Perlocutionary'. *Inquiry* (2020): 1–20. https://www.tandfonline.com/doi/abs/10.1080/0020174X.2020.1712231
Love, Heather. 'Close But Not Deep: Literary Ethics and the Descriptive Turn'. *New Literary History* 41, no. 2 (2010): 371–391.
——. 'Close Reading and Thin Description'. *Public Culture* 25, no. 3 (2013): 401–434.
Lucey, Michael. *Someone: The Pragmatics of Misfit Sexualities, from Colette to Hervé Guibert*. Chicago: University of Chicago Press, 2019.
Lucey, Michael, Tom McEnaney and Tristram Wolff, eds. 'Language-in-use and the Literary Artifact'. *Representations* 137 (2017).
Lynch, Deidre. *The Economy of Character: Novels, Market Culture, and the Business of Inner Meaning*. Chicago: University of Chicago Press, 1998.
McCormick, Samuel. *The Chattering Mind: A Conceptual History of Everyday Talk*. Chicago: University of Chicago Press, 2020.
McGee, Patrick. 'The Politics of Modernist Form; or, Who Rules The Waves?' *MFS Modern Fiction Studies* 38, no. 3 (Fall 1992): 631–650.

McNeill, Dougal. 'Ali Smith and the Art of the Epigraph'. *Critique: Studies in Contemporary Fiction* 60, no. 3 (2019): 357–367.
Marcus, Jane. 'Britannia Rules The Waves'. In *Decolonizing Tradition: New Views of Twentieth-Century 'British' Literary Canons*. Edited by Karen Lawrence, 136–162. Urbana: University of Illinois Press, 1992.
Marx, Karl. *Capital: Volume I*. Translated by Ben Fowkes. London: Penguin, 2004.
May, Theresa. 'Theresa May's Conference Speech in Full'. *The Telegraph*. 5 October 2016.
Mee, Jon. *Conversable Worlds: Literature, Contention, and Community 1762 to 1830*. New York: Oxford University Press, 2011.
Meredith, George. *The Egoist*. New York: Penguin Books, 1968.
Miller, Andrew H. 'Implicative Criticism, or The Display of Thinking'. *New Literary History* 44, no. 3 (2013): 345–360.
——. *The Burdens of Perfection: On Ethics and Reading in Nineteenth-Century British Literature*. Ithaca, NY: Cornell University Press, 2011.
Mills, Charles Wade. *Black Rights, White Wrongs: The Critique of Racial Capitalism*. New York: Oxford University Press, 2017.
——. 'Retrieving Rawls for Racial Justice? A Critique of Tommie Shelby'. *Critical Philosophy of Race* 1, no. 1 (2013): 1–27.
Milner, Ryan. *The World Made Meme: Public Conversations and Participatory Media*. Cambridge, MA: The MIT Press, 2016.
Milton, John. *The Doctrine and Discipline of Divorce and the Judgement of Martin Bucer; Tetrachordon; & An Abridgment of Colasterion*. London: Sherwood, Neely, and Jones, 1820.
Mishra, Vijay. 'Rushdie-Wushdie: Salman Rushdie's Hobson-Jobson'. *New Literary History* 40, no. 2 (2009): 385–410.
Modood, Tariq. 'Muslims, Race And Equality In Britain: Some Post-Rushdie Affair Reflections'. *Third Text* 4, no. 11 (1990): 127–134.
Moi, Toril. *Revolution of the Ordinary*. Chicago: University of Chicago Press, 2017.
Moreillas, Alberto. *The Exhaustion of Difference: The Politics of Latin American Cultural Studies*. Durham, NC: Duke University Press, 2001.
Moses, Michael Valdez. 'Magical Realism at World's End'. *Literary Imagination: The Review of the Association of Literary Scholars and Critics* 3, no. 1 (2001): 105–133.
Mouffe, Chantal. 'Which Public Sphere for a Democratic Society?' *Theoria: A Journal of Social and Political Theory* 99 (2002): 55–65.
Mouffe, Chantal and Ernesto Laclau. *Hegemony and Socialist Strategy: Towards a Radical Politics*. London: Verso, 2001.
Mulhall, Stephen. 'Inner Constancy, Outer Variation: Stanley Cavell on Grammar, Criteria, Rules'. In *Varieties of Skepticism: Essays after Kant, Wittgenstein, and Cavell*. Edited by James Conant and Andrea Kern, 291–310. Berlin: De Gruyter, 2014.

——. 'On Refusing to Begin'. In *Contending with Stanley Cavell*. Edited by Russell B. Goodman, 22–36. New York: Oxford University Press, 2005.

Negt, Oscar and Alexander Kluge. *The Public Sphere and Experience: Toward an Analysis of the Bourgeois and Proletarian Public Sphere*. Translated by Peter Labanyi, Jamie Daniel and Assenka Oksiloff. Minneapolis: University of Minnesota Press, 1993.

Ngai, Sianne. *Theory of the Gimmick*. Cambridge, MA: Harvard University Press, 2020.

Nguyen, C. Thi. 'How Twitter Gamifies Communication'. In *Applied Epistemology*. Edited by Jennifer Lackey, 410–436. Oxford, UK: Oxford University Press, 2021.

Norris, Andrew. *Becoming Who We Are: Politics and Practical Philosophy in the Work of Stanley Cavell*. Oxford, UK: Oxford University Press, 2017.

Norval, Aletta J. *Aversive Democracy: Inheritance and Originality in the Democratic Tradition*. Cambridge, UK: Cambridge University Press, 2007.

——. '"Writing a Name in the Sky": Rancière, Cavell, and the Possibility of Egalitarian Inscription'. *American Political Science Review* 106, no. 4 (2012): 810–826.

Nussbaum, Martha. *Not For Profit: Why Democracy Needs the Humanities*. Princeton, NJ: Princeton University Press, 2010.

——. *Poetic Justice: The Literary Imagination and Public Life*. New York: Beacon Press, 1995.

——. 'The Window: Knowledge of Other Minds in Virginia Woolf's *To the Lighthouse*'. *New Literary History* 26, no. 4 (1995): 731–753.

Oakeshott, Michael. *The Voice of Poetry in the Conversation of Mankind: An Essay*. London: Bowes & Bowes, 1959.

Oliphant, Margaret. [Review of *The Egoist*], *Blackwood's Edinburgh Magazine* 128 (September 1880). In *George Meredith: The Critical Heritage*. Edited by Ioan Williams, 237–238. London: Routledge and Kegan Paul, 1971.

Ong, Yi-Ping. *The Art of Being: Poetics of the Novel and Existentialists Philosophy*. Cambridge, MA: Harvard University Press, 2018.

O'Toole, Sean. 'Meredithian Slips: Embodied Dispositions and Narrative Form in The Egoist'. *Victorian Literature and Culture* 39, no. 2 (2011): 499–524.

Paige, Nicholas. *Technologies of the Novel: Quantitative Data and the Evolution of Literary Systems*. New York: Cambridge University Press, 2020.

Pariser, Eli. *The Filter Bubble: How the New Personalized Web Is Changing What We Read and How We Think*. New York: Penguin, 2011.

Phillips, Whitney. *This Is Why We Can't Have Nice Things: Mapping the Relationship Between Online Trolling and Mainstream Culture*. Cambridge, MA: The MIT Press, 2015.

Pinch, Adela. 'Lost in a Book: Jane Austen's *Persuasion*'. *Studies in Romanticism* 32, no. 1 (1993): 97–117.

Plotz, John. *The Crowd: British Literature and Public Politics*. Berkeley: University of California Press, 2000.
Puckett, Kent. *Bad Form: Social Mistakes and the Nineteenth-Century Novel*. New York: Oxford University Press, 2008.
Purifoy, Christie. 'Melancholic Patriotism and *The Waves*'. *Twentieth Century Literature* 56, no. 1 (2010): 25–46.
Quigley, Megan. 'Modern Novels and Vagueness'. *Modernism/modernity* 15, no. 1 (2008): 101–129.
Rancière, Jacques. *Disagreement*. Translated by Julie Rose. Minneapolis: University of Minnesota Press, 1999.
———. *Dissensus: On Politics and Aesthetics*. Edited and translated by Steven Corcoran. New York: Continuum 2010.
Rathje, Steve, Jay J. Van Bavel and Sander van der Linden. 'Out-Group Animosity Drives Engagement On Social Media'. *Proceedings of the National Academy of Sciences* 118, no. 26 (2021): e2024292118.
Rawls, John. *A Theory of Justice*. Rev. ed. Cambridge, MA: Harvard University Press, 1999.
———. 'Two Concepts of Rules'. *The Philosophical Review* 64, no. 1 (1955): 3–32.
Remnick, David. 'Obama Reckons with a Trump Presidency'. *The New Yorker*. 28 November 2016. http://www.newyorker.com/magazine/2016/11/28/obama-reckons-with-a-trump-presidency
Ritzer, George and Nathan Jurgenson. 'Production, Consumption, Prosumption: The Nature of Capitalism in the Age of the Digital "Prosumer"'. *Journal of Consumer Culture* 10, no. 1 (2010): 13–36.
Robards, Brady. 'Belonging and Neo-Tribalism on Social Media Site Reddit'. In *Neo-Tribes: Consumption, Leisure and Tourism*. Edited by Anne Hardy, Andy Bennett and Brady Robards, 187–206. Cham: Palgrave Macmillan, 2018.
Rogers, Hannah Lee. 'Philosophy in Austen's Pump Room: How Enlightened Tolerance Became Disgust'. *Eighteenth Century Fiction* 32, no. 2 (Winter 2019–2020): 317–340.
Rombes, Jr., Nicholas D. '*The Satanic Verses* as a Cinematic Narrative'. *Literature/Film Quarterly* 21, no. 1 (1993): 47–53.
Rorty, Richard. *Philosophy and the Mirror of Nature*. 30th anniversary ed. Princeton, NJ: Princeton University Press, 2009.
Rudrum, David. *Stanley Cavell and the Claim of Literature*. Baltimore, MD: Johns Hopkins University Press, 2013.
Rushdie, Salman. 'In Good Faith'. *Imaginary Homelands: Essays and Criticism 1981–1991*. London: Granta, 1991.
———. 'Is Nothing Sacred?' *The Herbert Read Memorial Lecture*. *Granta* 31 (1990). https://granta.com/is-nothing-sacred/
———. *The Satanic Verses*. New York: Random House, 2008.
Russell, Bertrand. *An Outline of Philosophy*. London: Taylor and Francis, 2009.

——. *Our Knowledge of the External World: As a Field for Scientific Method in Philosophy*. London: Routledge, 2009.
——. *The Problems of Philosophy*. Oxford: Oxford University Press, 2001.
Sainsbury, R. M. and Timothy Williamson. 'Sorites'. In *A Companion to the Philosophy of Language*. Edited by Bob Hale and Crispin Wright, 734–764. Oxford: Blackwell, 2001.
Schrödinger, Erwin. 'The Present Situation in Quantum Mechanics: A Translation of Schrodinger's "Cat Paradox" Paper'. 1935. Translated by John D. Trimmer. *Proceedings of the American Philosophical Society* 124, no. 5 (1980): 323–338.
Schudson, Michael. 'Why Conversation is Not the Soul of Democracy'. *Critical Studies in Media Communication* 14, no. 4 (1997): 297–309.
Searle, John R. 'Reiterating the Differences: A Reply to Derrida'. *Glyph* 1, no. 2 (1977): 198–208.
Sen, Amartya. 'What Do We Want from a Theory of Justice?' *The Journal of Philosophy* 103, no. 5 (2006): 215–238.
Shanley, Mary Lyndon. '"One Must Ride Behind": Married Women's Rights and the Divorce Act of 1857'. *Victorian Studies* 25, no. 3 (1982): 355–376.
Shelby, Tommie. 'Race and Social Justice: Rawlsian Considerations'. *Fordham Law Review* 72, no. 5 (2004): 1697–1714.
——. 'Racial Realities and Corrective Justice: A Reply to Charles Mills'. *Critical Philosophy of Race* 1, no. 2 (2013): 145–162.
Shifman, Limor. *Memes in Digital Culture*. Cambridge, MA: The MIT Press, 2014.
Simmons, A. John. 'Ideal and Nonideal Theory'. *Philosophy & Public Affairs* 38, no. 1 (2010): 5–36.
Simpson, David. *The Academic Postmodern and the Rule of Literature*. Chicago: University of Chicago Press, 1995.
——. 'The Cult of "Conversation"'. *Raritan* 16, no. 4 (1997): 75–85.
Siraganian, Lisa. *Modernism and the Meaning of Corporate Persons*. New York: Oxford University Press, 2020.
Slater, Avery. 'Chatbots: Cybernetic Psychology and the Future of Conversation'. *JCMS* 61, no. 4 (Summer 2022): 181–187.
Smith, Ali. *Autumn*. London: Penguin, 2016.
——. *There But For The: A Novel*. New York: Pantheon, 2011.
Solomos, John, Bob Findlay, Simon Jones and Paul Gilroy. 'The Organic Crisis of British Capitalism and Race: The Experience of the Seventies'. In Centre for Contemporary Cultural Studies, *The Empire Strikes Back: Race and Racism in 70s Britain*, 7–44. London: Hutchinson, 1982.
Srnicek, Nick. *Platform Capitalism*. Cambridge, UK: Polity, 2017.
Standish, Paul. 'Rigour and Recoil: Claims of Reason, Failures of Expression'. *Journal of Philosophy of Education* 52, no. 4 (2018): 609–626.
Standish, Paul and Naiko Sato, eds. *Stanley Cavell and the Education of Grownups*. New York: Fordham University Press, 2012.

Stegman, Charles E. 'The Problem of Numeracy: Mount Everest Shrinks'. Letter to the Editor, *The American Statistician* 36, no. 1 (February 1982): 64–67.

Stonebridge, Lindsey. *Placeless People: Writings, Rights, and Refugees*. New York: Oxford, 2018.

———. *Writing and Righting: Literature in the Age of Human Rights*. New York: Oxford, 2020.

Stout, Daniel M. *Corporate Romanticism: Liberalism, Justice, and the Novel*. New York: Fordham University Press, 2016.

Tait, Theo 'The Absolute End'. *The London Review of Books* 34, no. 2 (2012). https://www.lrb.co.uk/the-paper/v34/n02/theo-tait/the-absolute-end

Taussig, Michael. *Shamanism, Colonialism, and the Wild Man: A Study in Terror and Healing*. Chicago: University of Chicago Press, 1987.

Taylor, Charles. *A Secular Age*. Cambridge, MA: Harvard University Press, 2007.

Terada, Rei. *Looking Away: Phenomenality and Dissatisfaction, Kant to Adorno*. Cambridge, MA: Harvard University Press, 2009.

Toner, Anne. *Ellipsis in English Literature*. Cambridge, UK: Cambridge University Press, 2015.

Tonn, Mari Boor. 'Taking Conversation, Dialogue, and Therapy Public'. *Rhetoric & Public Affairs* 8, no. 3 (2005): 405–430.

Trilling, Lionel. *The Liberal Imagination: Essays on Literature and Society*. New York: Scribner, 1950.

Tufekci, Zeynep. 'Capabilities of Movements and Affordances of Digital Media: Paradoxes of Empowerment'. *Connected Learning Alliance* (blog). 9 January 2014. https://clalliance.org/blog/capabilities-of-movements-and-affordances-of-digital-media-paradoxes-of-empowerment/

———. 'Social Media Is a Conversation, Not a Press Release'. *Medium* (blog). 13 January 2014. https://medium.com/technology-and-society/social-media-is-a-conversation-not-a-press-release-4d811b45840d

———. *Twitter and Tear Gas: The Power and Fragility of Networked Protest*. New Haven, CT: Yale University Press, 2017.

Turkle, Sherry. *Reclaiming Conversation: The Power of Talk in a Digital Age*. New York: Penguin, 2015.

Tuters, Marc. 'LARPing & Liberal Tears: Irony, Belief and Idiocy in the Deep Vernacular Web'. In *Post-Digital Cultures of the Far Right: Online Actions and Offline Consequences in Europe and the US*. Edited by Maik Fielitz and Nick Thurston, 37–48. Bielefeld: transcript Verlag, 2019.

Tuters, Marc and Sal Hagen. '(((They))) Rule: Memetic Antagonism and Nebulous Othering on 4chan'. *New Media & Society* 22, no. 12 (2020): 2218–2237.

Valentini, Laura. 'Ideal vs. Non-Ideal Theory: A Conceptual Map'. *Philosophy Compass* 7, no. 9 (2012): 654–664.

Walker, Eric C. 'Austen and Cavell'. In *Stanley Cavell and British Romanticism*. Edited by Eric Lindstrom, *Romantic Circles Praxis Series*, ed. Orrin Wang (online), July 2014.
———. *Marriage, Writing, and Romanticism: Wordsworth and Austen After War*. Palo Alto, CA: Stanford University Press, 2009.
Walzer, M. 'A Critique of Philosophical Conversation'. *The Philosophical Forum* 21, nos 1–2 (1998–1990): 182–196.
Watt, Ian. *The Rise of the Novel*. Berkeley: University of California Press, 2001.
Weatherby, Luke. 'Irony and Redundancy: The Alt Right, Media Manipulation, and German Idealism'. *b20*. 24 June 2019. https://www.boundary2.org/2019/06/leif-weatherby-irony-and-redundancy-the-alt-right-media-manipulation-and-german-idealism/
Wheatley, Catherine. *Stanley Cavell and Film: Scepticism and Self-reliance at the Cinema*. London: Bloomsbury, 2019.
Wittgenstein, Ludwig. *The Blue and Brown Books: Preliminary Studies for the 'Philosophical Investigations'*. 2nd ed. New York: Harper Torchbooks, 1965.
———. *The Philosophical Investigations*. 3rd ed. Translated by G. E. M. Anscombe. Oxford: Basil Blackwell, 1963. Reprint of English text with index, 1986.
Wolf, Maryann. *Proust and the Squid: The Story and Science of the Reading Brain*. New York: HarperCollins, 2007.
Wong, Amy R. 'Late Victorian Novels, Bad Dialogue, and Talk'. *Narrative* 27, no. 2 (2019): 182–200.
Woolf, Virginia. *A Room of One's Own*. New York: Harvest Books, 1989.
———. *Mrs Dalloway*. New York: Harvest Books, 1990.
———. *Selected Essays of Virginia Woolf*. Edited by David Bradshaw. New York: Oxford University Press, 2009.
———. *The Diary of Virginia Woolf*. Edited by Anne Olivier Bell and Andrew McNeillie, vol. 3. London: Hogarth Press, 1977–1984.
———. *The Voyage Out*. New York: Barnes and Noble Classics, 2004.
———. *The Waves*. New York: Harvest Books, 1978.
———. *To the Lighthouse*. New York: Harvest Books, 1989.
———. 'Walter Sickert: A Conversation'. London: Hogarth Press, 1934. Project Gutenberg Canada, 2012. https://www.gutenberg.ca/ebooks/woolfv-waltersickert/woolfv-waltersickert-00-e.html
Wright, Daniel. *Bad Logic: Reasoning about Desire in the Victorian Novel*. Baltimore, MD: Johns Hopkins University Press, 2018.
Zerilli, Linda M. G. *A Democratic Theory of Judgment*. Chicago: University of Chicago Press, 2016.
———. '"We Feel Our Freedom": Imagination and Judgment in the Thought of Hannah Arendt'. *Political Theory* 33, no. 2 (2005): 158–188.
Zuboff, Shoshana. *The Age of Surveillance Capitalism: The Fight for a Human Future at the New Frontier of Power*. New York: Public Affairs, 2019.
Zumhagen-Yekplé, Karen. *A Different Order of Difficulty: Literature After Wittgenstein*. Chicago: University of Chicago Press, 2020.

# *Index*

acknowledgement, 16–18, 20–1, 22, 27, 32, 36–8, 42, 49–50, 63–7, 74–9, 82–3, 98, 143, 188
  reading as (Moi), 8, 27, 188
aesthetic theory, 4, 20, 23–4, 28–30, 95, 97–104, 107–18, 120, 122, 141, 143–9, 158, 164, 177–84, 186, 189–92, 204n, 205n, 213n
  as a model for political judgement, 141, 143–54, 158–61, 177–8, 182–5
agreement in criteria, 20–1, 36, 41, 61, 64, 75, 161, 164, 169–77, 181, 183–5, 187, 189–90
allegories of interpretation, 43–5, 47–51, 52–4, 59–62, 87, 89–90, 94, 180–5
Alsop, Elizabeth, 9–10, 103
Arendt, Hannah, 5–6, 8, 16, 18–21, 23–4, 119–20, 136–9, 141, 143–53, 157–61, 163–4, 173–6, 177–8, 180, 182, 184–5, 188–90, 196n, 205n, 209n, 212n
Austen, Jane, 39–41
  *Persuasion*, 13, 22, 31–3, 42–54, 57–62, 140–1, 152, 189
Austin, J. L., 2, 22, 63–4, 66, 68–72
autonomy (aesthetic), 26, 181, 214n;
  see also 'purposiveness without purpose' (Kant)

Bakhtin, Mikhail, 9–10, 155;
  see also novels (history and theory)
Banfield, Ann, 104, 108
Baucom, Ian, 132–3, 135, 141–2
blockchain, 162
Bloomsbury group, 23, 97, 104, 107, 203n, 204n, 205n
Butler, Judith, 66, 139, 141, 154, 201n

Cavell, Stanley, 2–3, 5, 7–9, 11–18, 20–3, 25–30, 31–42, 45–6, 49–62, 63–5, 70, 72–82, 84, 93, 98, 101, 108–9, 117, 137–8, 141, 143, 148–9, 171, 173, 175, 180–1, 186–91, 195n, 196n, 197n, 199–200n, 201n, 202n, 213n
class (economic), 6, 11, 22, 25, 33, 47–55, 58, 99, 125–7, 142, 165, 198–9n, 200n, 206–7n, 211n, 212n
comedies of remarriage, 12, 14, 16, 18, 25, 31–2, 34, 36–8, 41–2, 53, 63, 73
common world, 6, 18–19, 23–4, 29, 85, 97–8, 104, 106, 117–19, 136–9, 141, 146–9, 157, 163, 174–8, 182, 184–5, 189–92;
  see also public realm; public sphere; scepticism

consent, 58–62, 68–9, 84, 91, 101, 173
conventions (ordinary language philosophy), 7, 12, 16–18, 56, 60, 64–6, 67, 71–6, 78–85, 89, 91, 101, 143, 164–5, 188–9; see also normativity
conversation
 etymology of, 21, 34, 96–7, 109–10, 113, 119, 136–8, 159, 178
 idealisation of, 2–5, 15, 60–1, 189–91, 193n
 in contrast to discussion and debate, 7, 20–1, 122, 137–8, 140, 143
'conversation of justice' (Cavell), 22, 32–3, 54–62, 78, 81, 94, 137, 140, 199–200n
conversational criticism, 2–3, 8, 12–15, 25–30, 59–62, 72, 184–5, 187, 190–2, 196n; see also acknowledgement: reading as (Moi); responsiveness
conversational outlook, 7–8, 10, 12–21, 23, 25, 29, 32, 57, 60–3, 64, 97–8, 142–4, 153, 161, 189, 192
counterpublics, 23, 28, 122–9, 136, 155–6, 158, 163, 174–5, 206–7n
criteria see agreement in criteria

democracy, 1, 5–6, 12, 15, 19–22, 24–5, 29, 57–61, 119–20, 122, 125–6, 137–9, 141–4, 146, 148, 153, 157, 159–61, 162–3, 173, 177, 200n, 207n, 210n
 literature and literary criticism's relation to, 11, 53, 157, 159–61, 177, 189, 191, 195n
 see also aesthetic theory: as a model for political judgement
Derrida, Jacques, 69–70, 201n

Descartes, René, 5–6, 119, 138, 195n
digital 'conversation' see form(s) of life: online discourse and; memes; platform capitalism; social media

education see instruction
Eliot, George, 25, 37, 200n
Emerson, Ralph Waldo, 13–14, 35, 41, 56, 196n
empathy, 4, 53, 145–6, 178–9, 195n
epistemology see scepticism, epistemological
ethics, 3, 5, 11, 21, 23–4, 35–6, 70–2, 75–8, 118, 143, 204n
 in literary theory and criticism, 4, 28–30, 186–9, 213n

family resemblances, 7, 8, 17
feminism and feminist critique, 40–1, 51, 54, 65, 80–2, 98–9, 120, 125, 131, 202n, 203–4n, 206n, 210–11n; see also patriarchy
formalism, 9–10, 143, 181–3, 186
form(s) of life, 7, 17–18, 22–3, 28, 32, 36–7, 67, 75–6, 79–80, 99, 109, 171–3, 188–9
 conversation as (Cavell), 18, 32, 36–7, 39, 41, 63, 76, 137
 literary and interpretive conventions as, 28, 32, 42–5, 48–50, 54, 60–2, 93–4, 155–6, 183–4, 191, 200n, 209n
 online discourse and, 171–3, 175, 183–4
 political implications of, 54, 65, 80, 82, 84–5, 121, 137–8, 140–1, 143, 147, 152–3, 160
Fraser, Nancy, 125–7, 133, 206n
freedom of speech and expression, 4, 155–6, 209n

Goffman, Erving, 4
gossip, 46, 48, 50, 54, 67, 86–7, 89–91, 94

Habermas, Jürgen, 4, 9, 19, 124–5, 137, 147, 207n
Hall, Stuart, 133, 206n
Ho, Janice, 131–2, 156–7, 206n
hybridity, 25, 123, 132–3, 142, 155–6; see also magical realism

ideal theory (political philosophy), 55–7, 199n
illocutionary acts/utterances see performativity; promises
imagination (in judgement and interpretation), 108–12, 117–18, 145–55, 159, 164, 177–84, 191
initiation into language, 17–18, 60, 80
instruction, 13, 33–5, 37, 39–40, 45–6, 54, 59–60, 93–4, 179–82, 203n, 213n; see also initiation into language
intention, 8, 26, 69–71, 73–4, 77, 80, 83, 91–2, 99, 117, 159, 172, 197n
interdisciplinary/interdisciplinarity, 2–3, 11, 25–6, 186, 188–90, 192, 196n
Internet, 1, 5–6, 162, 164–7, 169, 170, 183, 210n; see also form(s) of life: online discourse and; memes; social media

judgement, 20, 23–4, 56, 100, 107–18, 120, 122, 143–54, 157–61, 172–3, 177–8, 180, 182–5, 189–91, 205n, 213n
justice (and injustice), 22, 32–3, 35, 49, 54–62, 65, 78, 81, 83–5, 94, 133–4, 137, 143, 149–53, 177, 199n; see also 'conversation of justice' (Cavell); ideal theory (political philosophy); judgement

Kant, Immanuel, 4, 5, 20–1, 26, 35–6, 75, 78, 97, 98, 107–12, 114–18, 120, 122, 143–7, 149, 152, 159–60, 177, 179–82, 186, 204n, 205n
knowledge and acknowledgement, 5–6, 17–18, 49, 59, 65, 70, 75–6, 128, 187–8, 190, 196n

language-games, 17, 24, 89, 170–3, 175–6, 179, 183, 190, 204n
learning see initiation into language; instruction
liberalism/liberal theory, 1, 4–6, 9–11, 19–20, 22, 28, 32, 52–7, 80–1, 94, 122, 124, 125–6, 128, 132, 137–9, 143, 147, 162–4, 200n, 207n, 209n, 209–10n
 and the novel genre, 9–12, 32–3, 41, 52–4, 59, 61–2, 155–7, 189, 195n, 199n, 200n
Lynch, Deidre, 44–5, 53

magical realism, 24–5, 123, 129, 154, 156–61, 205–6n
Marxism/Marxist theory, 175, 192, 200n, 212n
memes, 24, 163–4, 169–77, 183–4, 185, 211n
Meredith, George, *The Egoist*, 18, 22–3, 64–71, 73–94, 95, 201n, 202n
Mills, Charles Wade, 55, 199n
Milton, John, 3, 36, 38, 63, 67
modernism (and modernist literature and culture), 9, 25, 65, 95, 103, 164, 202n
Moi, Toril, 8–9, 27, 194n, 201n
moral perfectionism see perfectionism

new formalism *see* formalism
newness *see* democracy
normativity, 57, 189
  in ordinary language philosophy, 6–7, 16–18, 64–6, 93–4, 143, 173, 197n
  in political philosophy, 16, 20, 23–4, 142–3, 145, 149–50, 153, 159–60, 177–8
  'universal voice' of aesthetic judgement (Kant), 20, 28, 108–9, 112, 145, 149, 159, 177, 182–3, 204–5n
  *see also* conventions (ordinary language philosophy)
Norval, Aletta J., 60–1, 142–3, 197n, 200n
novels (history and theory), 9–12, 32–3, 52–4, 61, 195n, 200n; *see also* liberalism/liberal theory: and the novel genre

ordinary language philosophy, 2–3, 5, 6, 7, 10, 14, 17–21, 28, 64–6, 68–73, 74–5, 77–80, 82, 84–5, 93–4, 108–9, 121, 143, 163–4, 169–73, 175, 180–1, 187, 188–9, 192, 193n, 197n, 201n, 201–2n
  in literary studies, 2–3, 8–9, 11, 187, 190, 193n, 194n, 198n
other minds *see* acknowledgement; scepticism

passionate utterances *see* perlocutionary utterances
patriarchy, 6, 11, 33, 40–1, 54, 65, 81, 98–101, 120
perfectionism, 7, 13–16, 20–2, 31–41, 45–6, 48, 54–61, 137, 143, 180–1, 188, 196n, 198n, 199n, 200n, 213n
  in contrast to moralism, 35, 40, 45–6, 48, 52, 189
  in contrast to deontological and utilitarian moral theory, 35–6, 58, 78
performativity, 7, 16, 18, 22–3, 63–73, 77–8, 80, 83, 87–9, 90–2, 94, 129, 135, 138–40, 148, 172–3, 183, 201n; *see also* promises
perlocutionary utterances, 28, 30, 71–3, 200n
platform capitalism, 175–6
politics *see* aesthetic theory: as a model for political judgement; common world; democracy; judgement; justice (and injustice); liberalism; public sphere
post-critique (and critique), 2–3, 186, 191–2, 194n
post-truth, 3, 6, 85, 90, 164
prejudice, 23, 144, 150–2, 162, 172–3, 178, 205n
private language fantasy, 74–5, 90, 118, 201–2n
promises, 60, 63–71, 73–4, 78–83, 91, 94, 136, 202n; *see also* performativity
public realm, 18–19, 21, 24, 98, 119–20, 122, 136, 138, 141, 143–4, 146, 151–3, 159–61, 164, 170, 174, 178, 180, 185, 189–90, 192; *see also* common world; public sphere
public sphere, 4, 9, 15, 121–2, 124–6, 128, 131, 134, 137–42, 147–8, 150, 155–6, 162, 207n, 209n; *see also* common world; counterpublics; Internet; scepticism
'purposiveness without purpose' (Kant), 21, 26, 116, 143, 181–2, 186, 191

Cavell's invocation of, regarding conversation, 20–1, 63, 85
*see also* autonomy (aesthetic); formalism

racism, 6, 11, 124–5, 129–31, 134–5, 144, 151, 158, 165, 172, 199n, 205n, 206n, 210n
Rancière, Jacques, 141–3, 145, 147, 153, 154, 200n, 213n
rationality *see* reason
Rawls, John, 19, 32, 54–6, 58–9, 137, 147, 199n, 202n, 209n
reality *see* common world; public realm; scepticism
reason, 4–5, 18–20, 68, 72, 108, 119, 122, 124–6, 128, 130, 132, 137, 139, 143–7, 149, 153, 156, 159–60, 177–8, 200n, 208–9n
remarriage comedies *see* comedies of remarriage
representative thinking, 109–12, 145–53, 161, 164, 177–80, 182–5
responsiveness, 3, 5, 18, 22, 26–7, 32–3, 36–7, 39–41, 46, 56, 58, 60–1, 72, 76–8, 82, 137, 143, 161, 186–92, 200n; *see also* acknowledgement; 'conversation of justice' (Cavell); conversational criticism
Romanticism, 9, 44, 45, 53, 196n
Rudrum, David, 26, 60–1, 141, 143, 200n
rules in language use, 7, 17–18, 20, 78, 93, 160–1, 202n
Rushdie, Salman, *The Satanic Verses*, 11, 23–4, 25, 120–37, 139, 140–4, 149–50, 152–9, 161, 174–5
'Rushdie Affair', 155–6, 206n, 207n, 209n, 209–10n

Russell, Bertrand, 97, 104–8, 110, 112, 114–15, 117, 118–19, 204n

'scenes of instruction' (Cavell) *see* instruction
scepticism, 1–3, 5–8, 14, 16–25, 36–7, 61, 64–6, 74–9, 85, 92, 94, 95–8, 119, 143, 150, 169, 187, 188, 204–5n
  epistemological, 1, 5, 11, 16–17, 21, 23, 51, 97, 104–8, 110, 114–15, 118–19, 204–5n
  in literary criticism, 27, 187, 193n, 195n
  linguistic, 22, 75, 96, 104, 169
  regarding other minds, 1, 5, 16–17, 23, 36–7, 64–5, 75–6, 187–8, 196n
  threat to common world and democracy, 5–6, 19, 24, 85, 119–20, 138–9, 143, 148, 190
Schrödinger's cat paradox, 88–90, 93, 203n
*sensus communis*, 97–8, 108–12, 114–18, 120, 145–52, 159–60, 177–8, 180, 205n
Smith, Ali, *There But For The*, 1, 24, 163–72, 174–85, 189, 191, 211n
'social' (Arendt), 122, 139, 164, 173–6, 183–4, 212n
social media, 4, 6, 19, 24, 161–4, 170–2, 174–6, 184, 210n, 212n, 213n; *see also* Internet
sociology and sociolinguistics, 4, 9, 186
'speech', political (Arendt), 2, 6, 15, 19, 21, 119, 122, 136–9, 143, 147–8, 164, 174, 178
speech acts *see* performativity; perlocutionary utterances
surveillance economy, 175; *see also* platform capitalism

universalism *see* normativity

vagueness, 87–8, 90, 93, 202n;
    *see also* Schrödinger's cat paradox
voice, 3, 8, 10, 14, 22, 26–30, 37,
    42, 46, 59–61, 65, 70, 77, 81–5,
    89, 94, 96, 105, 108–9, 117,
    125, 128, 138–9, 149, 155, 161,
    187–92, 201n; *see also* consent;
    conventions (ordinary language
    philosophy); conversational
    criticism; normativity

'we' as an invitation, 6, 28, 109
Web 2.0 *see* social media
Wittgenstein, Ludwig, 6–7, 9, 13–14,
    17, 24, 74–5, 79, 93, 99, 153,
    164, 170–3, 180, 187–8, 192,
    194n, 196n, 197n, 201–2n,
    211–12n

Woolf, Virginia, 9, 11, 95–121, 190,
    203n, 204n, 205n
    *A Room of One's Own*, 98–9,
        101–2
    *To the Lighthouse*, 23, 96–103,
        111–12, 120
    *The Waves*, 23, 96–8, 103–7,
        110–21
'world we have in common' (Arendt)
    *see* common world
worldmaking, 6–7, 27–9, 37, 44,
    50–1, 61, 94, 120, 122, 143,
    151–3, 155–6, 160–1, 163, 174,
    177, 182–3, 188, 190
Wright, Daniel, 65, 78, 82, 202n

Zerilli, Linda MG, 138, 144, 153,
    173, 194n, 205n
Zumhagen-Yekplé, Karen, 9, 196n,
    204n

EU representative:
Easy Access System Europe
Mustamäe tee 50, 10621 Tallinn, Estonia
Gpsr.requests@easproject.com

www.ingramcontent.com/pod-product-compliance
Lightning Source LLC
Chambersburg PA
CBHW051121160426
43195CB00014B/2287